THE TWO WORLDS OF
MARCEL PROUST

THE TWO WORLDS

of

MARCEL PROUST

By

HAROLD MARCH

Philadelphia

University of Pennsylvania Press

1948

ACKNOWLEDGMENTS

ALTHOUGH this book is based chiefly on Proust's published writings and correspondence, my heavy indebtedness to predecessors will be evident from the text and is acknowledged in the Appendix on Sources and Bibliography. But certain debts of gratitude call for more conspicuous mention: to Professor Robert Vigneron, of the University of Chicago, for his "Genèse de Swann" and "Marcel Proust and Robert de Montesquiou," with the dating of letters involved, as well as for courtesies and advice personally extended; and to Dr. Philip Kolb, of the University of Illinois, for permission to use before publication his study of the chronology of Proust's correspondence. Proust did not date most of his letters, and many of those published have either been left undated or have been wrongly dated by their editors. By internal evidence and cross-correspondence, first Professor Vigneron and then Dr. Kolb have established the solid basis of chronology which is indispensable to an accurate treatment of Proust's life and ideas.

I should also like to thank Professor Henri Peyre, of Yale, for much kind help and several fruitful suggestions; Mrs. Donald Stroop, for welcome assistance in the early stages of the manuscript; and Mrs. Theodore Andersson, for her skill and care in its final arrangement.

Grateful acknowledgment is also made to Mr. J. Anker Larsen for permission to quote from his book *With the Door Open,* and to the editors of the *Romanic Review* for permission to use materials of my article "The Proustian Manner," which appeared in that review in February 1944.

Swarthmore College
December 1947

H. M.

CONTENTS

		Page
	MARCEL PROUST IN 1922 (From a photograph)	Frontispiece
1.	THE CLIMATE OF IDEAS	1
2.	THE CHILD	19
3.	ACTIVITY	33
4.	PROUST IN 1896	52
5.	THE RELIGION OF ART	81
6.	WRITING THE NOVEL	103
7.	A LA RECHERCHE DU TEMPS PERDU	135
	Structure	135
	Characters	148
	Marcel and Albertine	171
	Society	182
	Intellectual Themes	194
	Transcendent Reality	216
	Style	228
8.	THE MEANING OF PROUST	240
	APPENDICES	253
	Sources	255
	Correspondence	264
	Important Works on Proust	266
	INDEX	271

*There are two worlds, one the world
of time, where necessity, illusion, suffering, change, decay, and death are
the law; the other the world of eternity, where there is freedom, beauty,
and peace. Normal experience is in the
world of time, but glimpses of the
other world may be given in moments
of contemplation or through accidents
of involuntary memory. It is the function of art to develop these insights
and to use them for the illumination of
life in the world of time.*

✦ 1 ✦

THE CLIMATE OF IDEAS

FOR some readers Proust's novel is gloomy, decadent, dissociative, in itself a sufficient explanation of why the country that produced it went down to defeat in 1940; for others, a smaller number, it is radiant with youthful hope, poetry, and faith. One critic will say that Proust "fishes in the subconscious with a net of time," and another that he has produced a realistic panorama of society comparable to Balzac's *Comédie humaine.* He is likened to Saint-Simon, La Bruyère, Stendhal, or to Bergson, Joyce, Freud, and even Einstein.

The strange thing about these conflicting statements is that behind most of them there is some truth. And yet Proust himself, carefully read, is not really inconsistent. His apparent contradictions are intended parts of a long demonstration, the exposition of a personal philosophy which was at the heart of everything he had to say. And so the first step toward an understanding of Proust must be a preliminary examination of this philosophy and its sources.

In the case of Proust—or for that matter of any author of stature—it is idle to look for merely documentary sources. A writer with any claim to originality does not present, as his report on human experience, a patchwork of the opinions of others. What he reads does of course have its effect on what he has to say, and more particularly on his rationalization of experience. But there is a selective process at work. He remains impervious to some of the ideas to which he is exposed because they do not correspond to his temperamental prejudices; but others awaken an immediate inward assent, because they make explicit what he already obscurely believes.

1

One of Proust's observations—a generalization, but applied to himself—gives us a start toward an understanding of his temperament. "Complete natures," he says, "being rare, a person who is very sensitive and very intellectual will generally have very little will power, will be the plaything of habit and of that fear of immediate pain which condemns to perpetual suffering."

Implicit in this statement is the ancient triad of the complete man to which Proust frequently recurs: intelligence, sensibility, and the will. With this, as with any formula for partitioning human nature, there are difficulties. But if we translate the triad into terms of temperament, we find that it does in a measure correspond to observed facts: there is an intellectual type, an emotional type, and an active type (characterized by decisiveness, or the will in action). It is certainly true, as Proust says, that "complete natures"—persons who think, feel, and act in a harmonious proportion—are rare; rare, too, he might have added, are extremes of a single type. Far more common are those who are oriented toward two types, but not toward the third, and of these was Proust. If we think of the three extremes as apexes of a triangle, his type would lie along the line joining the emotional and the intellectual apexes. Circumstances may pull such a type toward the uncongenial third apex, but once the tension is relaxed he springs back to his normal line.

The indecisive, impractical man of ideas and feelings is a familiar figure in modern civilization, and is particularly common among artists and men of letters; so that to place Proust in this category may seem an unpromising start toward an explanation of his extreme individuality. But pushed a little farther it is surprisingly revealing, both negatively and positively.

Negatively it helps explain why he is so isolated from the social problems of his times, and why, when reason and emotion have involved him in such questions as anti-Semitism, anti-clericalism, and the nationalistic spirit, his activity is so short-lived. It illumines his pathological indecisiveness, which was a lifelong subject of self-reproach, and is embedded in his very style. It contributes to an understanding of that "fear of immediate pain" which lay at the root of his neuroticism, his claustration, his dread of insomnia, his addiction to medicaments. Positively Proust's position in the triangle of temperaments illustrates his relation to the two poles of his being: intelligence and sensibility. In a revealing episode of his novel he tells how his young hero, transported by the beauty of the world after the rain, brandishes his umbrella with ecstatic cries of "Zut! zut," but immediately feels that he ought not to have contented himself with these "opaque words," but should have inquired more deeply into the nature of his joy. The incident sets the pattern for Proust's response to the external world. First comes intuition, for which emotion is the accompaniment and to some extent the instrument. Second comes analysis, the effort of the intelligence to classify and explain what intuition has apprehended. Proust also found a value in the direct application of the intelligence to the problems of reality, and with the advance of years and experience this use of the analytical powers increased. But it increased because of the decline of his emotional response, a decline which he deplored. The intellectual mode brought with it doubt, scruple, revision, dissection; but perhaps the most remarkable feature of his temperamental dualism is that even when he is functioning in this mode, his reason defers to his emotional intuition as to the oracle of a higher truth, a fact that he recorded at intervals throughout his career, and up to the last year of his life. This preference for intuition is of great importance, for without it the demonstration of the novel collapses.

Proust's marked individuality is partly a matter of the extreme character of his relation to emotion, reason, and action. His powerful affective response to people and to things is matched by a compensatory and equally insistent need for solitude, and by a capacity for minute dispassionate analysis. Toward action he shows himself no less extreme, but negatively: once his character is formed, he is almost paralytically indecisive, until driven into action by necessity or strong emotion.

Such, then, was the basic temperament which was to mesh with the moving thoughts of the later nineteenth century. Opinions are to some extent the result of the temperaments of those who have them, and since Proust's prejudices were rooted in fundamental human nature, it is no surprise to find that his psychological dualism was reflected in the thoughts around him. Indeed, one of the most characteristic features of nineteenth-century ideas is their constant tension between various loosely related polarities, some under their age-old names, others disguised as contemporary concepts. There were reason and emotion, science and religion, materialism and spiritualism, necessity and liberty, the individual and the group, consciousness and the unconscious, estheticism and utility, decadence and the strenuous life, and many other pairs of opposed ideas. So diverse are they in sum that it is quite impossible to divide them into two great opposing armies of thought; if we tried to do so, we should find many men fighting on both sides at once.

And yet it is possible to single out an antithesis somewhat more comprehensive than the rest: the idea of man as potentially master of his fate and that of man as the eternal victim. The first, a characteristically eighteenth-century concept, represents man as perfectible through reason, eventually capable, by its means, of understanding and mastering both his environment and himself. According to the second idea, man is merely the pawn of forces which he cannot control. His actions, his apparent choices, even his thoughts, are dictated from within or from without, in either case without his understanding or consent. In the second half of the nineteenth century a migration of opinion from the first to the second of these conceptions took place, with curious results. Starting with confidence in reason and using reason as a tool, thinkers arrived at the conclusion that man was not free, not even in his thoughts, not even in the reason by which he arrived at this conclusion.

The nineteenth century opened with a strong surface reaction against the rationalism of the preceding "Age of Enlightenment," but before its middle the romantic wave had spent itself, and rational empiricism was reasserting itself, with a growing trend toward experimentalism. In so far as the statement can be made of any one man, it was Auguste Comte who set the tone of scientific rationalism for the mid-century. Comte distinguished three phases of human knowledge: the theological, or fictitious; the metaphysical, or abstract; and the scientific, or positive. In the modern, the positive phase, said Comte, "the human mind, recognizing the impossibility of arriving at absolute conceptions, renounces the search for the origin and destination of the universe and the inner causes of phenomena, and attaches itself solely to the discovery, by the judicious use of reasoning and observation, of their effective laws. . . . The explanation of facts, thus reduced to real terms, is henceforth only the connection established between diverse phenomena and general facts, whose number scientific progress tends increasingly to diminish."

Comte had many disciples in various lands, but in France Taine (whose influence was unrivaled from, roughly, 1860 to 1880, and was effective for much longer) eventually emerged as the most eloquent exemplar of the positivist spirit. His "master faculty," as he would have called it, was for the collection of "small true facts," and for the formulation of laws to explain them. Many of his ideas stemmed from eighteenth-century empiricism, but he was a much more dogmatic believer in causation than Hume. For him every phenomenon was at once and always a cause and an effect, part of a chain from which there was no escape. Every cause-effect relationship was governed by a law, groups of such laws were ruled by higher laws, and at the top of the pyramid there must be, logically, a master formula that explained the universe.

Taine's theories of literary criticism do not directly concern us, but in philosophical psychology his most noteworthy ideas, and the ones that came closest to Proust, were two. The first was the extension of the principle of causation from the physical to the moral domain. As he put it in an often-quoted passage: "Whether facts are physical or moral, they always have causes. . . . Vice and virtue are products, like vitriol and sugar." The second and closely related idea was the reduction of human personality to the mere sum of successive states (something like Hume's "bundles" of successive perceptions), each of them as much a result and a cause as any phenomenon of the physical world.

Taine's viewpoint was the basis, and the new German experimental psychology the example, for a group of distinguished French psycho-physiologists, Théodule Ribot among them, at whose hands the old idea of the will as a faculty suffered serious damage. If a man's choices were strictly determined by antecedent moral and physical causes, the exercise of will power was an illusion, at best a sense of friction between opposing desires, each of them predetermined in quality and quantity. "Volition," concluded Ribot in his *Maladies de la volonté* (1883) ". . . is for us only a simple state of consciousness. It is the result of that psycho-physiological working of which only a part enters into consciousness under the form of a deliberation. *Furthermore it is the cause of nothing.* The acts and movements which follow it result directly from the tendencies, feelings, images, and ideas which have finally become coördinated in the form of a choice. . . . '*I will*' *states a situation, but does not constitute it.*"

The publication of *The Origin of Species* in 1859, and of its French translation in 1862, furnished a further impetus to scientific rationalism. Although Darwin did not explicitly take up man's place in the evolutionary system until 1871 in *The Descent of Man,* he referred in *The Origin of Species* to the inspiration he derived from Malthus' *Essay on Population* for his theory of natural selection, he mentioned the possibilities for future investigation of man's origin and descent, and his whole argument went to show that all existing species were the product, not of special acts of creation, but of the operation of natural laws. The theory of evolution was not new, but its adherents had been few. The extraordinary impact of Darwin's work was due to his long and painstaking accumulation of evidence, to the cogency of his demonstration, and above all to the fact that the times were ripe. Biological evolution manifestly fitted in with the gathering conviction that man and the universe were governed by immutable laws, and not by a Deity who could be persuaded to change the rules of the game in favor of a petitioning individual. Survival of the fittest became the law of life.

Great as was the enthusiasm aroused by the rapid advances in science, their philosophical implications were a serious blow to the long-established beliefs and to the morale of the intelligent layman. Not for him were the almost religious ardors of the search for truth in laboratory and study. Taine could be stirred to austere enthusiasm at the spectacle of the endless and purposeless, but strictly regulated, spawning of facts by the universe; lesser spirits were merely depressed, and sought relief for their distress each in accordance with his own strictly predetermined nature.

Serious literature offered little relief. Parnassian poets, schooling themselves out of romantic nebulosities and exhibitions of personal emotion, described in impeccable verse the visual and tactile world about them, and, when they arose to the cosmic view, they stoically accepted the hostility of nature and a universe of blind impersonal law. The naturalistic novel, in Zola's hands, had a theoretic relation to determinism and an advertised connection with experimental science, although its success was due to the realism of his sordid scenes and to broad romantic images and concepts of which he never succeeded in ridding himself.

Meanwhile, if reason and science were for the moment on top, non-reason—faith, emotion, or mere dissatisfaction—was strongly and constantly present beneath the surface. The individual, as often as not, was divided against himself, and the ardent champion of science today might swing to the church tomorrow. Brunetière was strongly impressed by the theory of evolution and tried to apply it in literary criticism; yet when it came to an issue between science and morals, it was on the side of morals that he aligned himself. Renan—described as one who "thought like a man, felt like a woman, and acted like a child," a characterization that might well have been applied to Proust—was converted in young manhood to scientific skepticism and spent his life in its service; yet his heart remained with the church he had abandoned. The unresolved inner conflict led him continually to undermine his own arguments; in his famous *Prière sur l'Acropole,* a hymn of praise to the goddess of reason, he said, "I shall go farther, orthodox goddess, I shall tell thee the intimate depravity of my heart. Reason and common sense are not enough."

This same inner conflict had much to do with the outbreak of "decadence" and estheticism in the late nineteenth century. The earnest and simple-hearted believer, convinced in spite of himself that his faith was vain, said, "They have taken away my Lord, and I know not where they have laid Him," and sorrowfully searched for a new faith. The more sophisticated felt that if life had lost meaning and purpose they might as well cultivate the sensations which the self, even though illusory, could furnish. They were disposed to accept the advice of Barrès to "take the Self as a waiting ground on which to remain until some energetic person has reconstructed a religion for you." "Let us be ardent and skeptical."

Writing in 1889, Paul Bourget distinguished two types among the young men of his day. One was the prematurely cynical egotist, with himself for god, success and pleasure for the sole object of existence, and survival of the fittest for motto. This young man was a monster, Bourget said, but less dangerous than the second type, "the refined intellectual Epicurean, as the first was the brutal scientific Epicurean." No less cynical and selfish than the first, he was more intelligent, more cultivated. He toyed with esthetic emotions and intellectual curiosities in the same spirit as the other satisfied his grosser appetites.

This "dilettante of sensations" (as Croce called D'Annunzio, an outstanding later example of the type) is the esthete, made familiar to us in England by Pater and Wilde, in France by Barrès and Bourget himself (though both of them only for a time). The ironic, superior, precious, but deeply unhappy esthete is but one of a complex of attitudes commonly covered by the word "decadence."

One approach to the complex is through the idea of perversity, of which Baudelaire, deriving some of his inspiration from Poe, is an outstanding exponent. But Baudelaire did not "borrow" perversity from Poe, nor did Poe invent it; nor, for that matter, did the romantics and pre-romantics who had exploited it before them. Perversity, like any recurrent attitude, is rooted in human nature. For whatever reason, it seems to be a fact of experience that every urge—from within or from without, instinctive or social—has its counter-urge, which in some people, under certain conditions, acts with obsessive force. The instinct of self-preservation is matched by the death urge. Loss of support, one of the basic infantile fears, exerts a fascination on some, and the impulse to throw oneself from a height may be the counter-urge both to the instinct of self-preservation and to its derivative, the fear of loss of support. The pleasure principle is countered by the quest of pain. Resistance to social pressure impels some people to laugh at funerals, insult their friends, commit gratuitous crimes; the modest commit offenses against decency, the pious are irresistibly drawn to blasphemy. Why? Hysteria, said the doctors of Baudelaire's day, dismissing the problem with a label. "It is a kind of energy which springs from boredom," said Baudelaire with more discernment, adding—for to him the "démon de la perversité" was no mere figure of speech—"these impulses authorize the belief that mischievous Demons slip into us and make us accomplish, unwittingly, their most absurd wishes."

Perhaps perversity is latent in everyone, though introverts are certainly more susceptible to it than strongly active natures. But when it breaks out as a group phenomenon among gifted and articulate people, we have a minor epidemic like the decadence of the eighties and nineties.

In decadence, perversity—the impulse to like or to do "the other thing"—conforms in general to one of two associated types: anti-nature, and the substitution of means for ends.

Interest in life is natural, because it is founded on a basic instinct. In this sense a preferential interest in death, typical of the decadent, is anti-natural. In some it appears in a mild form, as a gentle autumn mood, finding satisfaction in twilight, the fall of leaves, and the contemplation of ruins. More extreme natures, not content with twilight and suggestion, push on to black night itself, revel in the macabre paraphernalia of death, aspire to extinction. Similarly decadents find an attraction in objects that are repulsive to the healthy-minded—in rotting corpses, in the manifestations of disease, in all forms of hideousness: "aux objets répugnants nous trouvons des appas," wrote Baudelaire.

In the same spirit crime, anarchy, and violence were extolled over peace and the settled order. Satan was preferred to God; if we are to believe Huysmans, black masses (combining obscenity with blasphemy), black magic, maleficent spells flourished as they had not done for centuries. Reason and the immediate testimony of the senses were ridiculed. In this context the new vogue for spiritism and the occult, although it extended far beyond the bounds of decadence, is noteworthy.

Homosexuality has often been associated with decadence, and naturally enough, for it is at least superficially anti-natural, and the appetite of the decadent for anything that was against nature appeared to be insatiable. But the notorious case of Oscar Wilde is misleading. The fact that he was a homosexual and also, because of his estheticism, classed among the decadents, does not establish a necessary connection between the two aspects. One dubious feature about such a connection is that homosexuality is a more or less constant phenomenon. It exists in a rudimentary form even among the animals, and it has apparently always been present in human societies. Another difficulty is that, not only were many homosexuals non-decadent, but many typical decadents were patently heterosexual.

It would seem that what varies is not so much the number of homosexuals as the public attitude toward the question. Such a change occurred during the second half of the nineteenth century and on into the twentieth; but it can more reasonably be correlated with the growth of the scientific spirit than with decadence. In a series of pamphlets published from 1864 to 1880, an Austrian, K. H. Ulrichs, pointed out the existence of a type of individual, male or female, to which he gave the name "Urning," or Uranian, and which by later writers came to be called the intermediate sex. An Urning, according to Ulrichs, was a female soul in a male body, or a male soul in a female body. Such persons tended (with psychic heterosexuality) to attach themselves to members of the same physical sex. In the prolonged discussion, both medical and lay, which followed, a new attitude began to be discernible. Homosexuality was coming to be considered no longer as simply a vicious and unspeakable depravity, but as an unfortunate psychological fact, abnormal only in that it was a minority impulse. Medical writers looked askance at the idea of a soul of one sex in a body of the other, not only because of its origin—Ulrichs was a layman, and himself an Urning—but because talk of "souls" in medicine was abhorrent to the professional mind; nevertheless Ulrichs' idea, expressed in other terms, gained much support. Krafft-Ebing, the most widely read of the medical writers on the subject, admitted in his *Psychopathia sexualis* (1886) his belief in the existence of a genuine congenital Urning.

One point made by Krafft-Ebing is peculiarly pertinent to decadence: his distinction between perversion, a disease, and perversity, a vice. According to this idea, genuine Uranism would have nothing to do with the moral phenomenon of decadence, but an occasional case of deliberate sexual perversity might.

Uranism remained anti-biological but, chiefly under the influence of Krafft-Ebing, the argument became current that if physical love for other than reproductive purposes were admitted at all, there was no moral distinction to be drawn between one biologically sterile form of love and another.

Another connection between decadence and homosexuality is the apparent effeminacy of the extreme esthete. But if the average reaction to estheticism is acute discomfort, it cannot be wholly due to the effeminacy of the male, for the female esthete, without any suggestion of masculinity, is just as absurd or painful. The basis of the objection to the esthetic attitude is rather that it is felt to be incongruous, disproportionate, an offense against common sense; probably because it makes sense impressions, usually considered as a means, an end in themselves. To the healthy-minded (to whose opposed standards decadence must inevitably be referred) there is something obscene in the passive acceptance of titillation, in the supine listening to the voice of one's nerves. Sensations are given us, they would argue, for the practical purpose of contact with our environment, and for new discovery. They are in over-supply, and there is no harm in taking pleasure in their surplus acuity, but only as a by-product. Sensation for the sole purpose of pleasure is felt to be immoral.

The cult of the word, generally considered as an instrument of communication, is another example of the substitution of means for ends. "The decadent," said an article in the *Figaro* of September 22, 1885, "has no ideas. He does not want any. He prefers words. The reader generally objects. Hence the scorn of the decadent for the reader." The symbolist Mallarmé was less extreme, but over him too the word as such, with its power of incantation, exerted an insistent fascination, and led, with him and his followers, to a new vocabulary, to the torture of syntax, and to the cultivation of obscurity.

The prototype of decadence in fiction is Des Esseintes, hero of Huysmans' *A rebours* (1884). That the author should have made of him an example of racial degeneration confuses the issue, for, as he himself is at pains to point out, the hypersensitivity of a decadent is less degenerate than the surrender of some declining noble families to a purely animal existence; less degenerate even than the smug mediocrity of many a bourgeois existence. Decadence is the result of a misapplication of a surplus of nervous energy, as Baudelaire said of perversity. Boredom is one of its symptoms rather than its cause. No doubt a highly evolved society, having achieved for some of its members a degree of security, comfort, and leisure, and having permitted them to run through the gamut of recognized pleasures, leaves them with time on their hands and unsatisfied desires. But this partial explanation of decadence is not enough to account for the timing of its outbreaks.

Decadence is, as Bourget suggested in his reference to the "survival of the fittest" motto, an aspect of the thought of the times. Whatever philosophy of life men's reason may work out, they have a deeply rooted need to believe in a life having significance, value, purpose. A mechanistic philosophy, with man become a cog in the machine and God a superstition or another word for natural law, leaves a void, which decadents, without quite knowing what they are doing, try to fill with their restless search for the new. Their extravagances, far from signaling an end, are the promise of a beginning. Their very instability proclaims their transitional character. Huysmans closed *A rebours* with these melancholy but prophetic words: "Lord have pity on the Christian who doubts, on the unbeliever who would believe, on the galley slave of life who embarks alone, in the night, under a sky no longer lit by the consoling beacons of the old faith!" And Barbey d'Aurevilly, reviewing the book with a discernment which Huysmans himself was later to applaud, wrote: "After such a book, there remains to the author only the choice between the muzzle of a pistol and the foot of the cross."

In its basic mood of perversity, and in most of its manifestations, such as the death urge, decadence is a revival of a part of romanticism. Like decadence, romanticism rushed in to fill a void, created, in the earlier instance, by the desiccating effect of eighteenth-century rationalism, the progressive anemia of classical literature, and the collapse of the principle of authority. But while romanticism had a positive side with a vigorous literature, decadence as such had none. As an attitude, it had symptomatic significance; as a literary movement it was stillborn. Baudelaire was a great poet who often assumed a decadent attitude. *A rebours* is a classic description of the decadent state of mind, but the man who wrote it was already on his way elsewhere. Any movement that boasts, like decadence and like its lineal descendant Dada, of having no ideas, and no program but destruction, is self-condemned. But the attitude of decadence survived its literary demise, just as the mood of Dada was a significant part of the climate of the nineteen-twenties.

Decadence and naturalism were two dissimilar outgrowths of scientific rationalism, and by the eighteen-eighties there were energetic manifestations of dissatisfaction with them and with their parent philosophy. As Huysmans pointed out in *Là-bas,* the poverty of the naturalistic novel's psychology, its blindness to the nuance, its unvarying brutality of cause and effect, were becoming monotonous. Or, as de Vogüé put it in his preface to *Le Roman russe* (1886), "in the beginning the Lord God formed man of the dust of the ground, and breathed into his nostrils the breath of life; and man became a living soul;" the realists (with whom de Vogüé grouped the Naturalists) described man as formed from the dust of the ground, but neglected his living soul.

Public taste had about reached the saturation point when, in 1887, Zola published *La Terre.* The outcry was immediate. *L'Assommoir* had created something of a scandal, but because it had succeeded in arousing pity and had drawn attention to needed reforms, it had been accepted. But *La Terre* seemed to have no mitigating features; it was sheer depravity. The most effective of the protests was a letter signed by five former followers of Zola, who, as a result of *La Terre,* publicly dissociated themselves from him and from his movement. Just at the moment when naturalism was beginning to be a force abroad, Zola had to admit a check at home. He pushed his Rougon-Macquart series to a close, but eventually he had to find new methods and new materials.

Bourget's *Le Disciple,* whose preface contained the description of the "refined intellectual Epicurean," appeared in 1889, and marked a break with his former master Taine. In it Bourget renounced his former estheticism and took his stand squarely for religion and the moral responsibility of thinkers and writers. The book touched off an explosion of feeling that assumed the proportions of a movement. Like its companion trend in England, counter-decadence in France urged a return to religion and positive moral values, and had nationalistic implications. Edouard Rod, a former naturalistic novelist of Swiss origin, had long been haunted by moral problems. In 1891 he came out with his *Idées morales du temps présent,* in which he distinguished the "positives," men of conviction and good will, from the "negatives," the skeptical drifters. Close on his heels came his friend Paul Desjardins, with his *Devoir présent* (1891), in which he declared war on the negatives. He demanded flatly: "Are slavery to animal instinct, selfishness, falsehood absolute evil, or are they merely 'inelegances'? . . . Are justice and love the certain good, the certain law, and the port of salvation, or are they possible illusions, probable vanities? Have we a destiny, an ideal, a duty, or are our activities without cause and without purpose, existing for the amusement of some mischievous demiurge or simply by the absurd caprice of the great god Pan? Such is the question. . . . Personally, I have chosen my side." Maurice Barrès, who in the series of the *Culte du Moi* (1888-91) had appeared as the ironic esthete, turned fiercely to his trilogy the *Roman de l'énergie nationale,* whose most important part, *Les Déracinés* (1897) was a vehement argument for attachment to one's provincial and national past.

The revolt against decadence and the skeptical philosophy

from which it sprang coincided with an acceleration of recovery from the national feeling of inferiority resulting from the Franco-Prussian War. The Republic had weathered its first storms and was now well established; the Exposition of 1889 had been a great success and had excited the admiration of the world; and in 1891 France achieved an alliance with Russia which gave her a new sense of security against Germany. Furthermore, her colonial empire was growing mightily. The resurgent "positives" showed a disposition to add imperialistic propaganda to moral and religious admonitions. Kipling's dynamic imperialism found many admirers in France, and Paul Desjardins combined his appeal for a return to religion and a rebirth of the moral sense with a challenge to his nation to develop her colonies and bring civilization to backward peoples.

Counter-decadence was essentially an unreflective moral explosion, but reaction against the complacency of scientific rationalism and its over-simplification was not lacking on a more philosophic level. In his *De la contingence des lois de la nature* (1874) Boutroux reasoned that science works in an abstraction from reality which is not reality itself, and that the "laws" of nature have validity in the abstraction, in the mind, but not necessarily in reality. This book paved the way for the more celebrated *Essai sur les données immédiates de la conscience* (1889) of Bergson, who made a distinction between chronometric time and "duration," or the psychic experience of the passage of time, and drew therefrom an argument for a relative human liberty. Man cannot be said, Bergson reasoned, to be entirely at the mercy of past causes because his acts spring from a state of mind which is the sum of his past states plus an ever-new present. Consequently, he said, the problem of necessity and liberty arises out of a misconception.

But the most serious sapping of confidence in the power of reason came from the development of the conception of the unconscious. The real founding father of this essentially modern idea was Schopenhauer, whose *World as Will and Idea* was published in 1818, but who did not begin to exercise an important influence until some fifty years later. Schopenhauer's basic idea was that blind unconscious Will is at once the ultimate reality and the prime motivating force in human conduct. This extremely important conception, at least in its aspect of motivation in the unconscious, lies at the back of the whole modern psycho-analytic movement; philosophically it makes man a victim, not of simple wholly exterior forces, but of his unconscious self.

This much of Schopenhauer's philosophy made him a complete determinist. But he did not stop there. By ordinary perception, he asserted, man cannot arrive at true reality, for "idea," founded upon perception, is necessarily and always an illusion. But for a man of genius (philosopher or artist), there is another form of knowing: contemplation. In this process the distinction between subject and object disappears, will and idea are fused, and at the price of his separate identity man can rise to eternity and freedom.

This side of Schopenhauer's philosophy—especially as it was developed by his successor Hartmann *(Philosophy of the Unconscious,* 1861), who, unlike his master, included in the unconscious both will and idea—had an influence almost diametrically opposed to his famous pessimism. His belief that the function of the artist is, through contemplation, to pierce beyond the phenomenon to the noumenon (or Platonic Idea) of which it is the objectification, goes beyond that of Plato in the *Republic,* where it is claimed that art imitates the phenomenon, and io conocquchtly an imitation of an imitation.

The symbolist movement in literature was in part a new romanticism, in part an aspect of decadence, in part a revolt against naturalism; but its theoretic core rested squarely on Schopenhauer and Hartmann. Symbolists differed widely among themselves, but their esoteric nucleus believed in the neo-Platonic doctrine that the phenomena of the visible world were symbols of an invisible reality; consequently the business of the poet was so to handle the symbols as always to suggest the ultimate reality behind them. The subconscious mind, rather than the superficial rational faculty, was the key to contact with transcendent reality.

Proust's formative years, the late seventies and eightes, coincided with the ideological upheavals and shifts of emphasis we have been describing. He knew personally many of the protagonists in the battle of words, and both sides—or perhaps one should say all sides—left their mark upon him. He read Ribot and Taine, but he also read Plato and Schopenhauer and Bergson. He met some of the leading naturalists of fiction, and respectfully conceded their eminence; but their example discouraged his early literary ambitions because he felt himself to be so unsuited temperamentally to do what they were doing. For his own reading he preferred to them the Russian and English novelists. His whole education for literature centered upon his attempt to find some meeting ground for intelligence and sensibility.

~~ 2 ~~

THE CHILD

MARCEL PROUST was born in Paris on July 10, 1871. Whether or not the recent bloody disorders of the Commune had so agitated his mother as to leave a permanent mark on the child's health, it is clear that the moment was one of the darkest in French history.

His mother was Jewish, the daughter of Nathée Weil, a wealthy broker of a family originally from Metz. Being addicted to city life, he lived in the heart of Paris, but frequently came out to Auteuil, where his brother Louis had a house at 96 rue Lafontaine. Here too the Proust family often came, from their apartment on the Boulevard Malesherbes. Around the house was a large garden, later cut in two by the laying out of the Avenue Mozart. It was probably of this garden that Proust was thinking when he described, in the early pages of his novel, the coming of Swann to dinner; here it was that the little bell rang, announcing the arrival, through the garden gate, of the elderly man-about-town Charles Haas, who was to serve as the point of departure for Proust's composite portrait of Charles Swann.

Parisian Jews of that period belonged to various strata of assimilation. Some, like Charles Haas, men of cultivation and social ease, moved in the most aristocratic circles and belonged to the most exclusive clubs. Others, like the Weils, were less clearly assimilated, but were at home in both Jewish and Gentile circles at the bourgeois level. Still others were glaringly at odds with their environment: rich or poor, orthodox or non-religious, their oriental appearance, their ostentation of dress and behavior, and their tribal family life set them apart from their fellow citizens. Yet across all these strata a certain clannishness was

19

discernible. Violent anti-Semitism did not break out until the Dreyfus affair, but it was latent, and even a Charles Haas liked to drop in at the home of such a racial compatriot as Louis Weil, though his house was furnished without taste and the owner was not exempt from a suspicion of vulgarity.

Early portraits of Madame Proust show her to have been a remarkably handsome woman, with large dark eyes and firmly modeled features. Advancing years, ill health, and suffering heightened the latent austerity of the face, but without reducing the gentleness of the eyes. She was modest to the point of self-effacement, totally devoted to her family, and profoundly conscientious. Her life with her son was an unending battle between her demonstrative affection and her dutiful preoccupation with the strengthening of his character.

Marcel returned her love in kind. When he was still quite a small boy, his mother asked him what he would like for a New Year's present, and he replied, "Your affection." "Little stupid," said his mother, "you know that you will have my affection in any case. I mean what object do you want?" But still the child could think of nothing more desirable than the assurance of her love. At fourteen he noted that his idea of misery was to be separated from his mother.

His demonstrativeness, his intense need to give and to receive affection, extended to all around him. He liked to fondle, and the clinging look of the beautiful eyes he had inherited from his mother was in itself a caress. To busy and unemotional people there was something sticky sweet about his personality; his fondness for the image of honey—"the delicious honey of our personalities," "the honey of your words"—is no accident. The same emotion went out to trees, flowers, a sunlit countryside. He did not observe nature, he bathed in it. His brother Robert, recalling his earliest memories, when he was three and Marcel five, wrote, ". . . I find constantly the image of my brother, watching over me with a gentleness that was infinite, enveloping, and almost maternal. And strangely enough this moving image . . . is almost always associated with a sunny countryside." And Marcel himself wrote, ". . . a roof, a reflection of sunlight on a stone, the odor of a road used to make me stop by the particular pleasure they gave me, and also because they seemed to hide, beyond what I saw, something which they invited me to come and take."

From his earliest years Marcel was of delicate health. Nervous, troubled with insomnia, he daily faced the coming of night with horror. He found it intolerable to lie alone in the dark, forbidden to read, seeking sleep but too agitated to find it, and, worst of all, to be shut away from his mother, the source of all comfort. If she relented and consented to pass some of the dark time with him, talking, or reading aloud, it only made the next night worse. Such dependence, Madame Proust conscientiously felt, should not be encouraged. But in the end, her earnest efforts for the strengthening of Marcel's character were often defeated, betrayed by disquieting symptoms in the delicate child, betrayed too by her own love, and his overwhelming response to it.

Sometimes the father, officially in favor of discipline but preoccupied with other matters, became aware for a moment of his son's unhappiness, capriciously ordered indulgence, and thought no more about it. To his wife his word was law, but the work of weeks had been undone.

Dr. Adrien Proust was a very different type of personality from his wife. Everything about him bespoke energy and forceful determination: his solid figure, his abundant jutting beard, his thick curly hair, the forceful directness of his eyes. This robust father of a sickly child was a distinguished apostle of hygiene; in 1884 he became inspector general of sanitary services, and in 1885 succeeded to the chair of hygiene in the University. A man of great and useful activity, he sat as technical adviser at many conferences on hygiene and sanitation: at Vienna in 1874, at Rome in 1885, at Venice in 1897, and in Paris in 1903, the year of his death. These travels reverberated in Marcel's imagination. Once there was even some question of a departure for Italy by the whole family; but the excitement of anticipation brought on a fever, and Marcel, and of course his mother, had to stay at home.

Shortly after his father's death, Proust wrote to the Comtesse de Noailles, "You who saw Papa only two or three times can have no idea of how kind and how simple he was. I tried, not to satisfy him—for I well realize that I was the dark spot in his life—but to show him my affection. Nevertheless there were days when I revolted against his too great positiveness, the too great confidence of his assertions."

Dr. Proust came of a Catholic family, but his wife, loyal to her family and her race, lived and died in the Jewish faith. The sons were raised as Catholics. This difference in the backgrounds of the parents was reflected in the daily life of the home. Many— and during his school days most—of Marcel's friends were Jewish, or partly Jewish, but to the home Dr. Proust's eminence and attainments drew distinguished political, professional, and artistic personages, without regard to race or creed. At Auteuil Marcel was in a Jewish setting, but visits to the home of Louis Weil were offset by trips to Illiers, where Dr. Proust's family on his mother's side had a home. To this village on the Loire, twenty-four miles southwest of Chartres, the Proust family, in Marcel's early years, usually went for Easter, and often for the summer. More than any other one place, Illiers is the original of Proust's fictional Combray—Illiers with its garden and park, its old church close to the family home, its river Thironne— suggestive of the fictional Vivonne—and with Combries a famil- iar place name of the vicinity. Here Marcel had an uncle, an aunt who was always ill, a grandfather, and an old family ser- vant Ernestine—characters who were to give him the basis for descriptions of family life at Combray.

At Illiers, in spite of a few family regulations, Marcel found abundant time for his favorite occupations of reading and revery. Often he would shut himself into the dining room with a book for a whole morning, immersing himself in fictional adventures and rousing with an effort to reply to Ernestine, who insisted on looking in occasionally to see if he was comfortable. After lunch he was supposed to take a rest, but he would take a book with him when he mounted the short flight of stairs to his room, and instead of seeking sleep, impossible and undesired, he would read and brood by turns. A martial picture of Prince Eugene of Savoy hung on the wall, and the small room was cluttered with bottles and china and covers and cozies, all touched with a rosy light filtered through the colored panes of a window. He could watch the scenes of the street, so close below that he could have jumped to it in safety: his devout aunt on her way to church, Ernestine on an errand to the grocer's, the arms maker smoking a pipe in front of his shop across the way. All too soon the rest period was over, and he had to go to the park at the end of the village for play with other children. Here too the book went along, and as soon as possible he would withdraw from the others, to read and dream alone. And at night, when he could not sleep, he would relight his candle—surreptitiously, for it was forbidden—and finish the book.

His revery—the solitary counterpart of his clinging to people—floated on a sea of sense impressions of which he was scarcely aware at times, but which he absorbed, and later used. And all these impressions were dominated by the village church, with its spire visible for miles around, with its priest walking the streets and carrying his breviary under his arm, with its choir boy carrying the Host to some deathbed, its festivals, its bells softly punctuating his readings in the park, or sonorously marking the passage of sleepless hours at night—sights and sounds that were Catholic, all, and intensely French. And all were drunk in by a small boy whose sensitive receptivity was an inheritance from his Jewish mother.

Unlike Robert, who took after his father in character and appearances, and later followed in his footsteps as a doctor, Marcel looked like his mother. With his pallor, his jet-black hair, and his large heavy-lidded eyes, there was something, if not specifically Jewish, at least oriental about his appearance; the word "Assyrian" has been used to describe it.

There have been several attempts to analyze his mind and character in terms of Jewish racial characteristics. Mention has been made of his appetite for suffering, coupled with an astonishing resistance to it; of his faculty for minute analysis, and an almost Talmudic pursuit of the fine point; of his talent for insinuating himself into intimate circles and adopting the views, seeing with the eyes of others; of his hypersensitivity, his passion for music and painting, his fatalism and pessimism. All of these traits may with some justice be attributed to Proust. Whether or not they can with equal justice be called Jewish, they do appear to be associated with the maternal heredity and influence.

Born and bred a French Catholic, there could scarcely be in Marcel's mind any question of assimilation. Yet he recognized and accepted his share in the Jewish side of the family, and even, at the time of the Dreyfus affair, went out of his way to point out his mother's race and faith. On the other hand, he was able to view Jews, both of his family and among his friends, with an objectivity that might have been more difficult had he felt himself to be wholly one of them.

The crucial event of Marcel's childhood was the onset of his asthma in his tenth year. Returning one day from an excursion in the Bois de Boulogne with family and friends, he was seized with an attack of suffocation so violent that even his doctor father feared for his life. The attack passed, but disciplinary scruples vanished before the continued precariousness of his condition. Madame Proust at once moved into the boy's room, and for months was prodigal with her affectionate ministrations.

Asthma was to be with him all the remainder of his life. It was to transform him from the dreamy boy who loved the sun and the country into the confirmed neurotic of thirty years later, the strange somnambulistic creature with luminous eyes, waxy pallor, and dank matted hair, who, shivering and drugged, had himself driven in a tightly closed limousine for a look through glass at his still beloved fruit trees in bloom. He still loved the sun, and although he knew that only the coming of rain would put a stop to some particularly agonizing suffocation, a part of himself was sad when the sky clouded over. In his childhood he had seen somewhere a barometer in the form of a monk who covered his head for rain and threw back his cowl at the promise of fair weather, and he compared the monk to a "barometric personage" within himself. "I believe that on my deathbed, when all my other selves are dead, if a ray of sunlight happens to shine while I am drawing my last breath, the little barometric personage will be very happy, and will throw back his cowl and sing, 'Ah! good weather at last!'"

And yet in a way asthma was but the physical seal to a situation already in existence: "the fear of immediate pain which condemns to perpetual suffering." Probably there had already occurred the crucial incident—in essence and perhaps even in detail a biographic fact—described in the first volume of his novel. Swann (or Haas) has come to dinner, and Marcel, banished to bed, resolves to stay up until his parents come upstairs. Expecting punishment, he is rewarded, for his mother stays with him that night, reading to him from *François le Champi*. "I ought to have been happy: I was not. It seemed to me that my mother had made me a first concession which was to be painful for her, that it was a first abdication on her part from the ideal which she had conceived for me, and that for the first time she, who was so brave, confessed herself beaten." And at the end of the novel, recurring to the same incident, he wrote: "It was from that evening, when my mother abdicated, that dated . . . the decline of my will, of my health." The little bell in the garden gate that rang Swann out, rang in for Marcel a lifelong yielding to "the fear of immediate pain."

But illness had its compensations. "When I was a little child," he wrote in the preface to his first book, "the lot of no character of sacred history seemed to me so wretched as that of Noah, because of the flood, which kept him shut within the Ark for forty days. Later I was often ill, and for long days I too had to stay within the 'Ark.' I understood then that never was Noah able to see the world so well as from the Ark, despite the fact that it was closed and that night was upon the world." His already established taste for solitary revery found scope and justification in his enforced seclusion. He could cultivate the acquaintance of what he later called "the fraternal stranger within himself," and he discovered that the images and echoes of the world, rising in the memory of a child in bed, might surpass in richness the more active experience of his fellows. He could enjoy his seclusion with a clear conscience.

The result was that the return of health was not an unmixed blessing. "When my convalescence began," he continued in his preface, "my mother, who had not left me, and even at night stayed near me, 'opened the door of the Ark' and went out. However, like the dove, 'she came back again that night.' Then I was wholly cured, and like the dove 'she did not come back any more.' I had to begin to live again, to turn away from self, to hear words more severe than my mother's; furthermore, her words, so continually gentle hitherto, were no longer the same, but were imprinted with the severity of life and of the duty which she had to teach me."

"Then I was wholly cured": these words, written at twenty-three, are a significant admission. Of the reality of his distress, then and in later attacks, there can be no question, as any sufferer from asthma could testify. But it is also clear that the conditions were ideal for the development of neuroticism: fear, justified by the evident alarm of his parents, aggravating the symptoms, the extreme nervousness and suggestibility of the sufferer, his dependence on his mother, his realization that a reappearance of the symptoms would result in the resumption of his mother's close attendance, the rationalized pleasures of his state.

As he gradually resumed contact with the outside world, it was natural that his viewpoint should have changed. He liked to be taken by his governess—he was then twelve years old—to the Champs Elysées to play. His anticipations were always of the keenest. He would scan the sky if the weather was uncertain, and hope that the sun, not yet the enemy of his health, would emerge in time to make the excursion possible. When all went well, he seemed to be enjoying his play with the boys, and the group games with the girls—which he preferred—and the opportunities he had for showing elaborate attentions to elderly ladies. And yet the result was a disappointment. All that he really achieved was a new stock of memories, which, glorified in revery, served as a basis for new and unattainable anticipations.

One of the chief attractions of the Champs Elysées was a girl, three years his senior, by the name of Benardahy. When she was there, she would appropriate him. "Let's start to play right away," she would say, "you're on my side." But she was often absent, kept away by classes, errands with her mother, parties, a matinée—a whole life from which Marcel, because he had not met her parents, was excluded. The glamour of this unknown existence, the heightened value which her occasional presence at the games acquired from her frequent absence, idealized memories—all this had the inevitable result: Marcel fell in love for the first time. Her parents became wondrous beings to him. The delight of hearing her family name pronounced by another led him into conversational ruses that baffled his parents.

Proust never forgot young Mademoiselle Benardahy. Long afterwards he referred to her in a letter as "the great love of my youth, for whom I wanted to kill myself." He also, at a time when he better understood the peculiarities of his temperament, confessed to a desire to meet her brother, but he, unfortunately for Proust's curiosity, was killed in the war.

A little sketch in *Les Plaisirs et les Jours* is based on this incident of Proust's first love. For the ten-year-old hero of this sketch, his divinity is a disappointment. When for days and weeks he has not seen her, and has built his memories of her into an impossible perfection, and when at last she returns, he is in despair:

she is not the person his imagination has created. He attempts suicide by throwing himself from a window, but succeeds only in turning himself into an idiot. His friend, with exemplary devotion and in spite of the fact that the boy no longer recognizes her, marries him. In real life Mademoiselle Benardahy married Prince Radziwill, and Proust, retaining both life and sanity, lost track of her. But she became—minus the physical love-making and subsequent elaborations—the Gilberte Swann of his novel.

In a sense this lesson in the disappointments of experience brings Proust's childhood to a close, for by now he was sufficiently recovered to enter the lowest class in the Lycée Condorcet and to continue in school—at first with frequent absences—until he passed his baccalaureate in 1889. The spring pilgrimages to Illiers were gradually replaced by visits to Auteuil, less irritating to asthma. But the summer following his first year at Condorcet was spent at Illiers.

The coddled boy just entering the great public school was naïve and vulnerable. The sickroom had been a hothouse for his affectionate and caressing nature, and he cultivated impossible ideals of loyal and devoted friendship, together with misty aspirations toward the Good and the Beautiful. When he was fourteen, some friend asked him to write in a souvenir album the answers to several personal questions. The resulting self-portrait, even with due allowance made for pose, is characteristic and convincing. His favorite qualities in men, he recorded, were intelligence and the moral sense; in women, naturalness, gentleness, intelligence (actually the latter word is written *sentilligence,* as if he had started to write *sensibilité* and had changed to *intelligence.*) His favorite occupations were reading, revery, the study of history, the theatre; his idea of happiness was to live near those he loved, with the charm of nature, a quantity of books and musical scores, and not far from a theatre; he would like to live in the country of the ideal, "or rather," he added conscientiously, "of my ideal." His tastes in literature, music, and art were not yet developed: among prose writers his preference went to George Sand (from whose country idylls his mother used to read to him when he could not sleep) and Augustin-Thierry; Musset was his favorite poet, Meissonier his favorite painter, and Mozart and Gounod his favorite composers. His pet aversion, he stated, was "people who do not feel what is fitting [*ce qui est bien*], who do not know the sweetness of affection."

Unfortunately there seemed to be a good many of his schoolmates who did not know "the sweetness of affection," for in his schooldays and for several years after—until, indeed, he lost faith entirely in friendship—he had continual difficulties in fixing upon a worthy recipient for his demonstrative and exacting devotion. "Tell me about D. H. [Daniel Halévy]," he wrote to Robert Dreyfus, ". . . what does he want? Why, after having been on the whole very nice [*gentil*] to me, does he drop me entirely, making me feel it very clearly, and then after a month come and say *'bonjour,'* when he is no longer speaking to me? And his cousin Bizet? Why does he say he is my friend, why does he drop me even more completely? What do they want with me? To get rid of me, annoy me, mystify me, or what? I thought they were so nice!"

The fact was that his fellow students mistrusted him on account of his effusiveness and his excessive desire to please. To abound in compliments and apologies came to be known at Condorcet as "to Proustify." He was hurt, but he came to understand what his critics meant. Before the end of his course, he was able to write of himself, in the third person: "I will confess to you that he displeases me a little, with his great bursts of enthusiasm, his busy air, his grand passions, and his adjectives. Above all, he seems to me quite mad or very insincere."

Already his power of detached self-analysis was remarkable. In a letter written at the age of seventeen he tried to analyze the always difficult problem of his relation to his fellow students, and found that his explanation of their behavior depended on which of the different "Gentlemen" of whom he was composed was in the ascendant. The romantic Gentleman was always inclined to find a charitable explanation for cold or mysterious attitudes. The suspicious Gentleman was more inclined to take an unfavorable view, but professed not to care very much one way or the other—except as a psychological problem. One is reminded of Proust's claim in *Du Côté de chez Swann* that as a child he learned "to distinguish between those states that succeed each other in me, at certain periods, to the point of dividing each day between them, one coming to drive out the other with the regularity of a fever; contiguous, yet so foreign to each other, so devoid of means of intercommunication, that I can no longer understand, or even imagine, in one, what I desired, or feared, or accomplished in the other."

But the point of view of the seventeen-year-old was neither that of the romantic Gentleman nor that of the suspicious Gentleman, but of a personality superior to both, the observer, the person he became when he sat down in his room alone. So far as he learned to accord permanence to any of his selves, it was to this one. "As for the pleasure [of being introduced to Albertine]," he remarks at one point in his novel, "I did not experience it naturally until a little later, when, back at the hotel, and alone, I had become myself again."

Whether or not the youth was aware of the observer whose viewpoint he adopted when he was alone, it is clear that he had been absorbing the theories of Taine and the psycho-physiologists on the self as a mere sum of successive states. Those were gloomy days in the philosophy class of the schools. Alphonse Daudet, observing his son Léon, Proust's contemporary, wrote in his notebook: "Note: the sadness, the fright of my big boy who has just entered his year of philosophy and has read the books of Schopenhauer, of Hartmann, Stuart Mill, Spencer. Terror and disgust with living; the doctrine is dead, the professor without hope, conversations in the yard despairing. The uselessness of everything appears to these youngsters and consumes them. . . .

Is it a good thing to initiate them so suddenly? Would it not be better to continue to lie, to let life do the disillusioning?"

The atmosphere at the Lycée Condorcet was less grim than at such Left Bank institutions as Louis-le-Grand, Saint-Louis, and Henri IV, especially for day scholars like Proust. True, the more serious-minded of these boys would come to school early and engage in earnest discussions of what they had been reading. But the discipline was mild, and literature was emphasized. One of Proust's teachers, Maxime Gaucher, even encouraged him in a distinctly unacademc style of writing. "I can still see," writes Pierre Lavallée, "and hear Marcel reading his themes aloud, and the excellent, the charming M. Gaucher commenting, praising, criticizing, then suddenly seized with uncontrollable laughter at the audacities of style which, in the bottom of his heart, delighted him."

Marcel's literary tastes were developing, and his preference went increasingly to more daring and more modern writers than Musset and George Sand. "What we have in common with several others," he wrote complacently to one correspondent, "is that we know something about the literature of today and that we love it, that we have other ways of understanding art, and that we judge translations of writers by rather different rules."

The "literature of today" that he loved was not naturalism, for which he had no stomach, but Baudelaire, Mallarmé, Henri de Régnier, and a little later Maeterlinck; among translations he liked Tolstoi and George Eliot.

In spite of his somewhat irregular attendance on classes and his precarious health, Proust on the whole did well at the Lycée Condorcet, and collected a respectable number of firsts and seconds. In addition to French composition, in which he always did well, and Latin and Greek, in which he had seconds, he had a liking for natural history, and for political history, particularly that of the age of Louis XIV, with Jallifier. But the teacher who left the deepest mark upon him was Darlu, mentioned in the dedication of *Les Plaisirs et les Jours* as having "engendered his thinking." With him he head Plato, and from him acquired a passing taste for conducting discussions in the Socratic manner.

When he passed his baccalaureate examination in 1889, he was a much more alert and sophisticated youth than the dreamy boy of six years before. He was about to enter upon the most active period of his life.

~~☙ 3 ❧~~

ACTIVITY

IN NOVEMBER of 1889, the last year in which it was still possible to accomplish military service on the volunteer system, he enlisted in the 76th infantry regiment at Orléans. It was a momentous step for one of his delicate health, but his year's service passed pleasantly and successfully. Colonel Arvers, a friend of the family, was indulgent to his frail recruit, sparing him, so far as possible, difficult and tiring tasks. Proust found the life of the regiment beneficial to his health; he discovered that fatigue makes sleep easy to attain. And the simplicity of the life and of some of his comrades was a pleasant change. The bodies of these peasants, he noted, "had remained more handsome, their minds more original, their hearts more spontaneous, their characters more natural than in the case of the young men with whom I had associated before and was to associate afterwards."

But military duties and rustic simplicity did not entirely fill his days, for on weekends and occasional evenings he managed to indulge his taste for social affairs. Even before leaving Condorcet he was showing a fondness for fashionable life that seemed to his literary friends unworthy of a genius. Yet it was his schoolmates themselves who got him started. Jacques Bizet introduced him to his mother, Madame Emile Straus, widow of the composer of *Carmen,* and daughter of Halévy, the composer of *La Juive;* and through the cousins Jacques and Paul Baignères he was received in the salons of their mothers, and was promptly taken up by these energetic bourgeois hostesses. His early conviction that he was a "hopeless little imbecile" yielded to the recognition that under the stimulus of social occasions he could talk volubly and wittily, tempering the sharpness of his tongue with the gentleness of his manner. He is pictured in the salon of Madame Straus, sitting on a hassock at her feet and looking up at her with large, soulful eyes, or moving about among her guests with his gallant and insinuating manner, at once flattering and ceremonious. In no time at all he had conquered the affectionate indulgence of at least the feminine side of society.

In one house he met those who would invite him to another, and so his reputation spread. He was to be seen at the British Embassy of Lord Lytton, at a formal ball of the Princesse de Wagram, in the salon of the Bonapartist Princesse Mathilde. He followed the circle of Madame Arthur Baignères to her seashore home "Les Frémonts" at Trouville, that of the painter Madeleine Lemaire to her castle "Réveillon," in the department of the Marne. He wore a frock coat, loosely knotted water-green ties, a top hat, pearl-gray gloves with black stripes, an orchid in his buttonhole, and carried a bamboo cane. No doubt what he called his "alert and frivolous self" was pleased by his popularity, and flattered at being admitted so easily to such high strata of society. But he dreaded causing pain or envy, and when, in the spring while the family was at Auteuil, he went after school to the Gare Saint-Lazare with other out-of-town students, he would try to conceal that he bought a first-class ticket, and he took good care not to let those who thought him without "connections" know that he was well known in circles to which they never aspired.

At Orléans he was received in the salon of the prefect of the department, and there met Robert de Billy, who was to be his lifelong friend, and who, raised a strict Protestant and a young man of firm ideas, later testified, "I owe in large part to Marcel Proust the joy of thinking otherwise than by principles." It was on a week-end leave from military service that he met Madame Arman (later Arman de Caillavet), in whose Paris salon he was presented to the reigning lion, Anatole France, and where he also met her son Gaston. With the latter he established a lasting friendship, only briefly marred by the jealousy he aroused by attentions to Jeanne Pouquet, who later became Gaston's wife. But Gaston used faithfully to drive him, those Sunday evenings, to the station in time for the 7:40 to Orléans.

The years immediately following Proust's release from military service were busy, social, and, by comparison with later years, full of movement. He visited Holland and Belgium, traveling in Holland by canal boat and seeing Dordrecht, Vollendam, and Delft. He also went to the Hague, where he saw Vermeer's "View of Delft," from then on his favorite painting. In the summer of 1893 he spent three weeks at St. Moritz, and a week on Lake Geneva, at Thonon and Evian. There was a trip to Germany with his mother, primarily to Kreuznach to take the waters, but probably also including Mainz and Münster; a tour of Normandy and Brittany in the fall of 1895; and numerous small trips—to Versailles, to Saint-Germain, to the farm of his friend Lavallée at Segrez, to Trouville, to Dieppe.

Meanwhile his connections were steadily mounting in the social scale. Artistic and literary salons led to the diplomatic circle and the Napoleonic aristocracy; in the studio of the painter Madeleine Lemaire—artistic, too, but heavily attended by the old aristocracy—he began to meet the older families. He was now received by the Comtesse Potocka, the Comtesse d'Haussonville, the Comtesse de Guerne, the Princesse Edmond de Polignac (*née* Singer, an American heiress). At Thonon he met the Princesse de Brancovan, whose daughters, later respectively the Comtesse de Noailles and the Princesse de Caraman-Chimay, became his fast friends.

Proust's long acquaintance with Count Robert de Montesquiou-Fezensac began at the studio of Madame Lemaire, in April 1893. The connection has considerable importance. For one thing, the Count was in a position to further Proust's social ambitions, and did so. Said to be a descendant of the d'Artagnan of the *Three Musketeers,* Montesquiou was fantastically vain of his ancient lineage, had the *entrée* of all the most exclusive circles, and enjoyed dispensing a severe and discriminating patronage. For another thing, he had literary and artistic pretensions in the decadent manner, and he exerted an enduring influence on some aspects of Proust's style. He was reputed to be the original Des Esseintes of *A Rebours,* an imputation which he indignantly denied, but which was widely credited because it was so reasonable. He was a dandy, an exquisite, an artist in perfumes, colors, sensations, and the giving of elaborate fêtes, and he collected portraits of himself. Recently he had decided to descend into the marketplace and reveal himself as the greatest poet of the age, and as a step in this direction had published two volumes of verse, *Les Chauves-souris* and *Le Chef des odeurs suaves.* His bid for recognition as a great poet was prolonged until his death in 1921, and at the end was farther from success than at the beginning, for, in so far as he is remembered at all, outside of his connection with Proust, it is as the poet of *Les Chauves-souris.*

Finally, Montesquiou is considered, with much justice, to be the original of some aspects of Proust's Baron de Charlus.

The friendship—if the word can be applied to a relationship based on condescension on one side and humility on the other—began with a reading at the Lemaire studio of verses by Montesquiou. The author noticed Proust, granted him permission to call. Proust did so, and shortly after received a copy of *Les Chauves-souris.* At once his difficulties with the exacting Count began. Flattered and pleased, confused at not being able to use his favorite adjective *gentil,* proscribed by Montesquiou, he wrote a hasty acknowledgment, then, with a characteristic afterthought, and feeling that he had said too much about the Count's card and not enough about the verses, he wrote again, and sent flowers. "Believe," he said, "that I feel how unequal is the exchange and how much more beautiful and real are your flowers. Never did vain garden flowers smell so sweet. What they tell us confusedly, and what we understand so badly, you say with divine clarity but without dissipating any of their delicious mystery. Your soul is a garden, rare and choice like the one in which you permitted me to walk the other day." Montesquiou, apparently satisfied, sent him *Le Chef des odeurs suaves,* and Proust replied, "I am too much moved to compare this book to *Les Chauves-souris.* . . . Your verses are that mysterious honey whose combs have the sweetness of heaven. I could thank you endlessly if I thanked you to the extent of my happiness. But in closing I must thank you for the lofty words you caused me to hear yesterday, and which still ring for me in the rich music of your voice. Know that you have in me a frank, tender, respectful, and true admirer. Marcel Proust. I wait impatiently for your photograph. . . ."

So the tone of the relationship was set: from Proust incense, from Montesquiou patronage, interspersed with sharp criticism. It is hard to read Proust's adulation without impatience. He was already a sufficiently clear-sighted critic, capable of writing a not over-indulgent review of a book whose author he did not personally know. Was he dazzled by Montesquiou's name and social position? Was he cultivating him to further his own aspirations? One is tempted to think so from certain of the letters. In one of these he wrote, ". . . since two of your friends, Mme Lemaire and the Princesse de Wagram, have done me the honor to invite me this week, will you be so kind as to bring me, Thursday or Saturday, to the Rue de Monceau or the Avenue de l'Alma, that photograph, promised, but impossible to get. I shall also ask you (if they are present at one or the other of those affairs) to have the kindness to point out to me some of those friends among whom you are most often mentioned (Comtesse Greffulhe, the Princesse de Léon). . . ."

The Comtesse Greffuhle, one of Montesquiou's favorite relatives, to whom he was particularly grateful for her share in bringing him out of the tubercular delicacy of his childhood, was greatly admired for her beauty and distinction, and her salon was noted for its exclusiveness. Proust did see her, probably at one of the affairs to which he referred in his letter, wrote effusively to

Montesquiou of his impressions, asked him to let her know of his admiration, and in a subsequent letter inquired whether his commission had been fulfilled. Later he met her, and was received in her salon.

But it would be a mistake to assume too readily that Proust was trying, cynically and exclusively, to further his own ends. Flattery was his natural medium; knowing that Montesquiou demanded it, he was glad to oblige. Furthermore, throughout his career, he was incapable of writing or speaking of the work of a friend without the most extravagant and often ill-founded praise, and this quite independently of any possible advantage to himself. For him, the writing of serious literature was one thing, and the ordinary commerce of friendship quite another. In literature he was uncompromising, but when it came to letters, or dedications, or the mention of a friend in a newspaper article, his sense of social obligation came to the fore, and he acquitted himself of it in his own way, just as he sent masses of flowers at the slightest pretext. "Flattery," he wrote in a piece published in 1893, "is often only the overflow of tenderness, and frankness the frothings of ill-temper." Perhaps he was rationalizing, for he was well aware that people mistrusted his compliments, and called him behind his back "a half-hysterical flatterer"; but there was a grain of truth in his remark. Proust gave, as he demanded, affection, and nothing distressed him more than to suspect that he had caused pain.

But this heaping up of praise became an irksome precedent. "All these bows in the vestibule," he wrote in 1905, "which we call deference, gratitude, devotion, and with which we mix so many lies, are sterile and wearying." They became a tissue of habits, or "like promissory notes which we must pay, or which we pay more dearly still for the rest of our lives if we refuse to honor them." In writing these words Proust may well have been thinking back over his long and difficult relationship with Montesquiou, for at the time the Count was showing himself particularly touchy, and Proust was complaining of him to Madame Straus.

The causes of disagreement between patron and admirer were many, and for the most part trivial: questions of deference and precedence, the censoring of lists of guests at entertainments which the Count was to grace with his presence, repetition by Proust of Montesquiou's sayings—the Count called him "the traveling salesman of my wit"—or, still worse, rumors reaching Montesquiou that Proust had exercised his talent for mimicry at his expense. One serious quarrel, the earliest, calls for more detailed mention.

In February 1894, Proust wrote for permission to present a handsome young pianist and composer, Léon Delafosse, and Montesquiou, always interested in handsome and talented young men, acceded to the request. He was charmed by the young man, dubbed him "the Angel," and invited him frequently to his home in Versailles to play and sing. Gabriel d'Yturri, the capable, devoted—and of course handsome—secretary of Montesquiou, arranged a special musical entertainment around Delafosse on March 16, and Proust was present. A few days later he sent the Count a present by Delafosse, writing, ". . . as I have only one criterion of certitude with you—having only once caused you pleasure, by bringing "the Angel"—I take the liberty of offering you the humble and mute symbol of him, in the likeness of what they called in the eighteenth century an angel of the Manger. Mute? For one who can hear him he probably sings like our little musician, with the same spiritual voice. The break in the body leaves to the imagination the absent frock coat, which uncovers, by its disappearance, the wings. The little nose is not in very good condition. But if intact, I fear it would not have all the dry expressiveness, the passionate thinness, the eloquent concision of the nose of our little musician."

The Count pointedly avoided any reference to the gift, and Proust wrote anxiously to discover what was amiss. His fears were only too well founded; both the gift and the manner of giving had seriously offended the Count. With somewhat more dignity than usual, Proust replied that he abandoned any further attempts at self-justification, "convinced that we cannot, at a certain depth, understand one another, and not, furthermore, taking this too seriously."

The chief importance of the incident is that parallels have been drawn between the Montesquiou-Delafosse relationship and that of Charlus and Morel in Proust's novel, and it is quite possible that Proust, as was his wont, took a real incident or character as the point of departure for a much larger fictional development. But Montesquiou should not be too hastily and too largely identified with Charlus. According to Proust himself—and those in a position to know confirm him—the physical appearance, the mincing gait, and the makeup of Charlus were suggested by Baron Doasan, a cousin of Madame Aubernon, a frequenter of her salon, and a notorious homosexual. Proust too was an intimate of this famous salon, with its firmly controlled topics of conversation, its ritual, its migrations of the "faithful," and from it, no doubt, took some aspects for the "little clan" of the Verdurins in his novel. But Montesquiou also, though in a less offensive degree, had a reputation for inversion, of which Proust, despite his denials, could not have been unaware. According to gossip repeated by Proust's painter friend Blanche, also an intimate of the Aubernon salon, Doasan and Montesquiou were at swords' points since Montesquiou had "stolen" from the Baron the handsome Gabriel d'Yturri. However this may be, it is probable that the maniacal family pride, the religious ideas, the touchiness, and the vocal peculiarities of Charlus owe something to Montesquiou.

Proust's relations with Montesquiou continued, after the incident of the Angel, much as before. He attended one of the Count's fêtes in May, and wrote it up, anonymously, for the society column of *Le Gaulois*. He continued to accept patronage and to burn incense, and the fulsome note returned to his letters.

Whenever Montesquiou published some verses in a review, Proust was ready with a letter of eulogy; and in return for the hospitality he received, he entertained the Count at his home, or elsewhere, taking care to invite only those whom the Count might approve.

To follow the complex ramifications of Proust's social life would require volumes and would add little to our knowledge of his essential character. But since he has been accused of snobbishness, something should be said of his attitude toward his social life.

As clearly appears in his novel and other writings, Proust was always peculiarly fascinated by names, whether of places or of persons. Experience taught him the disparity between the preconceived image and the reality. Places were invariably different from what he had imagined, but people, though different, continued to suggest their past, particularly if it had resounded in history. Princesse Bibesco writes of his interest in the name of a Bauffremont, a young woman connection of hers: "He immediately indicated his desire to meet this young woman, thanks to whom he could see reflected the spires of Scey-sur-Saône and, in the distance, the masts of frigates commanded by a grand admiral of France." And to Antoine Bibesco he wrote, "Just imagine, I have learned that one of your friends with whom you had invited me to dinner . . . M. Cosmo Gordon Lennox, is a descendant of the Duke of Richmond whose portrait by Van Dyck . . . was the object of one of my great admirations of former times, and the subject of verses in *Les Plaisirs et les Jours*. All this makes M. Gordon Lennox very interesting to me." As Princesse Bibesco points out, an "old" family is one whose history is known; a commoner, with exactly as many ancestors as an aristocrat, less readily gives rise to that imaginative conjunction with the history and art of the past that was so stimulating to Proust. Yet when the lower orders did make contact with art, as in the sculpture and stained glass of cathedrals, Proust hailed with enthusiasm the "great silent democracy" of "coopers, furriers, grocers, pilgrims, plowmen, armorers, weavers, stone carvers, butchers, basket makers, cobblers, money changers."

Also fascinating to Proust was the persistence of physical characteristics in a family with portraits and a known history. It was his esthetic imagination that was more involved than his heart in his adoration, shortly after his return from military service, of the handsome Comtesse Adhéaume de Chevigné, whose husband was descended from a noble vassal of Blanche of Castille and who was of ancient lineage herself. His description of her, suggestive of the later portrait of the Duchesse de Guermantes at the Opera, first appeared in 1892:

. . . her laugh impresses me infinitely, and the purest profiles leave me unmoved when compared with the line of her nose, too aquiline in your opinion, to me so moving and suggestive of a bird. Her head also is a little like that of a bird, still more her piercing gentle eyes. Often, at the theatre, she leans on the rail of her box; her white-gloved arm stands out straight to the chin, which is supported on her fingers. Her perfect body fills her dress, whose customary white gauze is like folded wings. One thinks of a bird in revery on a slender and elegant foot. It is charming also to see her plumed fan palpitate near her and beat its white wing. I have never been able to see her sons or her nephews, who all, like her, have aquiline noses, thin lips, piercing eyes, and too delicate skin, without feeling emotion at recognizing her race, sprung, doubtless, from a goddess and a bird.

Like the Marcel of *Le Côté de Guermantes* he used to watch for her to leave her house, plan to meet her "accidentally" on the street. And as the fictional Marcel tried to obtain an introduction to the Duchesse de Guermantes through her nephew Saint-Loup, so Proust cultivated the nephew of the Comtesse de Chevigné; and, as in the novel, Proust finally met, was received by, and entertained his idol—when it was no longer of importance to him.

Proust was also much interested in studying the mechanism of social etiquette: posture, bows, entrances and exits, invitations, the phenomena of exclusion from and aspiration to a select salon. And if, as is probable, his vanity was flattered at his successful penetration of exclusive circles, his complacency was short-lived. Late in his life he asserted that he had broken with aristocratic society at the age of twenty, but he is not to be taken too literally. The period of his greatest society fever appears to have been 1893-94, when he was twenty-two, and although it is true that he was thereafter progressively less assiduous in social affairs, he maintained to the end of his life friendly relations with a large number of aristocrats, entertained and was entertained by them, and occasionally put in brief appearances at receptions just as others were leaving. But it may well be true that by twenty he had ceased to attach much importance to the social events at which he continued to present himself.

Outside of the fashionable drawing rooms the young Proust was still hunting for the perfect friend. Several seemed briefly to qualify, but the higher his hopes the surer his disappointment. Robert de Billy, met at Orléans, was a good friend to him, as many a letter shows, but his diplomatic career kept him away from France too often and too long. Not without coquetry Proust wrote to Billy: "At last I have found the friend of my dreams, tender and a letter writer. It is true that he puts only one stamp on his letters and every time I have to pay thirty centimes at the post office. But what wouldn't one do when one loves?" The next summer he boasted, to the same correspondent: "I received by the same mail as yours a letter from Horace [Finaly?], one from La Salle, one from Gaston Arman, one from his mother, one from Jean Lazard, one from Robert de Flers, one from his grandfather." The following year he wrote: "You wouldn't believe how much I miss you. My frivolity, which often brings me back to the present, the existing, has not here hurt my friendship for you. And I think all the more despairingly of you in that I cannot see you, that your charm no longer perfumes my daily life, that your gayety or your wisdom no longer console me in my troubles, that your advice no longer directs me toward the true and the good." And again, "There is nothing very much changed in my sentimental life, except that I have found a friend, I mean one who is to me what I would have been to X . . . , for example, if he had not been so dry in heart. He is the young, and charming, and intelligent, and kind, and tender Robert de Flers."

Two of the closest friends of his youth died, the young Swiss Edgar Aubert, in September 1892, and Willie Heath, the English boy, a year later. He planned to dedicate his first book to the memory of both friends, but having failed to come to an understanding with the parents of Aubert, he dedicated it to Heath alone, writing, "We dreamed then, we almost planned, to live more and more with each other, in a choice group of high-minded women and men, far enough from stupidity, vice, and ill will to feel ourselves safe from their vulgar arrows."

Reynaldo Hahn, the brilliant young composer, three years his junior, was another of his intimate friends; so too were Léon and Lucien Daudet, sons of Alphonse Daudet, whose Thursdays in the Rue de Bellechasse he used frequently to attend, sometimes in the company of Hahn.

One of his sketches of 1893, entitled *Amitié,* is characteristic:

It is sweet when one is unhappy to get into the warmth of one's bed, and there, all effort and all resistance gone, with one's head under the blankets, to surrender utterly to moans like those of a tree in the autumn wind. But there is a better bed, filled with divine odors. It is our sweet, our profound, our impenetrable friendship. There I lay my shivering heart when it is sad and icy. Burying even my thought in our warm tenderness, seeing nothing outside, with no further desire for self-defense, disarmed, but by the miracle of our tenderness at once fortified and invincible, I weep from my sorrow, and from the joy of having a trust that will contain it.

With such passionate demands and expectations, it is small wonder that he should have lost faith in friendship, to the point of writing, many years later, to his intimate, Lucien Daudet: ". . . don't go supposing that there is any reproach or recrimination on my part, you have always been more than good to me. But then I believed in friendship; today you will see what I say of it in *Swann,* and that it no longer exists for me; and I don't say that any particular person is the cause, it would be too long to explain."

Of his sentimental attachments to the opposite sex, there is little to record. While still a schoolboy, he fulfilled the obligations of elegance by flaunting an interest in light loves. To Dreyfus he wrote nonchalantly of a "platonic passion" for a celebrated courtesan—perhaps Closmesnil—followed by "a not very complicated intrigue" with a young and pretty Viennese, and finally of an "absorbing liaison . . . which threatens to last for a year at least, to the greater profit of *cafés-concerts* and places of the same kind where one takes this kind of person."

A more important contact of this nature began about 1891, with Laure Hayman, who at that date was forty years old. This beautiful Creole, a descendant of the painter Francis Hayman, and with English, Belgian, and French blood in her veins, was born on a hacienda in the Andes. After losing her father, an engineer, at an early age, and after enduring poverty, which her mother tried to lighten by giving piano lessons, Laure made a truce with necessity, capitalized on her beauty and charm, and became well known in many cities of Europe. Some time after Proust made her acquaintance, she went into partial seclusion, took up sculpture, and achieved some success in the art. She was the original of Bourget's pastel "Gladys Harvey" and apparently admitted the identification, for she was referred to by this name among her men friends, and she sent Proust a copy of the story bound in the silk of one of her petticoats. It was she who introduced him to Paul Bourget.

She had been the good friend of Proust's great-uncle Louis Weil; apparently the attachment caused some feeling in the family, for when, in 1896, Proust wrote to inform her of his uncle's death, she replied that she would like to go to the funeral, but feared that her presence might be shocking to some. Proust assured her that she would shock no one, adding, however, that he feared it would be tiring for her and that few women would be going. Laure Hayman took the hint. She did send a wreath of flowers which, although floral offerings had been ruled out at the funeral, was laid, at the special intervention of Madame Proust, as the solitary tribute on the grave of Louis Weil.

Parallels between these incidents and those concerning Uncle Adolphe and "the lady in pink" (Odette) in *Swann* and *Guermantes* suggest themselves; another link between Odette de Crécy and Laure Hayman, through the admittedly authentic portrait of Gladys Harvey, is the taste for Anglicisms and the interlarding of French conversations with bits of English, an affectation common to both fictional characters. The parallels were striking enough to call forth protests from Laure Hayman, after the publication of *Swann,* and Proust replied, as was his wont in such cases, by a blanket denial. "Odette de Crécy not only is not you, but is exactly the opposite of you"; he went on to cite Closmesnil as one who had contributed something to the character and appearance of Odette.

Laure Hayman took an affectionate interest in the nephew of Louis Weil. She collected Saxe porcelain, and Proust liked to discourse on psychology, with the result that she called him "mon petit saxe psychologique." What was apparently his first letter to her is so characteristic and revealing that it is worth quoting:

Dear friend, dear delights,
Here are fifteen chrysanthemums, twelve for your twelve when they are withered, three to complete your twelve; I hope the stems will be excessively long, as I specified. And [I hope] that these flowers, proud and sad like you, proud to be beautiful, sad that everything is so stupid—will please you.—I thank you again (and if I didn't have my examination tomorrow, Saturday, I would have gone to tell you so) for your nice [*gentille*] thought for me. It would have been so diverting to go to that eighteenth-century fête, to see those young men whom you call witty and charming, united in the love of you. How well I understand them! That a woman who is

merely desirable, merely an object of greed, should be able to cause only divisions among her adorers, exasperate them against each other, is very natural. But when a woman, like a work of art, reveals what is most refined in charm, most subtle in grace, most divine in beauty, most voluptuous in intelligence, a common admiration unites [her admirers], makes brothers of them. They are co-religionists in Laure Hayman. And as this divinity is very particular, as her charm is not accessible to everyone, as, to appreciate it, one must have rather refined tastes, as it were an initiation in sentiment and wit, it is right that there should be an affection among the faithful, comprehension among the initiates. Also your shelves of Saxe (almost an altar!) seem to me one of the most charming things one could see, and one which must rarely have existed since Cleopatra and Aspasia. So I propose to call this century the century of Laure Hayman, reigning dynasty, that of the Saxe.—Will you pardon all these follies and will you permit me after my examination to go and carry you

My tender respects.

Apparently Laure Hayman felt some responsibility for her youthful admirer, and took him to task occasionally, for in another letter he wrote, "Fair sweet and cruel friend, You made me listen to some harsh truths yesterday. They are very dear to me because they are friendly and come from you"; he closed, "I cast myself at your feet for absolution, and embrace you tenderly and absent-mindedly."

In character, attainments, and social position, Madame Straus was a very different person from Laure Hayman, but the friendships of the two women for Proust have points of resemblance. Like Laure Hayman, Madame Straus used to take Proust to task, for reasons that are evident from the correspondence: for inattention to his studies, for his flowers and gifts, for his audacities of language and behavior. In November 1890, he wrote, "I am all the happier at your letter in that I thought you were angry with me. I don't know why. Don't scold me for my chrysanthemums and for my friendship. They are melancholy enough things without that and besides are of too little value for your attention." And in March 1891, "I am unlucky, in the one time that I break my resolution and come. My excuse was that, having left to work, I had seen on the way these lilac branches, and that I was anxious to bring them. It was my excuse, and I cannot tell it to you! But believe that I fully recognize its weakness."

The special character of Proust himself was the common denominator in his friendships. With all he was at first flattering and ceremonious. As intimacy advanced, the flattery remained, but the ceremony yielded gradually to affectionateness, varied by jealousy and extreme sensitivity to affronts, usually imaginary. To these characteristics, common to all his friendships, was added, in the case of women, an audacity of language which shocked and charmed them. Here, for example, is one of his notes to Madame Straus, who was the mother of one of his schoolmates, and who might, for age, have been his own:

My dear little Madame Straus,
You must not think I love you less because I no longer send you flowers. But Mlle Lemaire can tell you that I drive every morning with Laure Hayman, that I often take her afterwards to lunch— which costs me so much that I haven't another *sou* for flowers—and except for ten *sous'* worth of poppies for Mme Lemaire I don't think I have sent any since I did to you. You were in bed, beautiful as an ailing angel, that is, fit to turn mortals mad. And not having dared, for fearing of giving you a headache, do it really, I here, and fictionally, kiss you tenderly.
Your little

Marcel.

In another letter he wrote: "But you haven't sufficiently absorbed this truth (I think you haven't absorbed any truth!) that *one must make great allowances* for Platonic love. A person who is not sentimental at all becomes strangely so if he is reduced to Platonic love. As I want to follow your pretty precepts against bad taste, I will not go into details. Be a little indulgent to the keenest Platonic love, by which is attached to you, deign to believe and permit it, your respectfully devoted, Marcel Proust."

As has appeared from passages in the letters quoted, not all of Proust's time in the years immediately following his military service was taken up with social and sentimental matters. The family was wealthy, and it was not, economically speaking, indispensable that Marcel should earn his living; but neither of the parents was of the sort to admit that wealth relieved one from the obligation to do useful work. From his schooldays Marcel had wanted to be a writer; his father felt, as fathers in such cases are apt to feel, that only extraordinary talents justified the pursuit of literature as a sole profession, and that ordinarily writing should be backed up by some more solidly established career. In this judgment Marcel somewhat reluctantly concurred; meanwhile, the burden of proof rested on him.

From 1891 to 1893 he studied simultaneously in the Ecole des Sciences Politiques and the Ecole de Droit, possibly also at the Faculté des Lettres; he also took private lessons. His efforts were directed somewhat vaguely toward a diplomatic career, or some branch of the law. He listened with serious attention to Albert Sorel and Leroy-Beaulieu in the Ecole des Sciences Politiques, and took part in the meetings of the mock Chamber of Deputies, organized and run by André Lebon for students of the school. But his efforts and his interest were irregular; sometimes, in his correspondence, he reproached himself for laziness, and at others protested, too much, that he was working hard. Early in 1893 he wrote to Billy, who was already launched on his diplomatic career and was in Berlin, "Give me, if you will be so kind, the list of the four examinations I have to take and of the books I must read; I've lost it!" Shortly after, he wrote to the same correspondent: "I scarcely dare write you. I am not worthy of it, I'm not doing anything and fortunately Paul Baignères, by having me pose for a portrait, is now furnishing a pretext for my inaction. Otherwise, remorse for my sluggishness would have devoured me." But the summer before he had written to Madame Straus, "I am a hard worker. . . . And the virtues of work and concentration to which I lay claim, because you esteem them, it is not very bad, perhaps, to boast of having, because they imply great difficulty in understanding and in getting to the bottom of things."

The results of his studies, like his interest, were variable. He passed his examinations in the Ecole des Sciences Politiques, but in the summer of 1892 he wrote to Billy, "I have failed the second half of my law, and my family is in the depths." The following academic year he was still studying law, and the year after he was taking lessons of some sort. The question of a career was getting acute; in the fall of 1893 he wrote to Billy:

I am in the greatest difficulty, because I must decide about my career, Papa wishes it. The Cour des Comptes tempts me more and more. This is how I reason. If I don't want to have a career abroad, I would have, at the Ministry of Foreign Affairs, as boring a career as at the Cour des Comptes.

Perhaps the Cour des Comptes is, for me, harder to prepare for, but isn't this amply compensated for by the fact that when this stage, which will occupy all the attention of which I am capable, is over, the rest of the time I shall go and do as I please.

Ah! my dear Robert, more than ever now your advice would be precious, and I suffer much from your absence. . . . Is the magistracy not too badly thought of? What is left, determined as I am to be neither a lawyer [*avocat*], nor a doctor, nor a priest, nor . . ."

Two months later he wrote, "If you are coming to Paris, come quickly, before my career is decided." At about this time, probably, he tried working with an *avoué,* but gave it up after a two weeks' trial; he also thought of buying a notary's practice.

While he was studying and trying to adapt himself to the requirements of what society considered a substantial career, he was taking his first small but successful steps in literature. At Condorcet, and in association with such fellow students as Robert Dreyfus, Daniel Halévy, the Baignères cousins, Louis de la Salle, Robert de Flers, and Gabriel Trarieux, he made contributions to the *Revue Lilas* and other short-lived manuscript reviews founded at the school. His schoolboy productions earned him the respect of his young collaborators, but they feared that either over-subtlety or too much interest in social affairs might prevent substantial achievements by him in literature.

So far as we surely know, Proust first broke into print in *Le Banquet,* whose title was suggested by the French name for Plato's *Symposium,* and which was founded, perhaps in the salon of Madame Straus, in 1892, by a group of former fellow students of Condorcet, and some others: Fernand Gregh (the leading spirit), Proust, La Salle, Jacques Bizet, Daniel Halévy, Robert Dreyfus, Henri Rabaud, Robert de Flers, Gaston Arman, Gabriel Trarieux (by then a symbolist poet), Léon Blum (later the Socialist leader and Prime Minister), Henri Barbusse, Amédée Rouquès. Each of the founders contributed ten francs a month toward expenses of publication; eight numbers appeared, from March 1892 to March 1893. The original plan for an editorial committee gave way, after the second number and by general consent, to the single direction of Fernand Gregh.

Proust's contributions, which began with the first number and continued through the seventh, consisted of two book reviews, two articles, one short story, and a number of short sketches. All but one article were republished either in *Les Plaisirs et les Jours* or in the posthumous *Chroniques.* In "L'Irreligion d'état," the article not republished, he deplored the existence of a godless school, declared that France owed her greatest masterpieces to Christianity, and registered alarm at the progress of socialism.

He contributed a book review to the May 1892 issue of *Littérature et Critique,* and after the suspension of *Le Banquet,* he, like some others of its founders, transferred his contributions to the symbolist *Revue Blanche,* where, from July 1893 to July 1896, he published a series of studies and stories, concluding with an article, "Contre l'obscurité."

These efforts were not in themselves sufficient to justify the choice of literature as a sole profession; but there were other factors pushing him to this decision.

❧ 4 ❧

PROUST IN 1896

THE publication in 1896 of Proust's first book, *Les Plaisirs et les Jours,* marks the end of a stage in his career. It is the culmination of his first effort to justify his pretensions to being a writer. With this book in hand, one can gauge his progress toward his future major work, and one can form, with the aid of information from other sources, a picture of his state of mind in 1896.

As early as November 1893, Proust wrote to Billy of his desire to publish "this year a collection of little things of which you know already the larger part," and to dedicate the book to the memory of his friends Aubert and Heath, adding, "But the mediocrity of the work, the great license of certain parts, the uselessness of a public homage that is always less than the memory unexpressed, had dissuaded me from dedicating the book to them except in the impulse of my heart. But a little event has changed my mind. Madame Lemaire is going to illustrate this little book. So it is going to get into the libraries of writers, artists, people of importance everywhere who would not have known about it otherwise and will keep it only for the illustrations. I should be glad then that all this *élite,* who would have appreciated Edgar and Heath if they had known them, who would have admired them, loved them, should know at least by my humble testimony, by a short preface, who it is that they have lost."

The following July he wrote the preface, addressed to Willie Heath alone; but the book, which was to include most of what he had written to date, was apparently too slim, for he wrote in the summer of 1894 to Lavallée of doing a great deal of writing. He began "La Mort de Baldassare Silvande" at about this time, and published it in the *Revue Hebdomadaire,* in the issue of October 29, 1895, with a dedication to his close friend Reynaldo Hahn. Probably "La Confession d'une jeune fille," and "La Fin de la jalousie" were also written after the preface, but they did not appear in periodicals.

The four short poems on the painters Cuyp, Potter, Watteau, and Van Dyck, written from Proust's schooldays onward and completed by the spring of 1895, were set to music by Reynaldo Hahn, who sang them on May 28 at one of the Tuesdays of Madame Lemaire. Proust, who did not do this sort of thing by halves, issued invitations, imported an accompanist from Chartres, and had the poems, with facsimile of Hahn's manuscript, printed in album form as *Portraits de peintres.* On the day of the concert the *Gaulois* referred in its society column to the "delicate verses" of the "charming poet," and on June 21 published extracts from the album. These "portraits," augmented by four of musicians (Chopin, Gluck, Schumann, and Mozart) appeared in *Les Plaisirs et les Jours,* which was also accompanied by the original album.

To the Lemaire illustrations and the Hahn music was now to be added a third elegant accessory, a short preface extracted, with some difficulty, from Anatole France by Madame Arman de Caillavet. "Why," began France grumblingly, "have I been asked to present this book to curious minds? And why did I promise to undertake this very agreeable but quite useless task?"

The book at last appeared early in June 1896, in tall octavo format, complete with pale green covers, beautiful paper, and supporting artists. As it turned out, Proust's modesty overreached itself, for the make-up of the book, its dependence on sponsors, even its title—*Pleasures and Days,* a parody of Hesiod's *Works and Days*—all suggested the esthetic trifling of a dilettante rather than the serious effort of a young man with a sense of social responsibility. Ironically enough, of the then celebrated Madeleine Lemaire the *Journal des Débats* was later to say that

her fame would rest on having illustrated the first book of
Marcel Proust, and while the music of Reynaldo Hahn and the
writings of Anatole France have been much more durable in
their own right, there is little doubt that in the long run the
unknown youth they befriended outstripped them both.

Les Plaisirs et les Jours was, for the most part, received as
elegant trifling. *Figaro, Le Gaulois,* and *Le Temps* reviewed it
with conventional and empty praise. Proust's old friends of
Le Banquet were definitely unkind, Léon Blum in the *Revue
Blanche* admonishing him to avoid dilettantism, and Fernand
Gregh in the *Revue de Paris* ridiculing him and his dependence
on sponsors. The following year a group of these old friends,
who had taken to gathering in the apartment of Jacques Bizet in
the Ile Saint-Louis, put on a skit which included a little fun
poked at Proust and his expensive book. He was of course much
hurt at the incident, which was only the culmination of a
growing estrangement from his former collaborators.

One critic, Charles Maurras in the *Revue Encyclopédique,*
took Proust and his book seriously, saluting the classic purity of
his style and recommending it as a model to the younger generation. Proust's gratitude for this article was still active in 1919,
when he sent Maurras a copy of his Goncourt prize book, *A
l'Ombre des jeunes filles en fleur,* and in the dedication recalled
how Maurras, among the first, had spoken "delightfully" of the
earlier work.

One can scarcely blame the majority of the critics for not
having seen in *Les Plaisirs et les Jours* the first indications of a
major talent, for even today, and in the current plain edition
of the *Nouvelle Revue Française* there is much to obscure these
indications.

For one thing, a considerable part of the book is clearly imitative. Bits of "Violante" might have been lifted from Voltaire's
Candide. The portraits—of Myrto, Parthémis, Lalagé, Doris,
Cléanthis, Ercole—the pessimistic estimate of human nature
and the insistence upon vanity in motivation, the futility of the

world by comparison with the riches of solitude, the epigrams and the *esprit*—"the paradoxes of today are the prejudices of tomorrow" (p. 183), "ambition is more intoxicating than glory" (p. 185), "his eyes sparkled with stupidity" (p. 164)—all this is unadulterated French classicism, the ideas and the portraits recalling particularly the seventeenth century (which furnished, incidentally, epigraphs from Madame de Sévigné, Guez de Balzac, and Racine), and the concise and pointed language being more suggestive of the eighteenth. Maurras probably had such passages in mind when he praised the young author for his classicism.

The imitativeness extended also to authors of his own day. Two paragraphs of "La Mort de Baldassare Silvande" bear a remarkable likeness to a passage of "L'Ermitage du Jardin des plantes," from *Le Livre de mon ami* of Anatole France. The hands in "Keep upon your knees this cluster of fresh roses and let my heart weep between your closed hands" (p. 218) sound suspiciously like those celebrated by Verlaine in a poem another line of which is quoted a little beyond (p. 250). The unknown guest of "L'Etranger" bears an extraordinary resemblance to the young man dressed in black of Musset's "Nuit de décembre." And many other modern echoes, some immediate, some more remote, might be tracked down.

Another impediment to the appreciation of this book is its curious ambiguity of tone. Anatole France in his preface called Proust "a depraved Bernardin de Saint-Pierre and an ingenuous Petronius," and it is easy to see what he meant. The young author is now idealistic, romantic, naïve, moralistic, and now sophisticated as an old roué. A superficial reader might readily dismiss him as a mere hypocrite.

The styles are as discordant as the tone. That the pieces of classical inspiration should be precise, sententious, and urbane is almost inevitable. It is also natural enough that the more modern subject matter should be tuned to the prevailing key of esthetic prose: a misty emotionalism in which descriptions of nature are seasoned with pretty conceits and inflated with talk of "souls" and "harmonies." But how can the same author, short of being a sort of literary impersonator, write in both styles? What is this young man, a belated classicist, a romantic, or a late nineteenth-century esthete? Two examples will show the contrast:

Honoré drew near to Violante so that she should not be cold, hooked her fur piece around her neck with ingenious slowness, and suggested that he should help her put in practice the theories which he had just taught her in the park. He tried to speak very low, brought his lips close to the ear of Violante, who did not withdraw it; but they heard a sound in the thicket. "It is nothing," said Honoré tenderly. "It is my aunt," said Violante. It was the wind. But Violante, who had risen, opportunely cooled by this wind, refused to sit down again and took leave of Honoré, despite his entreaties. She felt remorse, had an attack of nerves, and for two successive days had difficulty in going to sleep (pp. 50-51).

That is pure Voltaire. Compare it now with this specimen of overripe estheticism:

Suddenly we started, we had just seen a little pink butterfly, then two, then five, leave the flowers of our shore and flutter over the lake. Soon they were like an impalpable pink cloud blowing away, then they reached the flowers of the other shore, came back and gently recommenced the adventurous crossing, stopping sometimes as if tempted above this lake delicately tinted like a great fading flower. It was too much and our eyes filled with tears. These little butterflies crossing the lake passed back and forth across our souls, stretched with emotion before such beauty, ready to vibrate—passed back and forth like the voluptuous bow of a violin. The light movement of their flight did not graze the waters, but caressed our eyes, our hearts, and at every stroke of their little wings we almost fainted (pp. 222-223).

The passage continues for some time in the same vein, but enough has been quoted to illustrate the manner. This is eighteenth-century pre-romanticism, this is Rousseau quivering with natural harmonies in the bottom of his boat, this is Werther and Lotte watching the spectacle of an approaching storm, their souls so saturated with harmony that the enunciation of the single, unmusical, but significant name of "Klopstock" precipitates a deluge of tears. It is this, plus a flaccidity, an anemia, that is the hallmark of nineteenth-century estheticism.

Compared with the critic of 1896, the reader of today has an easy time. Armed with more information about the young author than appears between the covers of his book, and with foreknowledge of what he was later to do in his major work, one can now see *Les Plaisirs et les Jours* as a milestone in Proust's literary development and as a human document of considerable interest.

As he was later to show more openly in his parodies, Proust was a clever imitator, a first-rate specimen of a third-rate class. Yet even in imitating he was not entirely unoriginal. At first glance, "Mondanité et Mélomanie de Bouvard et Pécuchet" seems to be the closest approach in the book to a direct imitation, but closer inspection reveals something quite different. Proust merely adopted Flaubert's ready-made characters as a means of satirizing the literary and musical snobberies of the day, just as Flaubert had done for an earlier time, just as, before him, Reybaud had done with his Jérome Paturot, and before Reybaud, Musset with his Dupuis and Cotonet. The method and the characters were imitative, but the subject matter was the result of personal observation.

Furthermore, Proust imitated authors whose words made some appeal to his experience, or his personality, or sometimes, perhaps, only to his intuition. He was one of those for whom, in his own phrase, "disgust with life and the attraction of mystery have preceded the first sorrows, as if they had a premonition of the insufficiency of reality to satisfy them" (p. 235). If his sarcastic onslaughts on society and human nature were expressed in the manner of the classical moralists, it was because these writers had said things which he, with his precocious experience of society, believed to be true. He needed no one to tell him of the joys of solitude; the uninvited guest of "L'Etranger" resembled Musset's "jeune homme vêtu de noir" and like him symbolized the solitary self, but he was no stranger to Proust, who had made his acquaintance in his sickroom. Even a bit of borrowing like the passage suggestive of "L'Ermitage du Jardin des Plantes" had a basis in fact, for he and Heath, as he tells in the preface, had planned to go and live "far from the vices and ill-will of the world." When he talks of "the machinations of his enemies" and the "arrows of ill-will," he sounds youthfully bombastic; but he did suffer, with unnatural acuteness, at real or imaginary slights from friends who showed themselves insufficiently *gentils.*

Proust's two extremes of style, the classical and the esthetic, correspond with the intellectual and the emotional poles of his temperament and of his approach to knowledge. The classical manner, with its related intellectual mode of knowing, is clear-cut, analytic, often clever, always pessimistic in its estimate of human nature; the esthetic manner, though far less successful as a form of expression, does correspond to certain vaguer ideas whose origin is in feeling, hope, and intuition, rather than in rational analysis. Thus already Proust may be said to have his themes, put forth hesitantly and unsystematically here, and later developed and organized more surely in *A la Recherche du temps perdu.* That they should be truly original, particularly in their earlier presentation, would be too much to ask; sources or parallels could be found for every one of them. But in combination and in the light of their subsequent elaboration, they form a large part of Proust's view of life, and they are so indisputably his own as justly to be called Proustian.

First for the intellectual themes of *Les Plaisirs et les Jours.*

Man, according to Proust, has great difficulty in coming to a true understanding of his fellows, a difficulty accentuated by happiness and mitigated by suffering. "In happy life, the destinies of our fellow men do not appear to us in their reality, whether it is because they are masked by self-interest, or because they are transfigured by desire. But in the detachment caused by suffering

. . . the destinies of others and even our own speak at last to our attentive souls the word, hitherto unheeded, of duty and of truth" (pp. 200-1). In ordinary social life judgments are hasty, ill-founded, and irrevocable; everyone is "very different by nature from the character which society has picked out for him in its storehouse of costumes and characters, and which it has bestowed upon him once and for all" (p. 94).

The dominating characteristic of people's behavior in the social group is falsity. "A socially elegant environment is one in which the opinion of each one is made from the opinion of the others. If it is the opposite of the opinion of the others, then you are in a literary environment" (p. 82). Behavior is dictated by the desire to conform, or the desire to be different; in either case it springs from vanity, the desire to be well thought of, never from a wish to appear as one truly is.

Proust is much concerned with the analysis of snobbishness, or rather with *le snobisme,* which is not quite the same thing. Lemaître defines a *snob,* in the French sense, as "a sheep who follows the leader with a conceited air," a description which applies well enough to some of Proust's characters, to his Bouvard and Pécuchet, for instance, who are not merely platitudinous bourgeois, but literary and artistic snobs, concerned above all with being smart, with being up to the minute, or even a little ahead, on esthetic fashions. There are also society snobs, capable of any treachery, any baseness, any sycophancy, to rise to a higher social sphere. And there is a snobbishness to which Proust shows considerable indulgence, because it is his own: an infatuation with ancient noble names. In a sketch addressed to a feminine snob of this type he says: "For you the soul of the Crusades animates banal contemporary figures, and if you so feverishly read over your visiting lists, is it not because at each name you feel awaken, quiver, and almost sing, like the dead arising from a heraldic tomb, the rich old past of France" (p. 79).

For the most part, however, snobbishness is misguided self-interest, a source to which must also be attributed the malicious gossip which is characteristic of man in society, and by means of which he hopes to rise while pulling his fellow down. When one has observed, says Proust, how people snipe at each other's reputations, and "when one has noticed that the weapons are the same and that the forces, or rather the weaknesses, are about equal, one ceases to admire the one who shoots and to scorn the one who is aimed at. That is the beginning of wisdom. Wisdom itself would be to break with both parties" (p. 83).

Desire is awakened by inaccessibility, by "the charm of things which are not ours" (p. 54); but if desire quickens, "possession withers all things" (p. 185). "Her truest beauty was perhaps in my desire" (p. 192). "A dream come true. . . [is] a dream disappointed" (p. 230). The best illustration of these principles is love, a subject which Proust examines repeatedly.

With love, as with other desires, a simple man of pleasure may find a certain gross satisfaction in present experience; but the man of imagination is excluded from enjoyment of the present, and must look only to the past and the future. "Why obstinately insist on trying to enjoy the present, and weep at your failure? Man of imagination, you can only enjoy by regret or anticipation, that is, in the past or in the future" (pp. 92-93). Anticipation, because of repeated lessons of disappointment, eventually becomes fruitless; there remain the resources of memory. "Love is dead, I am fearful on the threshold of forgetfulness; but calm, a little pale, close to me and yet far and already misty, here, in the light of the moon, are all my past joys and all my healed sorrows, watching me wordlessly. Their silence is moving, while their distance and their indeterminate pallor intoxicate me with sadness and with poetry. And I cannot stop gazing at this inward moonlight" (p. 229).

Proust is already aware that love is, to use his own later succinct phrase, "always the love of something else." In "Présence réelle" he describes the ecstasy of the loving harmony of souls, but concludes: "But already I have ceased to be concerned with you. Satiety has come before possession. Platonic love itself has its saturation point. . . . The sight of you retains only one charm for me, that of recalling suddenly those names of a strange sweetness, German and Italian: Sils Maria, Silva Plana, Crestalta, Samaden, Celerina, Juliers, Val de Viola" (pp. 226-27).

Love as an obsession, occasioned by the most trivial and sometimes irrelevant events, is the subject of several stories of varying length. In "Mélancolique Villégiature," for example, the heroine falls desperately in love with a man whose only title to her interest is the fact that chance has several times prevented an introduction. She accepts and indeed cultivates the originally trivial obstacle. While he takes his vacations at Biarritz, she continues to go to Trouville. Hoping against hope that he will one day appear at Trouville, she nurses her sorrow and goes into a decline.

Love, according to Proust, inevitably and invariably dies. "Often, indeed, when we begin to love, warned by our experience and our sagacity—in spite of the protest of our heart, which has the feeling, the illusion rather, of the eternity of its love,—we know that some day she, by the thought of whom we live, will be as much a matter of indifference to us as all the others have become" (p. 198). And elsewhere, "of the person who, after having made us suffer so much, is now nothing to us, is it enough to say, in the common expression, that she is 'dead to us'? We mourn the dead, we love them still, we long feel the irresistible attraction of the charm which survives them and which draws us often to their graves. But the person who has made us feel everything, with whose essence we are saturated, can now no longer give us even the shadow of pain or joy. She is more than dead to us" (p. 220).

Proust deals with the subject of jealousy in love in the last story in the book, "La Fin de la jalousie." It is easily his most mature story to date. Its ideas patently rest on personal conviction, and even—particularly in the parts about illness—on personal experience. Naturally it falls short in subtlety and in depth of his subsequent treatments of the same topic; but in the skill of its psychological analysis it is comparable to the work of much more mature writers. In it Proust traces the course of jealousy from its beginning in the casual remark of a third party, through obsession, cruelty, and self-torture, to its end in death. As he is dying the hero discovers that his body, the instrument of pleasure, is at the root of his jealousy; freed of his body, he could truly love. Seeing Françoise, the object of his love and jealousy, among the others weeping at his bedside, and more stricken than any, he feels for her at last a great pity and a great love; but it is a love directed equally at the servants, at his relatives, at the doctor. "And that was the end of jealousy."

Such are, in 1896, Proust's chief intellectual themes, the fruits of his observation, reflection, and analysis. For such thoughts he had no apologies to make; they had abundant literary precedent, they were solidly documented in visible and tangible reality, and they reflected the clever pessimism that at best is admired, and at worst escapes ridicule. Fewer and more tentative are the intuitional themes concerned with invisible reality. That he attached to them a higher value than to his intellectual themes is evident from a sentence in a dedicatory letter to Lavallée: "If I have succeeded in putting in [this book] the things to which I attach the most value—a certain feeling for metempsychosis which to you I need not define further—what among them can be liked which is not found, with more distinction and more purity, in yourself, and which, the common heritage of our souls, is not for us that homeland where our sympathies became allied, the very foundation of our friendship, older and more lasting than it?"

"There is something in us that can be without us, and will be after us, though it is strange that it hath no history of what it was before us, nor cannot tell how it entered in us," wrote Sir Thomas Browne, and Proust would have agreed with him; not only in 1896, but in the last few months of his life, when he wrote a passage about the death of Bergotte containing much the same idea. Since metempsychosis as such does not appear at all in *Les Plaisirs et les Jours,* it is evident that what Proust is referring to in his letter is a belief in invisible reality, in the soul as distinct from the body. Indications of such a belief appear in connection with revery and the contemplation of nature. For Proust, both are essentially solitary occupations.

The sketch about the little boy who threw himself out of a window because the girl he loved fell short of his idealization concludes in this way: "Life is like the little friend. We dream it, and we like to dream it. One should not try to live it; [if one does] one throws oneself, like the little boy, into stupidity, not all at once, for everything in life deteriorates by imperceptible degrees. After ten years one no longer recognizes one's dreams, or disavows them; one lives, like an ox, for the sake of the grass of the moment. And who knows whether of our marriage with death may be born our conscious immortality?" (pp. 186-87).

Here are a statement, a hint, and a question. The statement is that it is better to dream one's life than to live it; the hint, that a superior type of consciousness, which would be lost in active life, is developed by solitary revery; and the question is whether this consciousness will survive death. On survival this is as definite as Proust gets—in fact the subject does not directly reappear at all; but the advantages of solitude and the superior consciousness which it makes possible, either by simple revery or by contemplation of nature, are constant themes, both within the book and in previous publications not included. In one such article, for example, he notes, "From excess of dreaming, from the overflowing of the impossible, is born a very sufficient reality." And more specifically, and with Bergsonian implications, he wrote, in his first book review, of a suprarational intelligence, "one and infinite like feeling, at once the object and the instru-ment" of the meditations of philosophers.

Sometimes what he sees in the contemplation of nature is no more than the projection of his own emotions, a familiar and superficial phenomenon of romanticism: "Raising our eyes to the sky, we recognized, not without exaltation, in the spaces between clouds still flushed with the farewell of the sun, the mysterious reflections of our own thoughts" (p. 228). At other times he communes with an older and simpler form of life: "Straight and erect, in the great offering of their branches, yet restful and calm, the trees, by this strange and natural attitude, invite us with gracious murmurs to enter into sympathy with a life so ancient and so young, so different from ours, of which it seems to be the inexhaustible reserve" (pp. 233-34).

Much more significant is the state of consciousness described in "Sonate Clair de Lune." Meditating one evening by the Norman shore, he feels himself filled with a soft inward light, and his cares and problems, of which he is still conscious, lose their heaviness. When he opens his eyes, an external moonlight continues the impression of the inward radiance. "Never, indeed, had the woods slept so deeply, one felt that the moon had taken advantage of the moment to bring to sky and sea this pale and gentle festivity. My sadness had disappeared. I heard my father scold me, Pia make fun of me, my enemies plot against me, and none of it seemed real. The only reality was in this unreal light, which I invoked with a smile." (pp. 195-96).

Art, in *A la Recherche du temps perdu* so important an approach to invisible reality, here plays a minor rôle. Allusions and comparisons in *Les Plaisirs et les Jours* show a sufficient culture in music and painting, but as yet no philosophy of art. Sailing vessels in harbor are described with considerable pictorial effect, suggesting his later disquisitions on the art of Elstir; so too does a remark on the absence of a clear line of demarcation between sea and sky (p. 236). As for music a hint of his future ideas appears in the sentence, "It [the sea] enchants us like music, which, unlike language, does not bear the mark of things, which tells us nothing of men, but which imitates the movements of our souls" (p. 237). The association of a musical phrase with a person, like the Wagnerian leitmotif, appears in "Mélancolique

Villégiature." Such instances give scarcely a hint of the immense significance which art was soon to assume for Proust.

Other gaps in his panoply of ideas are evident. There is nothing like a general view of society and its mutations. Instead of character development and careful portraiture there are swift sketches of type. The force of habit is recognized, but not exploited; the same can be said of that counterpart of memory, oblivion (*l'oubli*). Memory itself, although already a subject of importance, as yet lacks the most striking feature of its subsequent elaboration: the sudden and ecstatic resurgence of the past through association of sensations.

Proust does, however, show interesting marks of development. The work of 1892, contributed for the most part to *Le Banquet*, is clipped, sententious, and classical in style; its substance reveals a facile pessimism and a clever, but not profound, psychology. A few of the *Revue Blanche* pieces of the following year continue the same trends, but the larger proportion represent experiments in new directions. There is a group of emotional pieces in the esthetic manner; there is a story on homosexuality, not reprinted; and there is, in "Melancolique Villégiature," an attempt at more elaborate and sustained psychology. The work of 1894 and 1895 contains some nature sketches that are more thoughtful, less vaguely emotional, than the earlier descriptions; it also includes the longer, more confident, more skillful "La Mort de Baldassare Silvande," and in all probability "La Confession d'une jeune fille" and "La Fin de la jalousie."

Accompanying this trend from the concise, the clever, the superficial, to the more sustained and complex, there is, of course, an inseparable trend in style. The epigrams of 1892 gradually yield to the involved constructions of "La Fin de la jalousie," in which he uses neither the classical nor the esthetic, but a third style, his own, recognizably the forerunner of that of *A la Recherche du temps perdu*. Yet in July 1896, Proust published in the *Revue Blanche* an article called "Contre l'obscurité," in which he attacked the "systematic obscurity" of the symbolists and praised classical principles and clarity. If he was himself tending toward obscurity, it was not through intention, but because of his enlarging view of the complex reality he sought to reflect.

Evidence from outside of *Les Plaisirs et les Jours* suggests that what he was later to call involuntary memory, though absent from his book, was not unknown to Proust in 1896. In the *Revue Blanche* of September 15 of that year, there appeared a story called "Mystères," by Proust's friend and former collaborator Fernand Gregh. It describes an incident of involuntary memory happening to Gregh's friend "V. . . ," to whose description and explanation most of the story is devoted. So striking a resemblance do the incident and the commentary bear to Proust's later treatment of the same subject that one is tempted to believe that "V . . ." is none other than Proust himself. The identification is unlikely, however, because Gregh later used the materials of "Mystères" as a factual contribution to a psychological investigation, with the implication that the incident happened to himself.

Nevertheless there is probably some connection between Gregh's story and Proust's ideas or experience. It is almost certain that Proust read the story, since he was a contributor to the same review, and an allusion in "Mystères" indicates that Gregh had read his colleague's "Contre l'obscurité," which had appeared in July in the same review. Of the numerous literary or psychological precedents for Proust's use of involuntary memory in *A la Recherche du temps perdu,* none is so close in detail as this. Yet to suppose that so important a feature of his novel should have evolved from a simple literary borrowing dating back to 1896 is improbable; there is too much evidence of personal experience in Proust's involuntary memory. Possibly we have here one of those comparatively rare cases of two men, confronted by the same facts, coming independently to the same conclusion. On the whole, however, it seems more likely that there was discussion and comparison of experiences between the two, before or after the writing of the story, but before the strained relations resulting from Gregh's unfavorable review of *Les Plaisirs et les Jours.* In any case "Mystères" must be considered in relation to Proust's ideas.

According to the story, the author and "V . . ." were walking in the park when they heard bells ringing. The author started to make a remark, but stopped, startled at the expression on V . . .'s face. Pale, eyes fixed, staggering a little, he seems almost to have lost consciousness. Assisted by the author and recovering a little, he says, "But for the help of your arm, God forgive me, I think I would have fallen. . . . I have just had that extraordinary moral distress that comes over me sometimes. . . . I call it an *uprush of unconscious memories.* The attack is at first mental, but it shakes me completely, body and soul. . . ."

Without the violence, the experience, as he further describes it, is merely an instance of *fausse reconnaissance,* the feeling that one has been here, seen this, heard this, before. The unusual feature of V . . .'s experience is the extreme "moral distress," accompanied by strong physical reaction. The first reason V . . . gives for this distress is very Proustian: it lies in the compulsion to explain and rationalize his experience. His second reason, also Proustian, is that he feels that the present moment is not merely *like* a past moment, but *is* the past moment. "I have perhaps, in this moment, the stupefaction of a mathematician when he suddenly sees 2 and 2 make 5. Unless one interprets my giddy feeling as coming from the terrible conviction of our automatism, the too sudden vision of what is mechanical and fated in the mind, the revelation that we are not free." And elsewhere, "I was a ghost beginning to live again by remembering his first existence, I was present as a simple spectator of my own life."

One of the differences between the "unconscious memory" of V . . . and the later "involuntary memory" of Proust, is that for V . . . the sudden onset is painful, whereas the "privileged moments" of Proust's novel are uniformly described as ecstatic. Yet the possibilities of happiness are in V . . .'s experience, and in a very Proustian way: "To tell the truth, I do not live any longer, I remember having lived. I pass my life in remembering it. I shall only extract the beauty of this Easter morning a few days later, seeing it in memory. Like the worst of snobs, but for other reasons, I do not travel in order to see, but in order to have seen. . . . The present never pleases me, the future leaves me indifferent, because it does not exist; only the past seems to me beautiful. I know that it was mediocre and imperfect when it was the present, but time has robbed it of its precarious character and of all its ugliness, and I do not tire of contemplating it." Or, as Proust was to put it later, "the true paradises are those that one has lost."

The sudden onslaught of the "unconscious memory," the conscientious exploration of its quality and antecedents, the conviction of the actual reliving of the past moment in the present, the preference for the past over the present and the future—all this is strikingly like a faint preliminary sketch for Proust's later detailed analysis of involuntary memory. Whether or not he discussed or contributed to Gregh's ideas in 1896, he was almost certainly aware of them. Had he at that time had personal experience of involuntary memory?

Reynaldo Hahn has recorded that when he had known Proust "only a short time" (not later than 1893, probably, since at that date they were intimate), he observed Proust in a trance-like state before a hedge of Bengal roses, blinking his eyes and apparently making an intense effort of concentration. Rather than evidence of involuntary memory, the incident was probably an example of the feeling, recurrent with him since childhood, that some natural object had a message to communicate, if he could but read it clear. Contemplation of nature and involuntary memory were not linked until, in 1909, he worked out his theory of their common perception of essence.

And yet, at the earlier date, Proust did feel that he had more to say. Immediately after the publication of *Les Plaisirs et les Jours* he wrote to Lavallée that he had begun another book. Three and a half years later, he wrote to Marie Nordlinger (Reynaldo Hahn's English cousin, met in 1896), "I have been working for a very long time on a very long work but without finishing anything. And at times I wonder whether I am not like the husband of Dorothea Brooke in *Middlemarch* and whether I am not amassing ruins." There are suggestions that in these years his mind is running on the past, and on the qualitative difference between affective memory and that of the intelligence. To Madame Straus he wrote in 1898: "This same Reynaldo [Hahn] by some chance or other sang me the other day the 'Eros' of Holmès [the composer Augusta Holmes] . . . which I had never heard since you used to sing it after lunch, on the Boulevard Haussmann, for the friends of Jacques, while thinking of something else, of your own friends, probably. It was the time when for two months I kept promising myself to kiss your hand the next day, and did not dare. I cannot tell how much this melody, not by recalling all this to me, for I think of it often, but by putting me suddenly in its presence, without preliminary revery, gave me the impression of a charm and a poetry of which it is itself devoid." In January 1899, he wrote to Miss Nordlinger to thank her for her Christmas card, and continued, ". . . in proportion as Christmas loses its truth for us as an anniversary, it takes on, by the gentle emanation of accumulated memories, a more and more sharp reality, in which the light of its candles, its snows which form a melancholy obstacle to some desired arrival, the odor of its mandarines drinking in the heat of the rooms, the fragrance of tea and mimosas, reappear to us coated with the delicious honey of our personality, which we have unconsciously deposited on them throughout the years when, under the spell of selfish ends, we did not feel it, and now, suddenly, it quickens our hearts."

Such is the record, beyond which we are reduced to suppositions. And if we must guess, the simplest and the most probable solution is to follow the experience of Marcel, the narrator of *A la Recherche du temps perdu,* who in so many other respects coincides with Proust himself. We can say, then, that Proust, like Marcel, had, from childhood up, frequent experience of being arrested by a hint of special significance in a natural object, but that he had no experience of involuntary memory until maturity. In 1896, approximately, but too late for it to affect *Les Plaisirs et les Jours,* the incident of the madeleine and the cup of tea (or its equivalent) occurred. Like the narrator of the novel, he was content for the time being to revel in the enriched sense of the past that it brought, without inquiring more closely into its cause and significance. In this spirit he writes at his novel for a few years. But he pays the penalty of his refusal to penetrate the mystery of his experience. "What we have not had to decipher, to clarify by our personal effort," he wrote in *Le Temps retrouvé,* "what was clear before us, is not ours. Only what we draw out of the darkness within us, what others do not know, comes from ourselves." And so inspiration, never very strong, flagged, and the novel was laid aside. Not until the spring of 1909 did the equivalent of the reception of the Princesse de Guermantes occur, and with it the sudden understanding of the significance of both involuntary memory and contemplation. Seized with inspiration, he took up his novel and wrote with a speed and a sureness he had never before known.

But we must return to 1896.

A part of the ambiguity of tone in *Les Plaisirs et les Jours* can be referred, as we have seen, to the difference between Proust's intellectual and emotional modes of apprehension. But it is equally clear that another part of its ambiguity is due to an unresolved moral conflict in its author.

In 1899 Proust sent a copy of *Les Plaisirs et les Jours* to one of his more recent friends, and wrote: "Our lives have been so affectionately mingled in these two years that you have a sort of retrospective right to my thoughts and imaginings of the past. . . . This book . . . presents to you a Marcel that you have not known. . . . It seems to me that, closely associated as you

were with the very sources of my joys and sorrows in the years
when you were my confidant and friend, you, better than
another, should feel in these pages what they still retain of
storms that will not return."

The mere prevalence in *Les Plaisirs et les Jours* of death, sui-
cides, and a generally pessimistic estimate of human nature is no
sufficient indication of "storms," for it is natural for a young man
to be somber, especially if he has a strong dash of romanticism
beneath his classical veneer. The real clue to the conflict is
the unusual combination of moral earnestness—apparent in the
choice of epigraphs as well as in the text—with a bland and
knowing acquiescence in the evil he denounces. The most consistent theme in the book is the superiority of solitude to society,
but he is worldly even while castigating worldliness. The sophisticated irony of "Violante, ou la Mondanité" is capped by an
epigraph from that least ironic of books *The Imitation of Christ:*
"Be seldom with the young and with strangers . . . nor willingly
seek the society of the great."

But why should Proust's characters remain in society while
disapproving of it? From vanity and the force of habit in "Violante" and "L'Etranger," from sexual temptation in "La Confession d'une jeune fille"; in all three from indecisiveness and
weakness of will.

And weakness of will, as we know from his self-analysis in
Albertine disparue, was in his own opinion, along with high
intelligence and sensibility, one of the cardinal features of his
temperament. Much earlier, in the preface to *Les Plaisirs et les
Jours* itself, he speaks of clinging to his mother after his illness
like "the protection implored by our weakness," and of his
despair at ever being able to fulfill all his obligations. Earlier
still he writes to Billy, half jocularly, of remorse for his laziness,
and of his unworthiness to correspond with so industrious a
friend. In a letter of 1890 to Madame Straus he mentions times
"when my will is too sick" (*quand j'ai trop mal à la volonté*).

Proust's early social aspirations, the vanity of his "alert and frivolous self," are too obvious to require further comment. But how about the sexual temptation?

The presence of this element in "La Confession d'une jeune fille"—and to a slighter extent in "Violante"—is not in itself particularly significant. The sense of guilt, the feeling of lost innocence, the despairing conviction of a secret sin that belies the favorable opinion of others—many a sensitive adolescent, nourished on ideals, has felt them, and later, when he has learned of the commonness of his experience, has felt that they were disproportionate to their cause. But in Proust's case there was something more than the ordinary "storms" of adolescence. For he was a homosexual, a "Uranian."

Under date of May 14, 1921, Gide (whose substantial veracity it is impossible to doubt) wrote in his *Journal:*

Passed with Proust an hour of yesterday evening . . . he complains that his life is nothing but a prolonged death agony and although having begun, immediately upon my arrival, to talk to me of Uranism, he interrupts himself to ask me if I can give him some enlightenment on the teachings of the Gospel, on which somebody or other has told him that I spoke particularly well. He hopes to find in them some support and comfort for his sufferings. . . . I bring him *Corydon* [at that time only privately printed] which he promises me to speak to no one about; and as I tell him a little of my memoirs [later published as *Si le grain ne meurt*]: "You can tell everything," he exclaims; "but on the condition of never saying 'I.' " Which doesn't suit me at all.

Far from denying or concealing his Uranism, he reveals it and I might almost say boasts of it. He says he has never loved women except spiritually and has never known love except with men. . . . I did not suppose that Proust was so exclusively [a Uranian].

This testimony—to which it is unnecessary at present to add the considerable corroborative evidence—casts a new light on the strong emotion Proust shows in the introductory section of *Sodome et Gomorrhe*. It is not only, not even primarily, of M. de Charlus that he is thinking when he writes of the "race over which hangs a curse and which must live in falsehood and perjury, because it knows its desire is considered punishable and shameful, not to be avowed . . . ; sons without mothers, to whom they are obliged to lie all their lives, and even at the hour of closing their eyes; friends without friendships, in spite of all those which their frequently recognized charm inspires and which their often kind hearts would appreciate; but can one call friendships those relations which subsist only by the favor of a lie, and from which they would be cast out with disgust at their first yielding to an impulse of confidence and sincerity?"

These words help us to understand Proust's remorse at living a lie to the mother he adored; to understand, also, some of the difficulties he had in making and keeping friends, between his natural affection, without ulterior motive, on the one hand, and his fear of suspicion, or even of self-betrayal, on the other. His worst sufferings must have come, first from what seemed like incredible moral lapses, and later from the gradual realization that he was not like others, just at an age when to be different was a source of shame. "For no one knows at first that he is an invert," he wrote. "The schoolboy, learning love poetry or looking at indecent pictures, if he pressed closely against a comrade, thought that he was merely sharing with him a common desire of women. How should he believe that he was not like everyone. . . ?"

In later years, when he was publishing the successive volumes of his novel, and talk had started about his relation to homosexuality, Proust was eager to defend himself against charges of effeminacy, pointing to his one duel as disproof of the accusation. It is true that he never brazenly indulged, like some, in feminine adornment and manners, but there was much in him that suggested a feminine nature: his passionate love of flowers, his intense interest in music and art, his delight in feminine fashions and the gossip of tea parties, his coquettish jealousies, his extreme sensitivity to changes of temperature, above all his special relation to women, who, no matter what their age, seemed unconsciously to adopt him as one of themselves, and to accept from him audacities of language that would have been impossible from another. We have seen something of his attitude toward Madame Straus in his letters; there is another even more revealing, but it is quite too startling to quote. Proust himself recognized his ambiguous appeal and its dangers. "The young man whom we have just tried to depict was so evidently a woman that women who looked at him with desire were doomed . . . to the same disappointment as those who, in the comedies of Shakespeare, are deceived by a girl disguised as a young man. The deception is the same, the invert himself knows it, he divines the disillusion the woman will experience when the disguise is removed, and feels how this error about sex is a source of poetic fantasy."

Proust seems to have been a genuine Urning. His was not a case of vicious perversity, but of spontaneous and at first unrecognized perversion, which is quite another matter. It was involuntary, but whether it was congenital or acquired is a question for the specialist. It is enough to note that his long pre-adolescent illness, possibly resulting in an arrest of development and certainly increasing his dependence on his mother, and the fact that he was coddled and accustomed to solitude and revery, suggest, by their parallel with other recorded cases, that his condition was acquired. On the other hand his extreme delicacy and nervous instability from the earliest years and his pronounced intellectual and artistic gifts may indicate a congenital character. Perhaps it was both.

The painful process of self-discovery was far advanced when, in the *Revue Blanche* for December 1893, he published "Avant la nuit"; he did not include it later in *Les Plaisirs et les Jours,* possibly because he thought it compromising. In this story, as in "La Confession d'une jeune fille," the heroine is lingering on after a remorseful attempt at suicide, and is trying to explain to her lover that she is not all he thought her to be:

"Do you remember how, when my poor friend Dorothy was caught with a woman singer whose name I have forgotten . . . how you explained to me that we could not scorn her? I remember your words:

How can we be indignant at habits which Socrates (it was a question of men, but it is the same thing, isn't it?) who drank the hemlock rather than commit an injustice, gaily approved in his preferred friends. If fertile love, intended to perpetuate the race, noble as a family, social, human duty, is superior to purely voluptuous love, there is, on the other hand, no hierarchy in sterile loves and it is not less moral—or rather not more immoral—that a woman should find pleasure with another woman rather than with one of the other sex. The cause of this love lies too exclusively in a nervous deterioration for it to involve a moral significance. . . ."

Probably Proust had been reading Krafft-Ebing, the seventh edition of whose *Psychopathia Sexualis* became available in French translation in 1892. That genuine Uranism was to be associated with nervous deterioration and was frequently hereditary, was the opinion of the learned German psychiatrist; and the argument about the Greeks and the equal moral value of all sterile loves occurs in the testimony of one of his patients, in almost the same words as those used by Proust (case 110 of the seventh edition). There is one significant difference: Krafft-Ebing's patient was talking of male homosexuality, and Proust, referring to female perversion, had to add, "But it is the same thing, isn't it?"

A better indication of his state of mind in this story is an allusion to Michelet, whose excursions into natural history he had been reading: "Most people withdraw in disgust from the medusa [jellyfish]. Michelet, appreciative of the delicacy of their colors, liked to pick them up." Proust suffered from belonging to a class that inspired repugnance in normal people, and wanted to point out that, just as the jellyfish, with its bizarre reproductive characteristics and its repulsive clinging, had its beauties, so Urnings too, if sympathetically viewed, had qualities that could be admired. So impressed was he by the analogy that he recurred to it, and to the Michelet allusion, in *Sodome et Gomorrhe*.

With this background we can return to *Les Plaisirs et les Jours* and its most authentic personal document, "La Confession d'une jeune fille."

The narrator is a young girl in delicate health, abnormally dependent on her mother's affection and on the ritual of the goodnight kiss. As a child she spends much of her time at the country home of one of her uncles, and is visited occasionally by her mother.

One day when, unknown to the girl, her mother is to arrive, a young cousin comes to see her. He is precociously vicious, and teaches her things which make her shudder "with remorse and with voluptuous pleasure." Terrified, she finds strength to run away, calling for her mother, whom suddenly she sees, smiling and opening her arms. The mother misunderstands the importance of the child's outpoured confession, but shortly she has other subjects of concern:

> What reduced my mother to despair was my lack of will power. I did everything under the impulse of the moment. As long as this impulse was still furnished by the mind or by the heart, my life, without being wholly good, was nevertheless not wholly bad. The accomplishment of all my fine projects of work, of calm, of reason, preoccupied my mother and me above all, because we felt, she more distinctly and I confusedly but strongly, that this accomplishment would only be the image, projected into my life, of the creation by myself and in myself of that will power which she had conceived and over which she brooded. But I kept putting off to the morrow. I gave myself time, I was sorry sometimes to see it pass, but there was so much before me! However, I was a little afraid, and I felt vaguely that the habit of getting along without will power was beginning to weigh on me more and more heavily with the passage of time; suspecting sadly that things would not change all at once, and that, for the transformation of my life and the creation of my will, I could scarcely count on a miracle which would cost me nothing (pp. 148-49).

During the girl's sixteenth year she passed through a severe illness, after which she was presented to society by her mother. She began to meet persons of her own age, among them a young man who took up the instruction in sensuality where the cousin had left off. She fell in love with him, and when the love was gone, the habit remained, and there was no lack of others to

exploit it. The example and the advice of her new companions
checked her desire to confess to her parents. Instead,

> To distract and drive away all these evil desires, I began to go
> much into society. Its desiccating pleasures habituated me to living
> perpetually in company, and I lost, with the taste for solitude, the
> secret of the joys which hitherto nature and art had given me. . . .
> It was then that, searching for an opposite remedy, and because I
> lacked the courage to will the true one, so close to me, and alas, so
> far away, in myself—it was then that I turned again to guilty pleas-
> ures, thinking thereby to revive the flame extinguished by society. It
> was in vain. Restrained by the desire to please, I put off from day to
> day the final decision, the choice, the truly free act, the choice of soli-
> tude. I gave up neither of these vices for the other. I mixed them. . . . I
> went into society to calm myself after a sin, and I committed another
> as soon as I was calm. It was at this terrible moment, after the loss
> of innocence and before the remorse of today, at this moment when,
> of all the moments of my life I was the least worthy, that I was the
> most admired of all. . . . While I was committing the greatest of
> crimes to my mother, I was considered, because of my tenderly re-
> spectful manner with her, the model daughter. . . . Besides, no one
> suspected the secret crime of my life, and I seemed to everyone an
> ideal girl (pp. 150-52).

Her mother arranged a marriage with a model young man.
The girl told her confessor all, but he recommended silence,
exacting, however, a promise of future purity. For a time all
went well. She was virtuous and she was happy. Then the accom-
plice of her former delinquencies returned, and she yielded to the
old temptation.

So far Proust has not strayed far from his own story. The end
is in the nature of a grim forecast. The mother oversees the
encounter, falls, and dies. The daughter commits suicide, lingering on just long enough to write the document we have just
read.

No wonder Proust told Gide that he could tell all, provided
that he did not say "I." He did use the first person, but hid behind a transposition of sex. And perhaps the feminine rôle seemed
to him a natural one, as well as a prudent disguise. But the trans-

position had the effect of somewhat distorting the situation: the girl's besetting weakness, and the subject of her profound remorse, is ostensibly no more than heterosexual play between persons who, until the end, are not otherwise pledged. However regrettable, it is more like a venial sin than a crime. But turn the girl into a young man, and remorse, resulting in suicide, is more understandable.

A few more details from Proust's life help to fill in the picture.

As in his story, he looked everywhere but in himself for the remedy to his distress. The current deterministic philosophy, with its conception of the will as a mere moral sensation, without directive force, offered small consolation. In a book review written close to January 1, 1892, he wrote: "The sweetest perhaps of those flowers of sentiment which reflection withers is what one might call mystic trust in the future. The unhappy lover who, repelled today as he was yesterday, hopes that the woman he loves but who does not love him will tomorrow suddenly begin to love him; the man who, with strength unequal to his task, says to himself, 'Tomorrow, I shall have by some enchantment the will power that I lack . . .' these have a mystic hope in the future in that it is the product of their desire alone and that no rational foresight justifies it. Alas! a day comes . . . when we understand that characters do not change all at once . . . when we understand that tomorrow could not be quite different from yesterday, because it is made from yesterday."

But there was Bergson, with whom he became related by marriage, and whose early work he followed with great admiration and interest. "Let us not trust reason," wrote Proust hopefully to Dreyfus in July of 1892, and to Montesquiou in 1893 he spoke, in Bergsonian language, of "spontaneous gushing forth, spring, true spiritual life, that is, liberty."

And there was the new moral earnestness. He read Paul Desjardins' *Devoir présent,* to which he alluded by name in a book review of 1892, and said, "To a generation concerned particularly with the splendid uselessness of things has succeeded one anxious above all to restore to life its purpose, its meaning, and to man the feeling that he creates in a certain measure his own destiny." For moral philosophy he read Emerson, Carlyle; for religion, he read the *Imitation of Christ,* and attended the 1893 Lenten lectures of the Abbé Vignot, later published as *La Vie pour les autres.*

Perhaps these readings and activities, as well as the sobering effect of the deaths of his intimates Aubert and Heath, did have a salutary influence. At least he was able to make himself work: from 1892 to 1895 he wrote practically the whole of *Les Plaisirs et les Jours,* as well as several articles and stories he did not reprint—no mean achievement, considering his health and his other preoccupations. Perhaps these years corresponded to the last period of virtue and happiness of the heroine of his story. Gravely and hopefully he wrote to Montesquiou, on January 5, 1895: "Three years ago I dared have no hopes for a new year, neither for myself nor for others. I had the feeling that if years change, characters remain, and that the future, the dream desire, were only fulfilled by that same past from which one would wish it so different, and which gave us the exact tone of all the good and evil bells which we had previously set in motion. It is with a keener sense of divine grace and of human liberty, with confidence in at least an inner Providence, that I begin this year."

And then—he wrote "La Confession d'une jeune fille."

The ambiguity of tone of *Les Plaisirs et les Jours*—accentuated, though more scattered, in *A la Recherche du temps perdu* is, then, the result of this unresolved moral conflict. He can rid himself neither of his moral viewpoint nor of what he cannot help considering his vice. In "Avant la nuit" there is clearly an intent to defend homosexuality. In "La Confession d'une jeune fille" the narrator accuses herself of a "crime." The introduction to *Sodome et Gomorrhe* is an eloquent plea for sympathetic understanding of the invert's problem, for which he is not responsible; yet here even, and elsewhere in the novel, M. de Charlus is presented as vicious and grotesque.

It was this apparent hypocrisy that shocked Gide. Some months after his recorded call on Proust, he noted in his *Journal:*

> I read the latest pages of Proust (December number of the N.R.F.) with, at first, a start of indignation. Knowing what he thinks, what he is, it is hard for me to see here anything but a pretense, a desire to protect himself, with a very skillful camouflage, for it could be to no one's advantage to denounce him. Still more: this offense indeed runs the risk of pleasing everyone: the heterosexuals whose prejudices it justifies and whose repugnance it flatters; the others, who will profit by the alibi and by their small resemblance to those whom he depicts. In short, I know of no work which is more capable, with the aid of the general cowardice, of confirming error than the *Sodome* of Proust.

Gide did not have Proust's fatalistic resignation, his willingness to acquiesce in a persecuted lot; he could not accept, like Proust, the necessity of concealment at a part of the curse hanging over the homosexual. Nor could he understand how anyone could accept both the condemnation and the extenuation of homosexuality.

Proust did not choose this difficult position; he found himself stranded in it, as a result of his deeply rooted temperamental indecisiveness, his habit of postponing decisions. Morally stranded he remained; but for his justification, he learned to look to art.

☙ 5 ❧

THE RELIGION OF ART

THE years from 1896 to 1899 were marked for Proust by a gradual deterioration of health, a progressive withdrawal from social affairs, and a creative inertia. Presumably he was working on his novel, but progress was unsatisfactory, and outside of this effort he could show, from July 1896 to January 1900, only four trifling pieces of journalism as evidence of literary activity.

In so far as we can judge from letters and from echoes of his personal life in his novel, his health was at its peak immediately after his military service, when his letters are gay and contain small reference to illness. Gradually, however, the pathological note creeps in: pleurodynia, rheumatic fever, grippe, bronchitis are added to the familiar asthma. Under the pressure of events and emotions his attacks of suffocation become more frequent and more painful, as in the spring and summer of 1896, with proof of *Les Plaisirs et les Jours* to correct, and with the deaths, first of his great-uncle Louis and then of his grandfather Nathée Weil. He took the waters at Mont-Dore, taking advantage of the occasion to visit churches in neighboring Clermont-Ferrand and Issoire, and returned to new sufferings, as was usually the case when his anxieties were increased and his routine broken by travel. Although there is as yet nothing comparable to the continuous dirge that issued from the cork-lined chamber of later years, there is evidently a steady deterioration.

Probably it is no coincidence that in the conflict between duty and desire with respect to a steady position, illness should have intervened in favor of desire. And his craving for a life permitting frequent solitude was reinforced by the growing conviction that such a life for him was more moral and that he had, despite his small success to date, something to say in literature. As yet he was too conscientious for deliberate malingering, but his nervous disease, peculiarly susceptible to suggestion, took care of the matter for him; not in any spectacular way, but by a continual reproachful demonstration of delicacy that was, for one of his temperament, a better answer to his father's insistence than a forthright, but impossible "no."

Yet he made one final, and somewhat ludicrous, attempt to place himself in the world of affairs. In 1895 three posts of attaché to the Bibliothèque Mazarine fell vacant; Proust presented himself for the competitive examination, and passed third. The post paid nothing, and called for five hours a day of not very exacting attendance at the library. The candidate who should pass third was designated in advance to be attached, not to the library itself, but to the Ministry of Public Instruction in the Rue de Grenelle, for the legal deposit service. This work did not suit Proust at all; he pulled some wires, and the head of a bureau wrote to the Director of the Mazarine that "number three" seemed to be of "languishing health," and that it would be better if number one or number two were sent to the Rue de Grenelle. The Director was inexorable; if number three was too weak to fulfill his duties, he should not have applied for the post, which he must either fill or resign. Proust countered by applying for leave for the remainder of the year. It was granted, and on its expiration he applied for and received a full year's leave in addition. Meanwhile he turned up at the quai Conti (not the Rue de Grenelle), met his "colleagues," perhaps did a little work. In 1896 he appeared at the library only to present copies of *Les Plaisirs et les Jours;* he felt that it would be indelicate to appear frequently when he was officially on leave, and the same scruple kept him from the Rue de Grenelle. He went on applying for leave and getting it, until a general inspection of the Mazarine revealed the administrative irregularity and resulted in an ultimatum, dated February 14, 1900, to return to his post. He did not do so, and his theoretical connection with the Mazarine came to an end.

Meanwhile his gradual withdrawal from formal social affairs did not prevent a somewhat relaxed continuance of relationship with old friends and the acquiring of new. He remained, and was long to continue, one of the faithful of Madame Lemaire's salon, though at times with some reluctance. Madame Arman de Caillavet he also continued to see, and Anatole France, for whom, just before his departure for South America in May 1897, he gave a dinner, inviting Montesquiou, whom he carefully informed of the others invited: the Marquis de Castellane, M. Béraud, M. de Turenne.

His relations with Montesquiou continued with their usual ups and downs. Incidentally, this friendship was the cause of Proust's duel in February 1897. "Jean Lorrain," one of the pen names of the Belgian poet and novelist Paul Duval, wrote a scathing article on Montesquiou's *Hortensias bleus,* and denounced his influence on "pretty little society gentlemen in literary heat," naming among them Proust. Feeling his honor attacked, and scrupulously anxious to carry the affair off correctly, Proust challenged Lorrain, obtained the services of Gustave de Borda, a celebrated duelist, as a second, and succeeded in having the meeting take place in the afternoon, when it would interfere less with the routine of his health. There was the traditionally ineffective exchange of shots, and honor was declared satisfied. But the affair long remained in Proust's mind, not only because he had, for once, achieved decisive action and disproved, he hoped, the suspicion of effeminacy, but because of the reflections which were inspired by the prospect of the duel. These appear in *La Prisonnière,* where he speaks of a procrastinating writer about to fight a duel: "Then there suddenly appears to him, at the moment when he is about perhaps to lose it, all the value of a life which he could have put to profit by beginning a work, or even by enjoying pleasures. . . . 'If only I can manage not to get killed,' he says to himself, 'how

I shall set to work on the instant and also how I shall enjoy myself.'" But the encounter, of course, had no such desired effect upon Proust.

His friendship with Laure Hayman, complacently ostentatious at first, and then suspended for a time, was renewed after the death of Louis Weil, and on a revised footing. And a short time later he began a new feminine friendship, this time with himself in the rôle of elder counselor. His letters to the young actress Louisa de Mornand reveal another extraordinary but characteristic relationship, a compound of physical familiarity and an almost feminine friendship. One of the earlier letters is interesting both because it shows us the cloistered Proust that was coming into being—the man in bed, sending out letters to summon friends to his bedside, fretting and imagining slights if they do not come—and because it recalls Marcel waiting for Albertine:

Oh! my little Louisa, how unkind! I get up expressly to see you. So as not to take up in advance your whole evening, if you wanted to go out to supper, I tell you that we can only be together half an hour, but mother, to leave me more free, when I told her, went to bed, and everything was arranged, when my naughty little Louisa (who meanwhile had probably been invited to a more interesting party and pretended she preferred not to disturb me—because she knows very well that when one is expecting somebody what is disturbing is not to see him) when my naughty little Louisa, whom I love with all my heart, paying no attention to the carriage and the concierge I had sent for her in all haste to the Vaudeville [theatre], let me down. I am none the less dying to kiss her on her two cheeks, and even on her pretty neck if she will permit (I will tell you why I made a correction). But when? Shall I be well enough to get up tomorrow? . . . Anyway, till one of these days, tenderly yours, my little Louisa,

Marcel.

He took a keen interest in her love affairs, suffered for her and for her lovers, remonstrated with her when he thought her in the wrong, made attempts to mediate—all accompanied, of course, by gifts and flowers. One of his friends gives us a glimpse of him with her: "Thereupon L. de M. [Louisa de Mornand], the mistress of R. G., joined us. Marcel felt immediately that there had been a rather sharp dispute between the young people. But he appeared not to have noticed it; and I still see the delicate way he put his hand on the back of her neck, stroking her like a young colt, but also enumerating, with a teasing, good-humored, interrogative air, all her faults that he knew so well. He scolded her severely with a very gentle, very measured voice, but with an ironic authority and a persistence that surprised me."

This interest in the love affairs of his friends—attributable in part, perhaps, to the pleasures of vicarious experience or to the desire to collect literary material, but largely and more simply to affectionate generosity—is well illustrated in a letter of several years later to Louis de Robert:

Finally and above all, I who have been so continually unhappy in love . . . I who am so incapable of moving hearts which I should like to unite to mine, as soon as I am not concerned, dear friend, have magic powers of which you should have some experience and which are due perhaps simply to a mixture of clairvoyance and a desire for the happiness of others raised to a higher degree than usual. I have reconciled not merely friends and lovers, but husbands and wives. . . . Oh! dear friend, if for you whom I love so much, I could do something, how glad I should be!

The Dreyfus affair put Proust in a difficult position, with his Jewish friends and relations on the one hand (partisans, naturally, of Dreyfus), and on the other his intimates among the aristocrats, almost as naturally, though with some notable exceptions, anti-Dreyfus. In a letter to Montesquiou he stated frankly his Jewish side, and, by implication, his sympathy with the Dreyfus cause, but added, somewhat ambiguously: "For if our ideas differ, or rather if I am not free to have on this subject the ideas I might perhaps have otherwise, you might have hurt me involuntarily in a discussion."

Despite interpretations one might put on this remark, it is clear that Proust aligned himself, and more vigorously than on any other issue of his lifetime, on the side of Dreyfus. He claimed afterward to have been the first *Dreyfusard,* to have organized the first list in the newspaper *L'Aurore* calling for a reopening of the case, and to have been responsible for obtaining the signature of Anatole France, who, in turn, asked Proust to get M. d'Haussonville to sign an address to Colonel Picquart. But Proust retained friends in both camps, and as late as 1907 was worrying about how to entertain together Reinach, in a way the incarnation of the Affair, and the Duke and Duchess of Clermont-Tonnerre; in the end he decided not to invite Reinach.

Except for his early efforts to get signatures, Proust refrained from active participation in the Dreyfus affair. But his social conscience, once aroused, remained available on occasion. Instead of following many of his fellow partisans of Dreyfus into anti-clericalism, he defended the church, and in a newspaper article of 1904 he attacked the Briand proposal for the secularization of churches. The following year he wrote to Georges de Lauris an unusually earnest letter, expressing concern for the state of France and protesting equally against anti-Semitism and anti-clericalism.

It would be idle to pretend that Proust had much of the social reformer in him; not only the small number of his interventions in public issues, but the occasions of them are against the supposition. In the Dreyfus affair he had a personal interest in the racial issue; his attack on the Briand project was on esthetic and historical grounds; his protest against anti-clericalism in the Lauris letter was occasioned by the exclusion of the priest of Illiers, sentimentally associated with his childhood, from the ceremony of the distribution of prizes at the end of the school year. And yet in all these cases there is evidence of sympathy for the underdog, a prime motive of the social reformer. One of the curious aspects of *Sodome et Gomorrhe I* is the frequent association of inverts with partisans of Dreyfus, on the ground that both groups were the object of public persecution. He speaks, for example, of inverts being served in a restaurant "with a politeness covering indignation, by a waiter who, as on the evenings when he waits on partisans of Dreyfus, would take pleasure in sending for the police if it were not to his advantage to pocket the tips." And the Church had been under more or less systematic attack by the Left since the foundation of the Third Republic.

One of the most important of Proust's group friendships was with various members of the Franco-Roumanian families of Brancovan and Bibesco, and with their friends, notably Count Bertrand de Salignac-Fénelon. He had known the Brancovans (the mother, the Princesse de Brancovan, and her daughters the Princesse de Caraman-Chimay and the Comtesse de Noailles) since 1893; with them, and with the brother and son, Constantin de Brancovan, relations were closer from 1901 onward. With their cousins, Antoine and Emmanuel Bibesco, he was still more intimate. Prince Antoine Bibesco was a career diplomat, in the early days of his friendship with Proust a secretary of the Roumanian Legation in Paris. He attended the salon of Madame Lemaire, and it was perhaps there that he and Proust met. At any rate, when the Proust family moved, in 1901, from the Boulevard Malesherbes to the Rue de Courcelles, they found themselves but a few doors from the Bibesco home, and dropping in at one or the other of the houses became a daily event. The friendship soon reached the stage of first names and the familiar second person singular. Almost immediately Fénelon was added to the intimacy, although Proust complained that he was too active, too dispersed in his friendships. Fénelon, like Antoine Bibesco a diplomat by profession, was an aristocrat to the fingertips, a great-grand nephew of the famous archbishop and author of *Télémaque;* his blue eyes, physical grace, and charming manners furnished some of the more attractive aspects of Proust's Saint-Loup.

Antoine Bibesco's older brother Emmanuel spent more time in Roumania, where he had a political career, and did not make Proust's acquaintance until somewhat later.

With these and with several others of his friends a strong tie was a common love of art in all its forms, tastes that with Proust were of long standing. Even before entering the Lycée Condorcet he was showing his lifelong disposition to view objects and events in terms of art—literary, musical, or visual—and to view art in terms of comparison or analogy with other art or with life. From childhood he spent hours before pictures and churches, preferably in the company of a friend from whom he could get explanations of what he saw, or to whom he could impart his own. During the years when he used to appear occasionally at the Bibliothèque Mazarine, he would accompany Lucien Daudet to the Louvre and delight in talking of painters' styles and subjects or in detecting a contemporary likeness in a face painted by an old master. In the same company he would go to concerts, and once, when they had heard Beethoven's Ninth Symphony and Lucien was trying enthusiastically to hum a passage, Proust began to laugh, and said, "But my little Lucien, your *poum poum poum* would never make anyone admit this splendor! It would be better to try to explain it." He was early caught up by the Wagnerian enthusiasm of the symbolist era, and followed the Colonne and Lamoureux concerts which were so instrumental in establishing the taste for Wagner in France.

Yet for a time even his love of art was contaminated by the apathy and discouragement that were impeding his literary work. But only for a time: under the influence of Ruskin, with whom he may have had some acquaintance in school, but whom he did not effectively discover until 1899, his artistic enthusiasm rose to new heights.

On his return in July of that year from a trip to Lake Geneva, he wrote to a friend that he had at last "found, read and liked the *Seven Lamps of Architecture* of Ruskin, in the *Revue générale.*" The return from his trip is accompanied by the usual bout of illness, but his studies continue. On the first of the following December he asks Lavallée to look up for him the *Queen of the Air;* on the fifth he tells Miss Nordlinger that he is writing "about Ruskin and some cathedrals." The next month he tells her that he is translating Ruskin, though his English is so uncertain that he has to accept help from his mother and from various friends. Miss Nordlinger is also interested in Ruskin, and helps with advice.

When Ruskin died, on January 21, 1900, Proust began assembling from his long article a shorter piece, which he entitled "Pèlerinages ruskiniens en France." It appeared in the *Figaro* on February 13, the first of his Ruskin publications. The chief theme of the article was stated at the beginning:

> Thousands of the faithful will be going to Coniston to pray before a grave where will rest only the body of Ruskin; I propose to his French friends to celebrate in another way the "worship of this hero," I mean in spirit and in truth, by pilgrimages to the places which hold his soul . . . and which entrusted to him their own, so that he might make them immortal by putting them in his books.

He continued with quotations from Ruskin and announcement of forthcoming articles of his own. A passage from one of these, which appeared in the *Mercure de France* the following April, gives an idea of the veneration, almost the idolatry, of his early attitude toward Ruskin:

> Ill comprehending the bearing of religious art in the Middle Ages, I had said to myself, in my fervor for Ruskin: He will teach me, for he too, in certain particles at least, is he not the truth? He will cause my mind to enter places to which it had no access, for he is the door. He will purify me, for his inspiration is like the lily of the valley. He will intoxicate me and give me life. And I felt indeed that the mystic perfume of the rose of Sharon had not entirely vanished, because we breathe it still, at least in his words.

Putting into practice his own advice in "Pèlerinages ruskiniens en France," he made a sudden trip to Rouen, with the aid and support of his friends the Yeatmans, especially to see a small figure mentioned by Ruskin. Almost as sudden and similarly inspired was his trip to Venice and Padua in May, supported this time by his mother. In Venice he was met by Reynaldo Hahn and Miss Nordlinger, and began almost at once to correct with her the proofs of his translation of *The Bible of Amiens.* They worked beside Saint Mark's; during a storm they took refuge within the basilica, and there read appropriate passages from *The Stones of Venice.*

The first, and idolatrous, phase of Proust's enthusiasm for Ruskin lasted barely a year, having apparently reached its peak at the time of the trip to Venice. The subsequent decline, resulting in 1903 in a decision, later reversed, to abandon the translation and annotation of *The Bible of Amiens,* is attributable to several factors. For one thing, the state of his health must be taken into consideration.

The indisposition following his trip to Lake Geneva in the summer of 1899 was succeeded by grippe and more suffocations; by the end of January 1900, he had been "sick for some time," and was dictating most of his letters. On his departure for Venice he believed his days were numbered, and the trip left him "broken in health." The year 1902 was particularly trying, for in February 1903 he wrote (with some exaggeration, as other letters show), "I have passed more than a year in bed, without even getting up for half an hour a day, and although I am much better now, I am often obliged to stay in bed several days in succession." And it was perhaps at about this time that he wrote to Louisa de Mornand, "Shall I continue to the day of my death to lead a life which even the gravely ill do not lead, deprived of everything, of the light of day, of air, of all work, of all pleasure, in a word, of all life? Or am I going to find a means of change? I can no longer delay the answer, for it is not only my youth, it is my life itself which is passing."

Yet illness in Proust's case was rarely a sufficient explanation of unproductivity. Given sufficient enthusiasm, he could work in the face of all but the most extreme obstacles, as shown by his activity in late 1899 and early 1900, and later by his prodigies of achievement when working on his novel. A much more probable explanation of his declining interest is a definite parting of the ways between his thought and that of Ruskin, a separation that was to be expected from the very excess of his early adulation.

As a matter of fact, if, after an acquaintance with *A la Recherche du temps perdu,* one turns to Ruskin, to the *Seven Lamps,* for example, one is struck, not so much by their common ideology as by their difference. Ruskin's didactic morality is a far cry from the supple amorality of Proust's novel. One would think that the preaching and the theology of Ruskin would have repelled Proust, and in the end they did. Not that Proust did not believe in the profound morality of art, but he objected to moralizing. "Whistler is right," he wrote to Miss Nordlinger, "when he says in *Ten O'Clock* that Art is distinct from Morals. And yet Ruskin also speaks the truth, on another plane, when he says that all great art is moral."

The first effect of Ruskin on Proust was something like a conversion—not to the religion of Ruskin, but to that of art. It was not, however, a decadent estheticism, in which sensations were cultivated for the sake of the pleasure they brought. "Beauty," wrote Proust in 1900, under the inspiration of Ruskin, "cannot fruitfully be loved if one loves it only for the pleasure it gives. And just as the search for happiness for its own sake can only attain weariness, and to find it one must look for something else, so esthetic pleasure is given us in addition if we love Beauty for its own sake, as something real, existing outside of ourselves and infinitely more important than the joy it gives us." The conviction of the external reality of art was what Proust needed, and what he believed he had found with the aid of Ruskin. And this faith survived his first infatuation with the master.

Even at the height of his first study of Ruskin, Proust's reading was by no means confined to him, and it is likely that comparisons between Ruskin and other writers on art contributed to his disillusionment. Emile Mâle, whose works he read as they came out, and whose advice he later asked about visits to churches, is mentioned by Proust as early as 1900. Billy, with whom he had discussed matters of art since early in their friendship, helped him considerably with suggestions and the loan of books, among others the first one by Emile Mâle. Other readings included the thirteenth-century Vincent de Beauvais and the nineteenth-century restorer Viollet-le-Duc.

On November 24, 1903, after Proust had decided to abandon his work on *The Bible of Amiens,* his father collapsed in the midst of his heavy work, and died two days later. Although not intimate with his father, he had a deeply respectful affection for him, and he suffered vicariously in the much deeper pain of his mother. Furthermore, this death was a first blow at the foundations of the home in whose shelter he had always lived.

Yet from the point of view of his artistic and intellectual development, the loss had a beneficial effect: it returned him to his Ruskin studies at just the moment when he was most threatened with relapse into apathy and discouragement. Shortly after his father's death he wrote to the Comtesse de Noailles: "I have not the courage to *think* what my poor mother's life can be. . . . She had given him, to a point that would scarcely be credible to one who had not seen it, every minute of her life. . . . Mother has such energy (energy without an energetic air, not letting one suspect the effort for self-control) that there is no apparent difference between what she was a week ago and today. But I know at what depths and with what violence and for how long the drama is to be played, and I cannot but be afraid. . . . Papa had so much nobler a nature than I. When he was sick he had only one thought, that we should not know it. But these are things of which I cannot yet think. It hurts too much. Life has begun again. If I had an objective, an ambition of some sort, that would help me to bear it. But such is not the case. . . . Mother, learning that I had given up Ruskin, has taken it into her head that that was all Papa wanted, that he was daily awaiting its publication. So I have had to reverse my orders, and here I am beginning my proofs again."

The translation of *The Bible of Amiens* did not appear until February 1904. The delay was due less to the difficulty of translating this short work than to the extent of the notes, which were equivalent in length to the text itself, and to the readings and investigations they entailed. In a note added to the preface when it was republished in *Pastiches et Mélanges* in 1919, Proust said: "If, in the course of this study, I have quoted so many passages of Ruskin drawn from other of his works than *The Bible of Amiens,* this is the reason. To read only one book of an author is to have only one meeting with him. Now by talking once with a person one can discern individual traits. But it is only by their repetition in various circumstances that one can recognize them as characteristic and essential. . . . And from the comparison of the different works we separate the different traits whose sum constitutes the moral portrait of the artist."

References to others of Ruskin's works are indeed numerous in these notes; some eighteen titles are quoted, including *Praeterita* and several volumes of *Modern Painters* and of the *Fors Clavigera* letters. Other English authors quoted or mentioned are Bunyan, Tennyson, Carlyle, Byron, George Eliot, and Pater; French men of letters and writers on art or religion are equally represented. It was natural and appropriate that his article of the following year should be entitled "On Reading." "Sur la lecture" appeared in the June 15, 1905, issue of the *Renaissance latine,* a review sponsored by his friends Constantin de Brancovan and his sister the Comtesse de Noailles; a year later it was published as the preface to the translation of *Sesame and Lilies,* which itself had received prior publication in *Les Arts de la vie.*

As his renewed interest in Ruskin was more guarded than his first lyric excitement, so the activity in which it involved him was more broad than before. Between 1903 and 1905, and in addition to his Ruskin work, he published in the *Figaro* seven articles on the salons with which he was familiar (these articles were signed "Dominique," "Horatio," or "Echo") as well as one entitled "La Mort des cathédrales: une conséquence du projet Briand"; in *Gil Blas* a pseudonymous review of a book by Gregh; and in *Les Arts de la vie* a review called "Un Professeur de beauté," about Montesquiou and his book *Professionnelles Beautés.*

He also made architectural excursions to Avallon, Vézelay, and Dijon—at the cost of many attacks of asthma and a trip to Evian to recuperate. Bertrand de Fénelon and the Bibescos—particularly Emmanuel, the Gothic expert and the one most skeptical about Proust's physical incapacity—prodded him into risking further pilgrimages, among them a spring excursion to Coucy, Laon, and Senlis, in the additional company of Billy and Georges de Lauris. "He even climbed," writes de Lauris, "to the platform of the great tower [of Coucy], the one the Germans destroyed. I remember that he climbed leaning on the arm of Bertrand de Fénelon, who, to encourage him, hummed the Good Friday Spell. It was, in fact, a Good Friday, with the fruit trees in bloom under a young sun. I also see Marcel attentive in front of the church of Senlis, listening to Prince Emmanuel Bibesco, who, with much modesty and as if protesting that he was not teaching him anything, explained what characterizes the spires of the Ile de France."

Specific marks of Ruskin's thought are to be found in *A la Recherche du temps perdu*: the intense, almost tactile attention to the material in which an artist has worked, the symbolic significance—the soul—in statuary and architecture, the combination of the local and temporary with the general and universal in the models who served for statues, Ruskin's exposition of Turner in *Modern Painters,* which served as a background for the impressionist theory in Proust's novel.

Furthermore, one can scarcely read the notes that accompany Proust's translation without being struck by the resemblance of the style to that of Ruskin, and at the same time to that of

Proust's later manner. It is not that the sinuous parenthetical constructions of *A la Recherche du temps perdu* are an imitation, but rather that in dealing with Ruskin's ideas, and possibly even encouraged by his example, Proust began to dare to be himself, to "follow the meanderings of his thought" with something of the same voluminous attention to details, the same scrupulous anxiety for completeness, that characterized the author he was translating.

More significant than specific ideological parallels and resemblance of styles, however, is the transmission from Ruskin to Proust of an attitude toward objects of art. As Proust put it, "The universe took on again in my eyes an infinite value. And my admiration for Ruskin gave such importance to the things he made me love, that they seemed of greater value than life itself." And later in the same article, "There is no better way to begin to realize what one feels oneself than to try to recreate in oneself what a master has felt. In this deep effort it is our own thought as well as his which we bring to light."

Of the psychological benefit which Ruskin, whatever his intrinsic merits, had conferred upon him, Proust, who had his own reasons for being interested in the pathology of the will and had read Ribot on the subject, was well aware, for he wrote, in 1905:

It is known that, in certain disorders of the nervous system, the patient, without damage to any of his organs, is mired in a sort of incapacity to will, as in a deep rut from which he cannot extricate himself alone, and in which he would finally perish, if a powerful helping hand were not extended to him. . . . Now there are certain minds which may be compared to these sufferers, and which a sort of laziness or frivolity prevents from descending spontaneously into the deep regions of the self where the true life of the spirit begins. It is not that, once they have been led there, they are incapable of discovering and exploiting the true wealth, but, without this external intervention, they live on the surface in a perpetual forgetfulness of themselves, in a sort of passivity which makes them end by suppressing in themselves all feeling and all recollection of their spiritual nobility, if an external impulse did not come and reintroduce them, as it were, into the life of the spirit, where suddenly they rediscover the power of thinking for themselves and of creating. Now this impulse, which the lazy mind cannot find in itself, and which must come from another, must, it is clear, be received in the heart of solitude, outside of which, as we have seen, cannot be produced that creative activity which, precisely, must be resurrected. From pure solitude the lazy mind could get nothing, because it is incapable by itself of setting in motion its creative activity. . . . What is necessary, then, is an intervention which, while coming from another, is produced in the depths of ourselves, an impulse, indeed, of another mind, but received in the heart of solitude. Now that, we have seen, is precisely the definition of reading, and to reading alone is the definition applicable.

This pathological inertia, this frivolity of life, this compensatory longing for solitude, coupled with an incapacity to profit from it, apply very well to Proust; add to them dutiful efforts regularly ending in failure and consequent remorse, and you have a fair picture of his state between the publication of *Les Plaisirs et les Jours* and his discovery of Ruskin. He was living in a superficial part of himself, in which plans and resolutions remained ineffectual against the dead weight of the torpid remainder of his being. The enthusiasm awakened by Ruskin stirred the depths, reconciled contradictions, and made possible the previously impossible.

To have sent him back to Ruskin when, too soon, he was ready to drop work and confess that he had no object in life, must be reckoned as one of the many services of Proust's devoted mother. But the service had its limitations. It led him, it is true, into a happier and better adjusted way of life. He took much interest in late 1904 and early 1905 in the articles of Robert Dreyfus (with whom his estrangement was at an end) on Gobineau, made efforts to place articles by another friend, worked on his translation and preface of *Sesame and Lilies,* and organized a severely exclusive gathering at his home to listen to Montesquiou read from his works. His eyes troubled him a little from excessive reading and writing, but his general health was, for him, fair. In May he wrote to Dreyfus, "I go out about once a month for an hour, and then have—not to mention attacks of asthma—a week of bed, fever, etc. . . . I am not too unhappy now. I can work a little—except during my last attacks —and I lead a very pleasant life of repose, reading, and studious intimacy with Mother."

From the personal point of view, such conditions were an improvement upon apathy and discouragement, but they were not a favorable climate for the production of the original work which he was now eager to undertake. At times the Ruskin work and the newspaper articles irked him. As he wrote to Antoine Bibesco,

> All that I am doing is not real work, but only documentation, etc. . . . It is enough to arouse my thirst for achievement, but naturally without quenching it at all. From the moment when, for the first time since this long torpor, I looked inward, toward my thought, I have felt all the emptiness of my life; a hundred characters for a novel, a thousand ideas beg me to give them body. . . . I have awakened the sleeping bee and I feel its cruel sting much more than its impotent wings. I had subjected my intelligence to my repose. In freeing it from its chains I thought I was merely liberating a slave, [but I find] I have given myself a master whom I have not the physical strength to satisfy and who would kill me if I did not resist him.

As was becoming usual with him, Proust's health became an obstacle to his desires only when there existed some other impediment, which, in a way, his illness symbolized. The end of his Ruskin commitments was in sight, and he did not need to do small articles for the newspapers if he did not so choose. Why then should he feel frustrated, and unable to undertake his novel?

A part of the reason is that the "thousand ideas" teeming within him were not yet harmonized and fused by the necessary emotional experience that was to launch him on his major work. But another reason probably existed, although no direct evidence in Proust's published work or letters can be produced to support it, and although it is even unlikely that he should have so much as mentioned it in conversation. It is that the "studious intimacy" in which he lived with his mother and her strong interest in his work were not conducive to the unhampered handling of sexual and homosexual materials. The treatment of the homosexual theme in the story of 1893 was a model of circumspection, and the "extreme license" which he admitted to exist in certain passages of *Les Plaisirs et les Jours* was an anemic foreshadowing of his later language, which his mother was never to see. We can scarcely doubt that Madame Proust would have been pained, and it is a natural inference that her son, in his boundless affection for her, would have censored himself.

The new dilemma into which he was heading was solved by the death of Madame Proust.

For some time her health had been failing. The death of her parents had been such a blow to her "that," Proust noted in 1902, "I still wonder how she survived." He went on to describe the change in her voice in words that recall the conversation of Marcel with his grandmother in *Le Côté de Guermantes:* ". . . in the telephone suddenly there came to me her poor broken voice, bruised forever, a different voice from the one I had always known, full of cracks and breaks; gathering up in the receiver its broken and bleeding fragments, I had for the first time the horrible feeling of what had been forever broken in her."

In the summer of 1898 she had a serious operation, which caused her son great anxiety, but she was apparently recovered by the end of the year. The death of her husband, in November 1903, was another blow, such that when the first—and for her the only—anniversary of his death came around, Proust felt that he could not leave her alone. In September 1905, when he accompanied her to Evian, she was already seriously ill with uremia, but made heroic efforts to conceal the gravity of her condition. Two hours after their arrival she was seized with such a violent attack of illness that she had to be brought back to Paris, and there, on September 23, she died. To Montesquiou, who, both before and after her death, had written sympathetically, Proust replied,

My life has now lost its only objective, its only sweetness, its only love, its only consolation. I have just lost her whose incessant vigilance brought me—in peace, in tenderness—the only honey of my life, which I taste still at times with horror in this silence which she could make so deep all day around my sleep, and which the habit of the servants whom she had trained still causes inertly to survive her finished activity. I have been steeped in all sorrows, I have lost her, I have seen her suffer, I can believe that she knew she was leaving me and that she was unable to make recommendations that it was perhaps anguish for her to suppress, I have the feeling that by my bad health I have been the sorrow and worry of her life. The very excess of my need for her has for the last two days prevented my seeing anything before my eyes when I think of her but two particularly dreadful visions of her illness. I can no longer sleep and if, by chance, I doze off, sleep, less sparing of pain than my waking intelligence, overwhelms me with atrocious thoughts which at least when I am awake my reason attempts to measure out, and, when I can no longer stand them, to contradict. Only one thing has been spared me. I have not had the torment of dying before her, and of feeling the horror which that would have been for her. To leave me for eternity, feeling me so little able to maintain the struggle of life, must have been a severe trial for her also. She must have understood the wisdom of parents who, before dying, kill their little children. As the Sister who tended her said, I was still four years old to her.

This profound grief, and the dislocation to his habits resulting from it, naturally had their repercussion in his always sensitive health. For several months before his mother's death he had been making inquiries about doctors and possible courses of treatment, and was thinking seriously of putting himself in the hands of Dr. Sollier, a specialist in nervous diseases. Madame Proust's death did not change his intention. In January 1906, he entered Dr. Sollier's institution, intending to stay perhaps six weeks. He was reluctant and pessimistic about the step, and got off to a bad start. The doctor engaged him in conversation, in the course of which Bergson was mentioned. "What a confused and limited mind," he said in a superior way. Proust only smiled, but, as he noted later, "that did not contribute to the success of the psychotherapeutic treatment." While in the institution he wrote to Billy, "I am not climbing the hill, alas! I am going down at a gallop, but I want to prolong the trial." Nevertheless he did not stay out his time. On January 27 a mutual friend wrote to Billy that Proust was at home, and more ill than ever.

In June he wrote to Dreyfus that he had not dressed for seven months, but was determined "next year" to dress and go out daily. In July he was making inquiries, in his usual complex and inconclusive way, about renting rooms at Cabourg or Trouville, but perhaps "the most reasonable would be Evian." In the end he stayed in Paris until well into August, and then went to the Hôtel des Réservoirs at Versailles, where his stay, almost entirely in bed, was prolonged until the end of the year. Having decided to leave the apartment at 45 rue de Courcelles occupied by his parents, and then by himself alone from late 1900 on, and dreading entirely new surroundings, he planned to move to 102 Boulevard Haussmann, an apartment house in which his greatuncle Louis Weil had lived and died. There were many difficulties about installations and repairs, so that he did not move to his new quarters until early 1907, and even after his occupancy he was driven frantic by the noise of unfinished work. It was in this apartment that he installed his famous cork-lined room; there he lived until 1919, and in it he wrote nearly all of his novel.

By summer his health was slightly improved. In August he went to Cabourg, and from there, in a sudden access of energy, he made automobile trips to see churches in Caen, Bayeux, Balleroy, Dives, Lisieux, and other places. For these trips he hired a *Unic* car (a company in which his friend Jacques Bizet was interested) and, with all windows tightly shut, set forth

upon his travels. Motoring was an adventure in those days; if
the driver handled his noisy and complicated machinery with
skill, if he accomplished his journey without serious mishap, he
aroused in his passenger an enthusiastic admiration unknown to
the motorist of today. Proust was enchanted with his chauffeur
Agostinelli, a handsome nineteen-year-old native of Monaco. At
Lisieux they had a breakdown which delayed them till nightfall,
and before leaving Proust wanted to have another look at some
carving on the façade of the cathedral. It was already too dark
to see, but he got out of the car and went forward to pass his
hands over the object of his interest. Suddenly the façade was
flooded with light: "It was my driver, the ingenious Agostinelli,"
Proust wrote in "Impressions de route," "who, directing to the
old sculptures the salute of the present . . . turned in succession
on all parts of the porch the searchlight of his automboile. And
when I came back toward the car, I saw a group of curious
children, who, their heads bent over the searchlight and their
curls dancing in this supernatural light, made a new composition of Angels of the Nativity, projected, as it were, in a ray
from the cathedral."

   Night had fallen when they left Lisieux, and Proust, watching his young chauffeur admiringly from the back seat, continued
his esthetic comparisons. Agostinelli had put on a rubber cape,
which, with his beardless face enclosed in a hood-like helmet,
made him look "like some nun of speed." When his hand moved
to the gear shift lever and from the depths of the 1907 model
there issued the extraordinary musical effects of low gear, he
became a Saint Cecilia at the organ. But generally he kept his
hands on the wheel, as on the cross of consecration held by the
Apostles in the Sainte Chapelle in Paris, Proust thought, or the
stylized wheel of medieval art. It was an appropriate symbol
of his ministry, but Proust hoped that it was not an omen of
the death by which he should die.

   Agostinelli drove him back to Paris at the close of the season, and for a short time remained at his employer's disposition. But then he had to leave for Monaco, and it was there that he read the description of himself in "Impressions de route en automobile," published in the *Figaro* for November 19. Proust received several letters about that article, but the "prettiest," he wrote Madame Straus, was from Agostinelli.

~ 6 ~

WRITING THE NOVEL

AT THE beginning of "Matinée chez la Princesse de Guermantes," the last chapter of *A la Recherche du temps perdu,* the narrator, Marcel, is in a deeply discouraged state of mind. At a stop of the train that is carrying him back to Paris after his trip to Venice he looks out at the trees that line the track, and mournfully reflects that they no longer arouse any emotion in him. " 'Trees,' I thought, 'you have nothing more to say to me, my chilled heart no longer understands you. . . . Perhaps in the new and so desiccated part of my life which is beginning, men might inspire in me what nature no longer can. . . .' But in substituting a possible observation of humanity for an impossible inspiration, I realized that I was merely trying to console myself, and that the consolation was without value."

These words, probably written in 1909, describe Proust's own state of mind after finishing with Ruskin. The emotional inspiration originally derived from the study of the master had cooled. As he wrote in 1904, in the preface to his translation of *The Bible of Amiens,* "Being unable to reawaken the fires of the past, we wish at least to gather up their ashes. In default of a resurrection of which we are no longer capable with the frozen memory we have of these things . . . we wish at least to describe it scientifically." In other words, he believed he had lost forever the power of affective memory.

He continued to occupy himself with journalism. Just after moving into the Boulevard Haussmann apartment in 1907 he had managed on very short notice to write a commissioned article for the *Figaro;* other articles followed in March, June, and July. After his summer excursions he wrote two more articles, one of

103

them the "Impressions de route en automobile," which was in part founded upon some pages written in childhood, long before the day of the automobile. In 1908 he began a series of parodies, a type of writing at which he had already tried his hand in 1904 with "Fête chez Montesquiou à Neuilly."

But such work was scarcely more satisfying than translation and annotation. He felt that the *Figaro* articles were of small interest to the majority of its readers, and that its editor, Calmette, only published them out of friendship. In an attempt to even the score he gave for Calmette an elaborate dinner at the Ritz on July 1, 1907, with entertainment by professional musicians and with celebrities and aristocrats among the guests.

The original material which he felt within him remained intractable, but he was still thinking about it, and alive to the possibilities of new subject matter. In 1907 and 1908 considerable publicity was given to homosexual scandals in German aristocratic circles, and it is probable that Proust followed them with interest, for in May 1908 he consulted Dreyfus about the possibility of an article or a story, in terms that suggest, as Dreyfus confirms, a treatment of homosexuality. The article as such never appeared, but its materials were very possibly used later.

Finally, in 1908—still with his "frozen memory," still without emotional inspiration—he got around to the novel again. In July he wrote to Montesquiou, in words that recall the efforts of 1899, "I struggle without progress, when I am not suffering too much, on a novel which will perhaps give you a little more esteem for me if you have the patience to read it." By March 1909 he had evidently written a considerable amount, for he wrote to Princesse Bibesco of sacrificing "almost a volume on Brittany," because of involuntary resemblances in his language to that of Madame de Noailles.

But still the newspaper work went on. On March 6 he published a parody of Henri de Régnier in the *Figaro,* and in a letter of the same month to Lauris he referred to two others, on Chateaubriand and Maeterlinck, not yet ready for publication;

to studies in Sainte-Beuve, to much other reading. On April 17 he accepted Dreyfus' suggestion for a parody of Nietzsche, and mentioned a project of publishing a collection of these *pastiches*.

In another month, however, all is changed. The miracle had occurred. What, exactly, it was, we do not know—probably an incident of involuntary memory, a vivid resurgence of the past, and with it the needed inspiration for his novel. It was the real life equivalent of Marcel's experience at the "Matinée chez la Princesse de Guermantes."

On May 23 he asks Lauris about the availability of the name Guermantes for a novel; in the latter half of June he writes to Montesquiou of having undertaken a long work, "a sort of novel whose beginning will perhaps appear shortly. Until it is finished, if I can work—for my strength is declining very perceptibly and I know exactly how much—I shall be very preoccupied. And my hand is so tired that I avoid letters." In July he informs Dreyfus that he has not put out his electricity for sixty hours, to the amazement of his valet. "Who would have believed it?" As for the parodies, he dismisses them with an inelegant but expressive monosyllable.

By August he is worn out; he drops work and goes to Cabourg. But from there he writes to Madame Straus, "I have just begun—and finished—a whole long book." What he means, as appears from other passages of his correspondence, is, not that he has finished the book, but that he has written the first and last chapters—"Combray" and "Matinée chez la Princesse de Guermantes"—of *A la Recherche du temps perdu*. At Cabourg he is able neither to work nor to go out on the beach; but he enjoys coming down to the Casino of the Grand Hôtel in the evenings and listening to the conversation of some very young men, to whom he reads poetry and for whose entertainment he makes plans.

When he returned to Paris in the fall, his belief in his work was strengthened by the favorable opinion of friends—among them Hahn and Lauris—who had read his opening chapter.

Convinced that he had only a short time to live, he resolved to claustrate himself in his apartment and dedicate his remaining strength to the completion of his work, and this, with as few interruptions at possible, he did. Systematically protecting himself by excuses about his extraordinary hours, his attacks, his fumigations for asthma, he kept his friends at bay. By the spring of 1912 the whole of his novel, as originally conceived, had been set down, and he began to revise and to enrich it by additions. He began to go out more, questioned friends, checked on costumes, gestures, and conversations, or refreshed his impressions of landscapes and fruit trees in flower.

As early as the summer of 1909 he had begun sounding out publishers; but in the fall of 1912 nothing was yet settled, and he had seriously to set about getting his book printed. Fasquelle, the Nouvelle Revue Française, and Ollendorff begged to be excused; finally, and not till March 1913, he concluded arrangements with the enterprising young publisher Bernard Grasset. Wearied with the long negotiations with other firms and seriously concerned that he might not live long enough to see his work in print, he stipulated at once with Grasset that the edition was to be at his own expense. The novel, which he had originally thought of as a single large volume, had been growing by successive revisions, and he had had to admit the necessity first of two and finally of three volumes, to be called respectively *Du Côté de chez Swann, Le Côté de Guermantes,* and *Le Temps retrouvé;* the trilogy was to be covered by the title *A la Recherche du temps perdu.*

If the three volumes had appeared at once, and simultaneously, they would have totalled some 1,500 dense pages. *Du Côté de chez Swann* appeared in November 1913, and the following June the second volume was set up. But it was never published, for the war intervened. Grasset was mobilized, and no new volumes of the series appeared until after the Armistice, and then by a new publisher, the Nouvelle Revue Française. During the war

Proust set about revising and enlarging the two unpublished parts of his work, and he continued the process after publication was resumed, with the material remaining in his hands. The result was that between 1914 and 1922, the year of his death, he added some 2,500 pages to his original second and third volumes —considerably more than the total length of the work in 1912.

Naturally such an enormous expansion was not accomplished without change, not only in the dimensions but in the character of the work. Its proportions were disturbed and its structure— already complex in the original version—was seriously obscured. Unintentional repetitions and contradictions were introduced, as might be expected from the fact that, with cutting, pasting, marginal insertions, and changes of order, the manuscripts got into such a state that Proust himself could scarcely read them. Yet the basic philosophy and the methods of the original remained intact in the revision.

This statement is possible not only because Proust is abundantly on record as to his intentions and his methods at the time of the publication of *Swann,* but because we can reconstruct in considerable detail the three original volumes and compare them with the final version.

The first volume, *Du Côté de chez Swann,* is common to both versions. The fly leaf of the original edition carried an announcement of the two remaining volumes "to appear in 1914," with a brief analysis of the contents of each, sufficient to make possible the identification of the episodes. Furthermore, a set of proofs of the second volume, set up in June 1914, was discovered and studied in detail by Albert Feuillerat, who appended to his book *(Comment Marcel Proust a composé son roman)* a list of the additions to the original second volume, as they appear in the corresponding volumes of the final version, *A l'Ombre des jeunes filles en fleur* and *Le Côté de Guermantes* Part I. The contents of the second volume as revealed by the proofs correspond precisely to the analysis given on the fly leaf of the original edition of *Swann;* in all probability the analysis of the third volume shown on the same fly leaf is as accurate as that of the second, although a detailed comparison in this case is not possible.

The most important of Proust's intentions and methods in his original novel result from what happened in the spring of 1909: a profound emotional experience which convinced him that the past was still living, still essentially present. The mechanism of this revelation was a chance association of sensations which made a moment of the past suddenly relive in all its forgotten details, and he was left with the feeling that beneath the fleeting surface of experience there was an immortal substratum, a timeless essence. On reflection he decided that this essence was what he had sensed when some natural object seemed to challenge him to read its secret; had sensed, too, in the emotion engendered by great art.

These ideas were not for him mere literary capital; they were the truth, and a way of life. In 1910 he wrote to Dreyfus: "Furthermore by continuing to live in this way [a life devoted to writing] you will live in a region of yourself where the barriers of the flesh and of time exist no more, where there is no death, because there is no time, nor body, where one lives sweetly in the immortal society of what one loves." To Princesse Bibesco he wrote in May 1912: "Nothing is more foreign to me than to seek the essence of happiness in the immediate sensation, still less in material realization. A sensation, however disinterested it may be, a perfume, a light, if they are present are still too much in my power to make me happy. It is when they recall to me another [sensation], when I savor them between the past and the present (and not in the past, impossible to explain here) that they make me happy."

Again in 1912, he wrote to Madame Straus, "What you say about a 'victory over the past' is one more proof that as you say our sensibilities are in tune, and I can give you no better proof of it than that one of the titles I have thought of for my book is for the first volume *Time Lost* and for the third *Time Regained.*

But you are wrong in thinking it only imagination. . . . The philosophers have indeed persuaded us that time is a process of numbering which corresponds to nothing real. We believe it, but the old superstition is so strong that we cannot escape."

Translated into terms of literary practice, this philosophy of the living past meant an insistence on the use of the involuntary memory, the sensibility, and the subconscious. "It is chiefly of the involuntary memory," Proust said in an interview in *Le Temps* of November 13, 1913, "that the artist should ask the raw materials of his work." And again, "It [my book] is in no sense a work of reasoning . . . its slightest elements have been furnished me by my sensibility." These statements may be true enough of the "Combray" chapter, but as applied to "Un Amour de Swann" they are an obvious exaggeration; the satiric tone and the psychological analysis of this part are an intellectual performance which could scarcely spring from involuntary memory, pure sensibility, or the subconscious.

His conception of style was based on the same theories. "Style," he said in the same interview, "is by no means an adornment as some people think, it is not even a question of technique, it is—like color for painters—a quality of vision, the revelation of the particular universe which each of us sees, and which is not seen by others."

The sense of the continuing past affected his portrayal of character. "There is plane geometry," he said, "and there is solid geometry. Well, for me, the novel is not only plane psychology, but psychology in time. . . . Like a city, which, while the train pursues its winding way, appears now on our right, now on our left, the different aspects which the same character has assumed in the eyes of another—to the point of being like successive and different characters . . . will give the sensation of time elapsed." And in a letter to Blum in February 1913, he said, "There are many characters; they are 'prepared' from the first volume, that is they will do in the second exactly the opposite of what one expected from the first. . . . And as for composition, it is so complex that it doesn't appear until late when all the 'Themes' have begun to combine."

Such are Proust's main principles at the time of the publication of *Swann*: the living past revealed by involuntary memory, the importance of sensibility by contrast with pure intelligence, style as a quality of vision, psychology developed in time, systematic reversals of character, a structure so complex that it will seem like haphazard discontinuity until the "Themes" have begun to combine.

If Proust believed in the use of the involuntary memory and the subconscious, he believed too in revision. As long as a manuscript was in his hands he kept touching it up. He corrected the manuscript of *Swann* and had it typed; he corrected the typescript and had it retyped. He continued the process with the proofs, to the annoyance of printers and at considerable expense to himself. As he wrote to Vaudoyer, "My corrections up to now (I hope this won't continue) are not corrections. Not one line in 20 of the original text (which has been replaced incidentally by another) remains."

And yet, contrary to his past and his future practice, and for reasons that will shortly become apparent, a full year elapsed between the publication of *Swann* and the beginning of his new revisions. When, near the beginning of 1915, he took up his manuscripts again, he had some new material and new ideas, and most of it was analytical in manner and pessimistic in purport. He seemed to have become more suspicious, and his estimate of human nature in general, never of the rosiest, and of the servant class in particular, had become gloomier.

Part of the change was due simply to the fact that he was growing older. He was well aware that in himself, as in other writers, the passage of time brought a gradual change from poetic sensitivity toward critical skepticism, for he noted in his last volume: "Often writers in whose hearts no longer appear these mysterious verities [intuitively perceived], write, after a certain age, with their intelligence alone, which has grown progressively stronger; on this account the books of their maturity are stronger than those of their youth, but they no longer have the same bloom." And in *La Prisonnière,* more personally, "Across from the sensitive child that I had wholly been, now stood a man of opposite character, full of common sense, of severity for the morbid sensibility of others."

But one should not jump to the conclusion that the Proust of 1909 to 1913 was dreamy, poetic, emotional, and that the Proust of 1915 to 1922 was a pessimistic intellectual who superimposed upon his first novel a second which in effect canceled his original message. His satirical and analytical powers and his generally low estimate of human motivation are abundantly apparent in "Un Armour de Swann," and even as far back as *Les Plaisirs et les Jours.* On the other hand, in additions after 1915 there is clear confirmation of his earlier belief that involuntary memory, the subconscious, and the sensibility are of more value to his art than pure intelligence.

Of the series of incidents of involuntary memory that punctuate the novel and support its structure, one (the three trees, IV, 161-65) has received a significant addition, and another (the musty odor, III, 90, 93-94) is in its entirety new material. Both occur in the volumes of the final version corresponding to the original second volume, the only part where it is possible to trace detailed additions. Furthermore, in this part there are no other clear instances of involuntary memory.

It is not even true to say that all additions are pessimistic. One on Françoise (IV, 69-70) and another on Saint-Loup (IV, 177-78) are definitely favorable, and one on Bloch contains the astonishingly optimistic generalization that "it is not common sense which is the most widespread thing in the world, it is kindness" (IV, 194).

As for the sensibility, two of Proust's finest long emotional passages were additions, one written in 1915 and the other in 1921.

What happened was that he went through a period of doubt

and depression which reached its low point in 1918, and which left its mark on a part of his work, most of all on *Sodome et Gomorrhe;* but that before the end he partially emerged from the darkness into a reaffirmation of his earlier faith. He was older then, and tired—indeed dying, and he had lost faith in many things; but at least he felt sure that the philosophy and the literary principles which he had set forth in 1913 were at the heart of his best work.

The really interesting change in Proust's novel is that from 1915 on it became increasingly a living human document. He had talked of psychology in time, but he never could have foreseen the extent to which his writing was to mirror his evolution. Under pressure of personal experience and of the war, he was changing, and the change is recorded.

One of the most important chapters of his personal experience opened—or reopened—in 1912, after he had finished the first draft of his novel: Agostinelli, the young taxi-driver of Monaco, finding himself out of work, offered his services to his former patron. But Proust already had as chauffeur Albaret, the husband of his housekeeper Céleste, and proposed, somewhat dubiously, that Agostinelli should turn secretary and type *Swann* for him. Agostinelli accepted, and he and his wife Anna (or his supposed wife, for it later turned out that they were not married) came to live with their employer. If Proust had admired the young man as a chauffeur, he was dazzled by him as a secretary. Later he wrote to Monsieur Straus, "Agostinelli (as I had not *imagined* at Cabourg where I had known him only as a chauffeur, and afterwards I hadn't seen him again for years) was an extraordinary person, with perhaps the greatest intellectual gifts I have known!" And in another letter, "I think you would have been amazed to read, from the pen of this chauffeur, sentences worthy of the greatest writers. You would certainly have found it hard to reconcile with these sentences the idea you could have had of him at Trouville (which was furthermore the idea I had of him too)."

By February 1913, there were signs of trouble in the Proust ménage. He urged correspondents to seal their letters with wax, to avoid telephoning (but if they did, to be sure to say nothing of his negotiations with publishers, especially if it was his valet who answered). In March he wrote to René Blum of a strong desire to get away, and go to Florence. "And then I lacked the courage, I waited too long and since because of hay fever I would have to leave Florence toward the beginning of April, it would scarcely be worth while." In further correspondence he mentioned "annoyances," "sorrows," "anxiety." He had lost confidence in his unharmonious domestic staff. Anna was jealous and rapacious; very likely Albaret and Céleste resented the newcomers. And there were hangers-on: Emile Agostinelli, a brother of Alfred, and like him a chauffeur, and in the background a sister who was the mistress of a baron. The Agostinellis had vulgar and expensive tastes; as Proust wrote to Monsieur Straus, "The Agostinellis are people who when they have fifty francs spend twenty on peaches, twenty on automobiles, etc., and have nothing left the next day . . . but if I told you their life in detail you *wouldn't believe me."* Proust was prodigally generous, so that his very considerable income, already damaged by naïve marginal speculations and by baccarat at Cabourg, became seriously strained.

Under these trying conditions he went through elaborate publicity maneuvers about his book, invoking friendship and influence and arranging for interviews and inspired articles. But by the time the first volume was ready to appear he had almost lost interest in it. In November 1913, he wrote to Vaudoyer, "Thank you for thinking of my book, it appears in two weeks, just at this time when I am so unhappy and when I cannot feel the joy which perhaps I would have felt at another time." Shortly after, he revived his plan to escape to Italy, but again couldn't make up his mind to it. To Madame de Noailles he wrote of his sorrow and added that he hoped she would read the second part of "Un Amour de Swann," which dealt with jealousy.

But worse was to come when Agostinelli resolved to learn to fly. Proust strenuously opposed the project, but the secretary, who, in spite of free spending, had put money aside, was feeling independent; besides, Anna was sure that there was a fortune in aviation. A break came, and Proust wrote to Agostinelli, "If you ever have the misfortune to have an airplane accident, be sure to tell your wife that she will find in me neither a protector nor a friend, and will never have a penny from me."

In the spring of 1914 Agostinelli went to the south of France and registered in an aviation school at Antibes under the name of "Marcel Swann." On May 30, during his second solo flight, his plane fell into the sea and he was drowned. And so the omen which Proust had feared to see as the young driver sat behind the wheel of his car in 1907 was fulfilled in 1914 by a more dangerous career than that of chauffeur.

Anna, who had been watching at the time of the accident, sent Proust a desperate telegram. Despite the warning she had received, she had well judged of his generosity, for he at once tried to secure financial help for her from the Prince of Monaco, and later to find her work. He even made efforts to place the brother Emile as a chauffeur. And when the distraught wife turned up in Paris he tried to calm her weeping and "to restore to her a courage which he lacked."

For Proust the two years that Agostinelli had spent with him were no mere tale of rapacity and abuse of confidence; the grief which he felt, and long continued to feel, after Agostinelli's death was deep and sincere. More than once, in the months and years that followed, he referred, although with the touch of secrecy that characterized most of his correspondence about the affair, to his "dear secretary" as the person whom, with his father and his mother, he had the most loved.

When *La Prisonnière* appeared in 1923, readers were puzzled by the anomalous status of Albertine. How could a young un-married woman in respectable social standing live with a man, be kept practically a prisoner by him, without apparently causing any scandal? And then gossip began to circulate that "Albertine was a man."

Such a statement, or its more precise variant that Albertine "was" Agostinelli, is too extreme, as we shall later see. But that the young chauffeur had an important influence on the elaboration of the fictional Albertine can scarcely be doubted.

As announced on the fly leaf of *Swann,* Proust's second volume was to contain nothing that suggests Albertine, nor did she appear at all in the proofs of this volume that were printed in June 1914. The episode of the band of adolescent girls at Balbec, originally scheduled for the third volume, now appears in *A l'Ombre des jeunes filles en fleur,* and there Albertine is mentioned. The material, which, although broken up, can readily be identified, has of course been revised, but even in its present form it merely shows Albertine as one of a group for which the narrator feels a poetic sentiment; he finally singles her out, but nothing like a serious love affair occurs.

Yet the announcement of the remaining material of the novel as printed on the fly leaf of *A l'Ombre des jeunes filles en fleur* in 1918 contains abundant reference to Albertine, and of a more important nature. "Albertine reappears," we read, and "Why I leave Balbec suddenly, with the intention of marrying Albertine," and "Life with Albertine," and "Disappearance of Albertine."

The clear inference that most of the Albertine material is new is strengthened if we read Proust's correspondence with Madame Scheikévitch. Late in 1914 she had lost her brother, and in January he sent her a letter of sympathy. During the course of 1915 she gave him her copy of *Swann,* apparently for his autograph, and on November 3 he wrote, "If you haven't yet got it back, it is because, in my great desire to reveal to you that part of myself which you know the least, which the first *Swann* contains in germ, but invisibly—and in spite of my dislike of taking the freshness off the new book, which I should have liked to give you intact—I have undertaken to summarize for you on the blank pages of your copy (already covered with my writing) an episode entirely different from the rest and the only one that could now find in your wounded heart affinities of sorrow. But as I must summarize in six pages the contents of six hundred, it is very hard work. As soon as it is finished, I shall send you back your copy, so it will contain, with the first *Swann,* that which, of the later ones, is at present known by *no one.* . . . So I shall ask you not to show it until the work has appeared."

The recommendation of secrecy was probably as much on personal as on literary grounds. In January 1918, he reminded her that she was the only person in possession of manuscript extracts of his unpublished work, and a year later he had against her grounds for complaint that were probably related to the same situation: "How could I believe that this complaint was unfounded, since it was a thing which I had written to you alone in the world which was divulged, to my great moral and material detriment." In 1921 he was still vindictive, and wrote bluntly, "You did not keep your promise to show no one the extracts made for you from my future volumes."

The long and minutely written inscription which Proust wrote on the blank pages of Madame Scheikévitch's *Swann* contained a page about Madame Swann and Madame Cottard, and another about Albertine at Balbec and later as "the captive." But by far the greater part of it was devoted to a careful account of the principal subject matter of *Albertine disparue*—the gradual encroachment of oblivion on the painful memory of loss. Nearly every sentence of this account is to be found, sometimes with trifling verbal changes and sometimes verbatim, in the final version of *Albertine disparue.*

Parallels between the story of Albertine, as told in the expanded novel, and that of Agostinelli are striking. In the novel Marcel first meets Albertine at Balbec (Cabourg), and there is a little sentimental dalliance between them. Later she reënters his life, and finally comes to live with him. Françoise (Céleste) is suspicious and irritated, thinking Albertine unworthy of her master. Marcel finds himself involved in expense, suspicion, and worry, and finally wishes his captive were gone, without having the courage to make a break. He thinks of going to Italy, but cannot quite make up his mind to it. When, however, Albertine takes the initiative and makes an abrupt departure, he is beside himself, and makes every effort to get her to return. Just after making an offer to accept any terms if she will only come back, he receives a telegram saying that she has been killed by a fall from a horse. Follows the extraordinary description of the rhythmic assaults of pain. But slowly, one by one, the "selves"—created by associations of acts and seasons—which had loved Albertine, drop away, and are replaced by new selves who know her only by hearsay; until at last memory is conquered by oblivion, and Albertine dies in his heart as she has previously died in the flesh.

The chief cause of Marcel's self-inflicted sufferings during the captivity of Albertine is jealousy, based on a suspicion that she has had homosexual experience. Some persons, Proust among them, are capable of jealousy on the slightest pretext, and any generalization about so capricious an emotion is risky. Still, it does seem to be the rule that a heterosexual is more disturbed by a suspicion of heterosexual infidelity in the loved one than by the idea that she may have had past homosexual experience. Homosexuality may shock him, may damage his idealization of the beloved, but a specific and overwhelming jealousy is not indicated. With a homosexual, the situation is reversed; he is more or less indifferent to heterosexual behavior in the loved one, and is jealous only of homosexuality. Yet in Proust's novel the ostensibly heterosexual narrator is jealous only of homosexuality, and wishes that Albertine had instead been unfaithful with Saint-Loup. One is tempted to believe that in writing the story of Albertine Proust transposed the sex of the original, thereby destroying the chief cause for the jealousy which he illogically retained.

Given Proust's character, it is inevitable that he was jealous during Agostinelli's two-year stay in his establishment, and probably his recommendation to Madame de Noailles to read the second part of "Un Amour de Swann" is significant. But of whom, or of what, was he jealous? To Monsieur Straus he wrote that Anna was insanely jealous of her husband, who deceived her, although she did not know it. Yet in the same letter he claimed that he had seen few couples so "affectionately united" as the Agostinellis. Personally, he said, he did not like Anna, but he had to admit that she adored her husband (or lover), and after his death had tried several times to commit suicide; Agostinelli, on his side, loved Anna more than anything in the world. Perhaps Proust was not jealous of Anna but of some suspected homosexuality in Agostinelli's past; perhaps he made investigations at Cabourg, as Marcel did at Balbec. Between Proust's bizarre emotions and his regrettable tendency to tell lies if he thought the occasion warranted, it is hard to get at the full truth; but what we do know is enough.

After receiving the proofs of his original second volume, in June 1914, Proust's prostration at the death of his secretary was such, he wrote Montesquiou, that he had put off correcting them: "I am incapable even of rereading myself." The outbreak of the war undoubtedly caused further postponement. Probably he never did correct these proofs, for the set that has turned up came from among his papers and are untouched; when he did get around to his second volume, the changes of order and the additions of new material were so extensive that the proofs would have been of little use as a working basis. But by 1915 at the latest he was back at work—not on the second volume, but on what was to become *Albertine disparue*. In the analysis of unpublished work given to Madame Scheikévitch, the quotations about Madame Swann and her conversations with Madame Cottard were old work from his second volume, and appear practically verbatim in the current *A l'Ombre des jeunes filles en fleur*. The captivity of Albertine is barely mentioned in the analysis, after which he plunges into long quotations about the death of Albertine and the progress of oblivion. Evidently by the end of 1915 the episode of the captivity has been roughly planned, but not written, whereas the most striking part of *Albertine disparue* is in a smooth and finished form.

Proust's own opinion in the spring of 1921 was that these pages were the best that he had done. When they were published in 1926 the public, expecting something picturesque and romantic, was disappointed, but from the point of view of sheer writing many readers can now agree with the opinion of the author. They are brilliantly clear, as all too often Proust is not, and they are transfused, even when the most subtly analytical, with pain.

The emotion which was the mainspring of such writing came from a fusion of his personal sufferings with those caused by the war. Shortly after its outbreak his brother Robert became an army surgeon, and Proust saw him off at the Gare de l'Est for the Verdun sector. In a few weeks his hospital at Etain was bombarded, and shell splinters pierced the table upon which he was operating. From then on he was in the thick of it, always seeking to be sent where there was the most to do, and consequently where there was the most danger. He was cited in the order of the day, and decorated several times.

In September Proust made a trip to Cabourg. Although he went with the dread of painful reminders of his excursions with Agostinelli, the war proved to be an effectual diversion. Having contributed all his available cash to work for the war wounded, he cut short his stay and returned to Paris—to bed, and a renewal of his physical and moral sufferings. His anxiety was constant about such intimates as his brother, Halm, Lauris, Lavallée, Vaudoyer, Maugny, all of whom left for the war. He himself was on the inactive list because of his health, but on his own initiative he brought his case up for reëxamination—not that he really wanted to go, because he felt that he would be of small use; but he wished to be correct. After much delay, he was rejected again. In his bed in Paris he wrote Madame Scheikévitch, "I bless illness for making me suffer, for, if this suffering is of no use to anyone, at least it relieves me of that greater one which would be caused by comfort and ease while those of whom I do not cease to think suffer and die."

He was exasperated by the war attitude of some stay-at-homes, many of them aristocratic acquaintances of his: their concern with the disappearance of someone socially prominent, their preoccupation with the trivial effects of the conflict, their callousness to the mass suffering. For his part, he told Lucien Daudet, "one loves even those one does not know, one weeps even for the unknown." There was nothing insular in his patriotism; he deplored the militant exponents of "French culture" who vilified everything German. "If we had had war with Russia instead of Germany, what would they have said of Tolstoi and Dostoievski?"

His intimates, at first spared in the general holocaust, began to disappear. One of the earliest was not a war casualty: his old friend Gaston de Caillavet died in Paris after a brief illness, in January of 1915. Proust was deeply moved, and wrote a letter of tender reminiscence to the widow. Late one night, after Gaston's death, Proust had himself driven to the familiar house. With the motor of the car still running, he waited in the street for some sign of life, looking up at the darkened windows and remembering the past. On returning to his home he wrote to the widow, "For me the dead live. For me this is true of love, but also of friendship. I cannot explain this in a letter. When all my *Swann* has appeared, if ever you read it, you will understand me."

At about the same time Bertrand de Fénelon was listed as missing in action and presumed killed; in April Proust wrote to Clément de Maugny: "[My heart], dear Clément, always full of affection for you, forgets its sorrows in thinking of yours. And yet mine are very great—you don't know it, our lives are so separated now—for a friend whom I lost a year ago, and whom, with my father and my mother, is the person I have the most loved. But since then the deaths have come in uninterrupted succession. Bertrand de Fénelon, who, when you stopped seeing me, became my Clément and showed himself an incomparable friend, Bertrand de Fénelon who did not have to be mobilized and was performing greater service where he was, wanted to go, and was killed. I had not seen him for ten years, but I shall always weep for him. The death of d'Humières hurt me greatly. My brother has just been decorated for acts of bravery, but they signify also the risks he runs. Altogether, I can say that it is with a bleeding heart that I think of you and of all that you must be suffering in this life that is glorious, but so full of mourning."

The first year of the war brought Proust suffering which he was able to transmute into artistic creation and which did not seriously disturb his basic philosophy. About May of 1915 he wrote to Jacques Emile Blanche that he found, as before, "images arising from an impression superior to those which serve only to illustrate reasoning," and spoke of the necessity of leaving the surface of himself and seeking "the depths of his being," in order to see clearly.

After writing of the death of Albertine, Proust turned to the complete reshaping of his original second volume. *A l'Ombre des jeunes filles en fleur* was in the hands of his new publisher, Gallimard of the Nouvelle Revue Française, by the fall of 1916; from then on he worked on his volumes, in general in the order in which they later appeared. But it should be borne in mind that his revisions and additions were of two sorts. He was steadily occupied with preparing long new passages in the natural order of his book; but at the same time, having all his manuscripts about him, he jotted down ideas, corrected, and made short additions as they occurred to him, and at any part of the story. In 1917 he worked on *Le Côté de Guermantes;* in 1918, in addition to revising the proofs of *A l'Ombre des jeunes filles en fleur,* he was working, as a letter of April clearly shows, on *Sodome et Gomorrhe II. La Prisonnière* was made up in 1921 and 1922 partly from passages not written until then and partly from material from his old third volume. The next on the list, *Albertine disparue,* was put together almost simultaneously with *La*

Prisonnière, and like it contained old third-volume material, plus the part written in 1915. It was as ready as it ever was to become in June of 1922.

Meanwhile *Le Temps retrouvé,* which Proust did not live to put in order, had been receiving large and somewhat confused additions at intervals. One entirely new chapter dealing with Paris during the war, and containing references to Gotha raids of the spring of 1918 and to events of 1919, was a recent addition. The final chapter, written originally in 1909, had grown greatly by becoming the repository of his current ideas, chiefly observations on changes within himself, on his feeling of approaching death, on his methods of work and the state of his manuscripts. New and old are so intricately combined that a detailed separation is impossible. Confusions of chronology are introduced. We are told, for example, that Marcel spent "long years" in a sanatorium, came briefly to Paris in 1914 for a physical examination, and then returned. In 1916 the sanatorium was shut down because of the mobilization of its personnel, and Marcel made another trip to Paris, where he saw something of Charlus. He then withdrew to another sanatorium; returning, twenty years later, he found everyone greatly changed. All this would push the events of the final volume on to something like 1936, fourteen years after the death of the author. While it is not inconceivable that Proust intended to do just this, it is far more likely that he unintentionally confused his chronology by his additions, just as he confused other details.

After 1915 Proust's morale and his faith steadily deteriorated. He seemed to lose his confidence that the past—and with it the dead—was still living. Writing at the end of May 1916, of Fénelon, still not officially dead, he said: "Since it has not been known what became of Bertrand, it has been impossible for me to stay in bed without quantities of veronal. . . . I did not ever expect to see him again. . . . But if I was r•signed to his absence, it was my joy to think that he was happy. . . . But the idea, practically certain alas, that he may be cut off from the happiness of living, that for him, who had so many aptitudes for happiness and success, no sweetness of thought or feeling exist any more—this is an idea which I cannot endure and to which, for that very reason, I keep coming back, as one repeats the movement that causes pain."

The relief of sleep came only by increasing resort to drugs, which brought strange dreams and an insuperable torpor on awakening. To stimulate himself for work or contacts he then took caffeine, or gave himself an injection of adrenalin. In his anxiety for quick effect, in that "fear of immediate pain which condemns to perpetual suffering," he took too much both of narcotic and of stimulant. The result was a slow rhythm that ignored the divisions of day and night; febrility succeeded semi-coma in stretches of as long as two days. In September 1916, he wrote to Lucien Daudet: "At the moment it is a strange character out of Wells who is writing you, for I have not gone to bed for 50 hours. And even out of Jules Verne, for I have not sat down either (one cannot sit down when it is too long since one has gone to bed); nor have I stopped talking, which doesn't mean that I have thought, for . . . when I talk, I do not think."

Through 1917 the gloom deepened. The suicide of Emmanuel Bibesco in August did not surprise him: "I had guessed it all, and had predicted it for a long time." From life nothing was to be expected but evil; from men, nothing but duplicity. To his chapter on Paris during the war he added these morose words: "At the time when I believed what I was told, I would have been tempted, on hearing Germany, then Bulgaria, then Greece, protest their peaceful intentions, to believe them. But since life with Albertine and with Françoise had accustomed me to suspect in them thoughts and plans which they did not express, I allowed no apparently just word of William II, of Ferdinand of Bulgaria, of Constantine of Greece, to deceive my instinct, which guessed the machinations of each."

Instead of exploring "the depths of his being" he was now living more on the surface, and yielding in solitude to his old tendency toward a persecution complex. In January 1918, he wrote to Madame Scheikévitch: "I write you this little word to say: first, that I was *very* hurt at things you said about me since we saw each other; next, that I would be even more so at continuing to be angry with you on that account. The first days I thought it was better to say nothing: 'Only silence is great, all the rest is weakness.' And then this silence was too painful to keep. . . . I didn't wish you a happy new year because I was very upset and angry, but let us consider all that, if you will, as a 'rest measure,' and let us change the calendar . . . let us suppose that the 1st of January is only today. In the book for which you have shown such indulgence, my little man counted on the first of the year to start a new friendship with Gilberte. I have no longer the same illusions as he, and like you I know that characters go on. But at this moment I can only think of the sadness which your country must cause you."

But this pessimism about human regeneration was no more new than his brooding over slights. In the discouragement of these the darkest years of the war, he was reverting to attitudes of twenty and more years earlier. As early as January 1892, he had written: "Alas, a day comes when . . . we understand that characters do not change all at once, that our desire cannot direct the wills of others, so many are the things behind them which push them and which they cannot resist; a day comes when we understand that tomorrow could not be quite other than yesterday because it is made from yesterday." And as in the days when he was writing *Les Plaisirs et les Jours,* he was reading the pitiless character dissections of La Bruyère. "I thought of you much last night," he wrote Madame Straus at the end of 1917, "while reading La Bruyère (contemporary authors being unbearable to me). It seems to me that he has some thoughts that you must like. . . ."

It was in this frame of mind that he worked upon *Sodome et Gomorrhe.*

He was never, however, completely obsessed by his delusions

of persecution, and even in 1918 he retained a certain detachment about himself, for he wrote to Comtesse de Maugny, "I have in myself unfortunately a friend who is sentimental and a judge who reasons: their eternal quarrel fills my life with unhappiness."

Nor did his pessimism involve insensibility. The war still caused him pain, and in April 1918, he wrote to Maugny, "The parents who suffer sincerely from the death of a child tear my heart. I must say that, little as it is to the credit of Society, this suffering is deeper in the common people than in social circles, where I find that people console themselves with a terrible facility. There are exceptions of course. I received from the Duc de Luynes a letter which is the most touching cry of distress which I have ever heard." He interested himself in the welfare of the troops, writing to some, making efforts to perform services for them, and sending regular packages of chocolate and cigarettes to the front.

Lacking the comfort of his severely shaken transcendental faith, he sought consolation in music. At great expense he hired a string quartet to come and play some of his favorite music, and invited friends to share the treat. He bought a phonograph, and a piano player; occasionally, with great difficulty and inconvenience, he doctored himself up enough to go out to a concert. On one such sortie he was caught in the streets in the midst of a Gotha raid, which he watched with great interest, and put into his book.

His perennial bad health took an alarming turn early in 1918: symptoms of aphasia and amnesia appeared, and he talked of a brain operation. It turned out, however, that his difficulties resulted from the abuse of drugs.

Despite his many handicaps, and even because of his grave condition, he sought to extract what poor remnants he could from active experience. He had been seeing something of Princesse Soutzo, to whom he paid homage at the close of the war in a parody of Saint-Simon: "It is sufficiently within the knowledge of everyone that she is the only woman who, for my misfortune, has succeeded in making me come out of the retirement in which I lived after the death of the Dauphin and Dauphine. . . . Her graces had enslaved me and I scarcely left my room at Versailles except to go to see her."

His usual place of meeting with the Princesse was the Ritz, where he often reserved a private dining room. Because of his long patronage, eccentricities, and royal tips, he was a privileged guest to Olivier, the headwaiter, and he was allowed to wander about the hotel at will, talk to waiters and bell boys, and even occupy a post of observation in the lodge of the *concierge*. He recruited from the Ritz staff, in 1918, a new secretary, a youth with "astonishing" dispositions for painting.

Till 1921 secretaries and youthful protégés continued to play a rôle in Proust's life. In May 1919 he invited Reynaldo Hahn and Vaudoyer to dine with him in his room, adding to Vaudoyer, "There will be only the two of you (except for a youth whom I took in a few months ago, but who will not bother us, as he says nothing)." Early in 1920 he again invited friends to dine at his bedside, this time with his secretary. A little later his secretary left him, and in July 1921, he wrote to Sidney Schiff, "As you are nice enough to be interested in my life, I had told you, I think, that I had a secretary who was to marry the daughter of a *concierge*. He gave up this marriage, and as I was afraid that, without this distraction, he would be bored at my home, I found him a very attractive position in America, [an achievement] which I assure you, if you knew him, is prodigious." From 1921 on he used the niece of Céleste as a typist.

Meanwhile affairs of the heart are on record. In November 1918, he wrote to Madame Straus, "My health is somewhat less bad, but I am embarked on sentimental affairs without outcome, without joy, and perpetual creators of fatigue, of suffering, of absurd expense." The following May he mentioned to Walter Berry "an unhappy love affair which is coming to an end." It would be idle to speculate about the nature of these affairs, or the identities concerned; complete information, if obtainable, would probably add little to our knowledge of his essential character.

The end of the war brought some alleviation to Proust's gloom by removing one of its causes. On Armistice night he wrote to Madame Straus, "We have thought too much together about the war not to say to each other on the evening of victory an affectionate word, happy because of it, melancholy because of those whom we loved and who will not see it. What a marvelous allegro presto in this finale after the endless slowness of the beginning and of all the rest. What a marvelous dramatist is Destiny, or man who has been its instrument!" But with remarkable clear-sightedness he saw the dangers of the peace, even that of the Armistice; a few days later he wrote: "Yet for my part, I, who am such a friend of peace because I feel too deeply the suffering of men, think just the same that since people wanted a total victory and a hard peace, it would have been better if it had been still harder. I prefer to all other peace settlements those which leave no rancor in the heart of anyone. But since there is no question of such a settlement, and since this one leaves the desire for vengeance, it would perhaps have been better to make vengeance impossible."

For the Germans he felt no rancor. "I do not like people who cry, 'To death with him' when a condemned man goes by, and it is not my custom to insult the defeated." Nor was he a supernationalist: when, a few months later, a group of writers (among them his friend Daniel Halévy) signed a manifesto favoring a "Party of Intelligence," one of whose purposes would be the "intellectual federation of Europe and of the world, under the protection of victorious France, guardian of all civilisation," he protested vigorously against what he called "a kind of 'Frankreich über alles,' the policeman of the literature of all peoples, a rôle whose offer by other peoples it would have been more discreet to await."

Shortly after the Armistice the Nouvelle Revue Française issued *A l'Ombre des jeunes filles en fleur* and *Pastiches et Mé-*

langes (Proust's long projected collection of parodies, with the addition of other previously published articles). He was now by no means the unknown he had been in 1913. Throughout the war *Swann* had become the favored reading of a small but growing group of discriminating readers, and Swann clubs had been organized. After the Armistice readers were tired of the war and all its sequels so that *Swann* and its successor, with their evocation of childhood and of a world that was gone, benefited by the general taste for literature of escape. Literary critics who were not personal friends of the author began to take his work seriously. Some praised and some blamed, but at least Proust had become a writer to be reckoned with.

But these discreet beginnings of attention were nothing to the celebrity which burst upon him in December 1919, when the Prix Goncourt was awarded, largely because of the efforts of Léon Daudet, to *A l'Ombre des jeunes filles en fleur.* The award was widely and severely criticized, and no less warmly, though less extensively, defended. But attack and defense served equally to focus attention on the newly discovered master. The novelty of his style and methods now appeared as the marks of genius; everywhere he was discussed, worshiped, ridiculed, and even read. Requests for articles, prefaces, extracts poured in. He was compared to other great men, and finally (to Proust's delight) to Einstein.

To all this he reacted with sarcastic amusement, but genuine pleasure. He went more than ever to the Ritz, and was said to have spent there, in a single evening's entertainment, his entire prize money. Taxis went out from the rue Hamelin (to which he had moved in 1919) to bring friends to his bedside. His correspondence with critics and with new admirers, French and foreign, grew mightily. But he continued to work at his chaotic manuscripts and to bedevil his publishers into greater efforts to increase sales.

It was his last fling at a life of successful activity. In the fall of 1920 he saw unmistakable signs that his end would not be long delayed. "I never write about my health," he frequently told correspondents, but it was his favorite topic, and now more than ever he would have found it impossible to keep secret the new development. But he had been announcing his imminent death for so long (since 1900 in fact) that it would be hard now to get anyone to take him seriously. As early as February 1913, he had been aware of the embarrassment of not dying on schedule, and had written to René Blum not to mention the gravity of his condition in talking to Grasset. "For if after that, one lives for a while longer people don't forgive you."

The method of announcement that he chose was by way of a preface, first published in the *Revue de Paris* for November 15, 1920, for a forthcoming book of Paul Morand. The book was to contain stories titled with women's names, and Proust wrote:

I should have liked to take the useless trouble of composing, for the delightful little novels which bear the names of these fair ones, a real preface. A sudden event has prevented me. An unknown woman took up residence in my brain. She went and she came; soon, with all the fuss she made, I knew her habits. Besides, like an over-friendly tenant, she insisted on entering into direct relationship with me. I was surprised to see that she was not beautiful. I had always thought that Death was. Otherwise, how would she overcome us? However this may be, she seems to be absent today. Not for long, no doubt, if one may judge by all she has left me.

The language was precious, and its purport did not seem to be new, but this time Proust was not posing. Gradually the process of disintegration had been making headway, until, quite suddenly, he felt his whole organism seized implacably by a strange and hostile presence, and before his startled eyes the presence was objectified as a hideous woman in the corner of his room.

It must have been at this time that he added the following passage to the last chapter of *Le Temps retrouvé:*

This idea of death installed itself definitely within me like a love. Not that I loved death, I hated it. But after having thought of it no doubt from time to time as of a woman one does not yet love, now the thought of it clung so completely to the deepest layer of my brain that I could concern myself with nothing without its being first crossed by the idea of death, and even if I was doing nothing and was in complete repose, the idea of death kept me company as incessantly as the idea of the self.

Yet still people did not take him seriously; they had exhausted their capacity for alarm about him. In December 1920, he wrote to Madame de Noailles, with a testiness that is almost comic, "What you took for an improvement is the seizure of my whole being by death."

But whether or not people appreciated at its true value his dying condition was with him a lesser concern than the completion of his work. Impressed with his new fragility, and realizing that if he died too soon the thoughts within him would never be set down, he devoted himself thenceforth unreservedly to his work. His whole life was in it. His subsequent correspondence which remains to us is increasingly feverish. He is always in a rush, always driving himself, yet still complaining of his health and trying to conserve it in unimportant ways, neglecting the essentials of a reformed diet and the abandonment of drugs. Except for an occasional night dinner at the Ritz he subsists largely on café au lait, and counters heart attacks with capsules of caffeine. His sleep, as always, is drugged.

Yet it is clear that he was taking stock of his achievement and trying to evaluate the relative importance of its constituent elements. He declared in 1920, as he had in 1913, that the structure, the "architectonic line," of his work was rigorous, if obscured. In the last year of his life he insisted on the fundamental importance of the subconscious in his novel; and "as for style," he said, "I have tried to reject everything dictated by pure intelligence . . . to express my deep and authentic impressions and to respect the natural movement of my thought."

Of *Sodome et Gomorrhe* he wrote in late 1921, when it was ready to appear, that except for the chapter "Les Intermittences du cœur," (an episode of involuntary memory from his original third volume) he did not like it; and when the installment appeared, in 1922, he wrote Sir Philip Sassoon that its three volumes were the worst that he had written.

Even the pessimism that is so characteristic of *Sodome et Gomorrhe* he seemed to disavow. In a letter of 1920 to René Boylesve thanking him for a book, he said: "Alas! I have known, directly or by hearsay, many satyrs. Just the same I have difficulty in believing that they were great men; and the complicity, at least tacit, of Titian and Sansovino in the crimes of Aretino seem to me an insult against which, even in the Venice you describe delightfully, there are protests from masterpieces which I separate with difficulty from a state, even if unexpressed, of morality. I know that they are both on the right side in your marvelous account, but so tepidly! They protest only for the sake of form, and the hell of your 'divine Aretino' is paved with their barely good intentions. Does history really confirm the truth of this? Or have you so pessimistic a view of humanity?"

The ideal of pictorial art revealed in this letter was one which had been seriously undernourished during the war, but in the spring of 1921 he managed to go to an exhibition of masterpieces in the Jeu de Paume. For this exhibition his friend Vaudoyer had been writing a series of critical articles in *L'Opinion*. Proust read them with interest, especially the two on Vermeer in the issues of April 30 and May 7; and, giving himself a hypodermic injection for stimulus, he wrote to express his enthusiasm. Early in the morning a few days later, he wrote again: "I have not gone to bed in order to go and see this morning Vermeer and Ingres. Will you conduct this corpse there, leaning on your arm? . . . If you say yes, I shall send for you at about quarter past nine." Vaudoyer came, and supported his friend's tottering steps toward Vermeer's "View of Delft." Proust had not seen it since he was a young man, thirty years before, and ever since it had been for him the greatest of pictures.

The result of this sortie was such that he feared he might die at the exposition, and become a news item in the afternoon paper, "along with run-over dogs." But he managed to get home alive, and write up the experience. He attributed it to Bergotte, and put it in *La Prisonnière,* but the emotions and reflections were his own, and the "last books" to which he referred were not by Bergotte; they were *Guermantes II* and *Sodome I,* just off the press, with *Sodome II* shortly to follow:

At the first steps which he had to climb he was seized with dizziness. He passed in front of several pictures and had the impression of the dryness and futility of such artificial art, which was not worth the open air and the sunlight of a Venetian palazzo, or even a simple house by the sea. At last he reached the Ver Meer, which he recalled as more striking, more different from everything else that he knew, but in which, thanks to the article of the critic, he noticed for the first time the small people in blue, the pinkness of the sand, and finally the precious material of the little patch of yellow wall. His dizziness increased; he fastened his eye on the precious bit of yellow wall, like a child on a yellow butterfly he wants to catch. "That is how I should have written," he said to himself. "My last books are too dry, I should have put on several layers of color, made my sentence precious in itself, like this little patch of yellow wall." Meanwhile the seriousness of his dizziness did not escape him. As in heavenly scales there appeared to him on one side his own life, on the other the little patch of wall so well painted in yellow. He felt that he had imprudently given up the first for the second. "But I should not want," he said to himself, "to be the news item of this exposition for the evening papers."

He kept repeating: "Little patch of yellow wall with a pent house roof, little patch of yellow wall." He collapsed on a circular divan; suddenly he stopped thinking that his life was at stake, and, returning to optimism, said to himself: "It's just an indigestion caused by the under-cooked potatoes, it's nothing." A new attack struck him down, he rolled from the divan to the floor, and visitors and attendants rushed up. He was dead.

The rest of the year Proust spent on new writing for *La Prisonnière,* where indeed he wrote with the careful attention to beauty which he had felt lacking in his recent volumes; and on last touches to *Sodome et Gomorrhe II.* Of the gravity of his state he had left himself little to say—but he said it; a slightly new slant on his condition may be obtained in a letter written in August: "Day before yesterday I really thought I had touched the *bottom* of physical suffering (and moral, because my book depends on it, and without that you can imagine that I care little for my 'life' itself). But for the last two days I have seemed to feel a little better. So I give myself a little treat: I write to you.—I hope you haven't suffered too much from the heat, since they say it is hot and that normal people suffer from it. Writing you in my bed under seven wool blankets, a fur coat, three hot water bottles, and with a fire in the room, I regret the heat only for you."

Sodome et Gomorrhe II appeared in the spring of 1922, and Proust started on the last drive to get *La Prisonnière* ready. But by September he was almost past the possibility of work. He was coughing badly, and if he moved a step away from his bed he fell. The last phase of his illness had begun.

In this same month he managed to dispatch a letter to his German admirer E. R. Curtius in which he made a final affirmation of his faith in a suprasensible reality: "True literature reveals the still unknown part of the soul. It is more or less the saying of Pascal that I quote, wrongly, for I have no books here: 'A little knowledge separates from God, much knowledge brings us back.' One should never be afraid to go too far, for the truth is beyond."

Despite increasing fatigue and pain, he finished with *La Prisonnière;* it was still not quite to his satisfaction, but he was resigned to compromise. *Albertine disparue,* however, was too much for him. In October he made an effort to go out, but had to return at once. "Death is pursuing me," he said to Céleste. Soon he refused to take any nourishment but iced beer, for which he sent Albaret to the Ritz; and he kept trying to work. Dr. Bize and Robert Proust urged him to rest and to eat, but he would not listen to them, and ordered Céleste to keep all doctors away from him. As an apology, he sent flowers to Dr. Bize.

In November he wrote his last letter to his publisher Galli-mard: "I think at the moment that the most urgent thing would be to hand over to you all my books. The sort of relent-lessness that I put in on *La Prisonnière* . . . has kept me from the succeeding volumes. But three days rest may be enough. I must stop, good-bye, dear Gaston.

Marcel Proust.

"Letter follows when able."

The image of death was back in his room. "Céleste," he cried, "she is huge and all in black. I'm afraid of her. Don't touch her, Céleste, she is implacable, and she gets more and more horrible."

On the 17th of November he felt a little better, and thought he might try to eat. But early the next morning, feeling that he was dying, he rang for the exhausted Céleste and dictated some additions to the scene of the death of Bergotte, commenting that he thought they were good.

Too late the doctors arrived with oxygen and stimulants. Robert tried to raise him in bed, saying as he did so, "I am dis-turbing you, dear little one, I'm hurting you," and Proust re-plied faintly, "Oh yes, my dear Robert." He did not speak again, and died at four that afternoon.

In the last scene which he had revised he had written: "They buried him, but all through the night of mourning, in lighted windows, his books, arranged in threes, watched like angels with spreading wings, and seemed, for him who was no more, like the symbol of his resurrection."

❦ 7 ❦

A LA RECHERCHE DU
TEMPS PERDU

STRUCTURE

A START toward an understanding of the plan, or complex of plans, of Proust's novel is furnished by the titles of his original three-volume work, titles that were overlaid but not obliterated in the longer version which finally appeared: *Du Côté de chez Swann, Le Côté de Guermantes,* and *Le Temps retrouvé,* the three to be covered by the common title *A la Recherche du temps perdu.* In other words, over Swann's Way (that is, on Swann's side of town) or the Way of the bourgeoisie, the Guermantes Way or that of the aristocracy, and Time—Time lost and rediscovered. It is no accident that the first word of the novel is *longtemps,* and the last, *temps.* One of Proust's basic ideas is to show the permutations of society in time.

The point of view in time from which the narrator begins is the present. He is looking back, and at the close of the story he will arrive again at the point of departure. But the opening pages are an overture to the whole work, and the impressions recorded are scattered through the whole of the "long time" which he is about to relate. Thus, the dinners and walks at Tansonville of which he speaks do not reappear until the end of *Albertine disparue* and the beginning of *Le Temps retrouvé,* whose events (if we disregard certain unintentional confusions in chronology) bring us very close to the present. Madame de Saint-Loup herself appears much earlier in another rôle: she is Gilberte Swann, the narrator's first love.

This narrator must be distinguished, provisionally at least, from the author. At no point in the novel do he or any of his relatives receive a family name, and throughout most of it he is simply "I," without Christian name. Only twice, in *La Prison-nière* and the first time with a slight apology, he is called "Marcel," and by this name it is convenient to refer to him, and to reserve "Proust" for the author.

The overture, by exploitation of the indeterminate state between sleeping and waking, methodically disorients the reader in time and space. We see experience from the point of view of the man who spends most of his life in bed, and for whom action is less real than the life of the mind. He sleeps and he wakes and he sleeps again; dreams, imagination, and sense perception are intertwined. "For when I awoke like this, with my mind trying in vain to find out where I was, everything would be revolving around me in the darkness: things, places, years." Past selves are briefly resurrected by an accidental position of the body, bringing with them the scenes in which they had lived. The sense of personal identity is intermittent: now he is one of those dead selves which his body remembers, now he is what he has been reading about—a musical composition, a church, the rivalry between Francis I and the Emperor Charles V. What time can it be? He strikes a match and looks at his watch: nearly midnight.

It is the moment when a man who is ill, obliged to travel and sleep in an unknown hotel, and awakened by an attack of his illness, is delighted to see under the door a ray of light. What joy, it is already morning! In a moment the servants will be up, he can ring, help will come. The hope of relief gives him courage to suffer. Sure enough, he thinks he has heard steps; they come closer, then pass on. And the ray of light under the door has disappeared. It is midnight; the gas has just been put out; the last servant has gone, and the whole night must be spent in suffering unrelieved. (I, 12)

So the narrator carries us with him through his half-waking consciousness. Flickering light alternates with darkness, a train whistles in the distance, the woodwork emits a muffled report, snatches from the past flit through his mind, the walls advance or recede and the furniture changes position in accordance with the sleepy images of rooms in which he has slept in the past and now momentarily believes himself to be. And with a mention of the five towns of Combray, Balbec, Paris, Doncières, and Venice, with which successively and in approximately the same order his recollections are to be associated, Proust brings the overture to a close and focuses his memory on his childhood at Combray.

In the next forty-eight pages he tells us what he remembers of Combray and his childhood there. Various members of the family begin casually to appear, without introduction or explanation; but we are gradually enabled to fit in the relationships. The home at Combray belongs to "my great-aunt"; she is a cousin of Marcel's maternal grandmother and appears briefly in the early pages of *Swann*. She teases the grandmother, she teases Swann, she is "the only somewhat vulgar person in our family." We later learn that she has died. Aunt Léonie (or Madame Octave as Françoise calls her) is her widowed daughter, a neurasthenic who spends her time in bed; although she dies in the first volume of *A l'Ombre des jeunes filles en fleur,* she is a character of considerable importance for the Proustian themes. Françoise, the servant first of "my great-aunt," then successively of Aunt Léonie, of Marcel's parents, and finally of Marcel himself, is an interesting and fully drawn character throughout the book. The great-aunts Céline and Flora, not to be confused with "my great-aunt," are a pair of precious old maids, sisters of the grandmother. As for the maternal grandparents "Amédée" and "Bathilde," the grandfather appears in person only in the first volume of *Swann,* where it appears that he was a friend of Swann's late father and now of Swann himself, but is suspicious of other Jews. The grandmother, one of the most engaging and sympathetic characters in the book, dies in the second volume of *Le Côté de Guermantes.* Marcel's parents, and usually his grandmother, live in Paris, coming to Combray only for the summer, or at Easter. The father, a busy and energetic man who has little to do with his son, fades from the scene after *A l'Ombre des jeunes filles en fleur;* we assume that he has died. The mother stands in a curious relation to the grandmother; until the death of the latter, she is a pale replica of her, though immensely important to Marcel; after this death she becomes, for practical purposes, the grandmother.

The central features of the forty-eight-page group of recollections following the overture are Marcel's dread of going to bed, and its corollary, the importance to him of his mother's goodnight kiss. Swann is introduced because, on nights when he came to dinner, the mother did not come upstairs to kiss the child good-night in bed. One such night became crucial in his life. After trying in vain, by means of a message through Françoise, to induce his mother to leave her guest and come up, Marcel formed the heroic resolution of sitting up, without trying to sleep and at whatever cost, until Swann had gone. At last he heard the steps in the garden, and the sound of the little bell that rang whenever the garden gate was opened; he knew that the guest had left. The parents came upstairs, and the father, for once indulgent, suggested that the mother spend the night with Marcel, and against her better judgment she obeyed. It was against Marcel's better judgment too, and for him this night that should have been so happy was poisoned by remorse.

Next Proust makes what is for his work a vital distinction between voluntary and involuntary memory. All that he has told us so far about Combray has been recalled by the voluntary memory; so remembered, every detail of his life there has some connection with the daily drama of his going to bed.

To tell the truth, I might have answered anyone who asked me that Combray included something else and existed at other times. But as what I would have remembered would have been furnished me only by the voluntary memory, the memory of the intelligence, and as the information which it gives about the past preserves nothing of it, I would have had no inclination to think of this residue of Combray. All that was in reality dead for me. (I, 68)

There follows the celebrated incident of the madeleine and the cup of tea. One winter day, when Marcel is cold, tired, and discouraged, his mother suggests a cup of tea. At first he refuses, then characteristically changes his mind. Mechanically he carries to his mouth a spoonful of tea in which he has soaked a morsel of the little cake.

At the moment that the mouthful of cake crumbs touched my palate, I started, attentive to the extraordinary thing that was happening within me. A delicious pleasure had invaded me, isolated, without a hint of its source. It had at once made the vicissitudes of life indifferent to me, its disasters harmless, its brevity illusory, in the same way that love operates, by filling me with a precious essence: or rather this essence was not in me, it was myself. I had ceased to feel mediocre, contingent, mortal. (I, 69-70)

Trying to get at the reason for this joy, he soon discovers that its cause lies within, the cake soaked in tea having served only as an awakener. It has evoked, independently of his conscious mind, a similar taste experience of his childhood in Combray, and with it the accompanying scenes. At once the detailed structure of that past life begins to take form and to unfold, as if from his cup of tea. The involuntary memory, set in motion by a chance association of sensations, fills in the gaps left by the voluntary memory, and much more: its contribution, unlike that of the other, is fresh, living, and poetic. He seems to be actually reliving the past. For the time being he is content not to inquire why a memory should cause so profound and unique an emotion. Instead, he makes a new start on his recollections of Combray, this time unhampered by the restrictions of the voluntary memory.

From this point on to the end of the novel, there is a general chronological trend that follows the life of Marcel. There are a few exceptions, and the more important of these are clearly indicated. "Un Amour de Swann" takes place just before, and just after, the birth of Marcel, as he tells us plainly. At the end of *Swann* there is a brief return to the present, again clearly marked. Throughout, there are brief returns to the past to pick up an item called for by an association of ideas or to round out an episode or a character, and there are occasional allusions to future events. These procedures are common enough in most novelists, and offer no particular difficulties.

What is more individual to Proust, and what is perhaps the chief reason why he is at first hard to read, is that he sees events, not as external, objective, and successive, but as internal images and echoes which come and go and come back again. He omits the usual small aids to orientation in action. "Not once," he wrote to Dreyfus in 1913, "does one of my characters open a window, wash his hands, put on an overcoat, utter a formula of social introduction. If there were anything new in this book, it would be that." As for the date of an external event, that is a mere convenience for the voluntary memory and the organized mind, which for Proust are of secondary importance; first place is given to spontaneous emanations from a past that is inaccessible to purposeful recollection. Such dates as those of Grévy's presidency and of the Dreyfus affair leave their external importance behind them when they enter Proust's inner world, and take a position proportioned to the resonance of the echo or the brightness of the image they have produced within it. Furthermore, inner time is not chronometric time. As he wrote in 1913, "Novelists who count by days and by years are fools. Days are perhaps equal for a clock, but not for a man." And again, "To relate events is like making an opera known by the libretto alone; but if I were writing a novel, I should try to differentiate the successive music of the days."

Another peculiarity of Proust's narrative method is that he breaks up his large blocks of material by interpolations which serve as extended metaphors and as a means of introducing his "themes." Among the dispersed units of the "Combray" chapter are: the village of Combray and its church; incidents and revelations concerning certain characters, notably Aunt Léonie, Françoise, Legrandin, the Vinteuils, and the Duchesse de Guermantes; walks about Combray, and the important distinction between the two "Ways"; esthetic and intellectual acquisitions of the young Marcel, particularly in connection with reading, revery, the theatre, names, love, and nature.

In "Un Amour de Swann," with an abrupt change of tone from the poetic to the satiric, we are introduced to the Verdurin "clan," intensely bourgeois and professing disdain for the "boring" society of the Guermantes. A long series of changes lies ahead, before the clan is completely incorporated in the Guermantes Way by the marriage of Madame Verdurin to the Prince de Guermantes. The principal subject of this chapter is, as the title indicates, Swann's love for Odette de Crécy, a love prepared by art, music, and flattery, precipitated by an obstacle, aggravated by jealousy, prolonged by habit, and ended by separation. Swann does not marry Odette until after he has ceased to love her; the reason for the marriage is later given as his desire to legitimize his daughter and to present her to his close friend the Duchesse de Guermantes. In this ambition he is frustrated, although after his death Gilberte is not merely received by the Duchess but ends by marrying into her family.

The third part of *Du Côté de chaz Swann* develops the theme of Names, and continues the story of the love of Marcel for Gilberte. This material runs far on into *A l'Ombre des jeunes filles en fleur,* for the reason that the space limitations of his original edition obliged Proust to cut short his *Swann* and carry the remainder over to his second volume. The sequel, greatly enlarged by additions, now extends to volume II, page 59 of the current edition of *A l'Ombre des jeunes filles en fleur,* and the impressive conclusion of *Swann* belongs by right at that point.

The scenes of *Swann* are first Combray and second Paris. At the beginning (the logical beginning) of *A l'Ombre des jeunes filles en fleur,* the scene shifts to Balbec (like Combray a fictitious name), a resort on the Norman shore. The basic events of this section are the experiences and encounters of the adolescent Marcel during one summer at the Grand Hôtel of Balbec. He meets various members of the aristocratic Guermantes family: Madame de Villeparisis, Baron de Charlus (who had appeared briefly in *Swann*), his nephew Saint-Loup, with whom Marcel lays the beginnings of an intimate friendship. He also becomes acquainted with a band of adolescent girls which includes Albertine, and with the famous painter Elstir, whose work is the basis for an exposition of Proust's ideas on painting.

In the "Combray" chapter of *Swann,* which was an episode of the country, flowers were prominent, hawthorn blossoms for Swann's Way and pond lilies for the Guermantes Way. *A l'Ombre des jeunes filles en fleur* is an episode of the seashore; the women at Rivebelle, the diners at the Grand Hôtel at Balbec, are compared to strange aquatic creatures, and the band of "jeunes filles en fleur," that gracefully amorphous group in which personal identities are lost in the whole, is compared to seabirds performing evolutions on the beach.

The extraordinary reappearance of Charlus, coupled with the declining health of the grandmother, whose loving devotion to Marcel is a symbol of the security of his childhood, is a warning that the disillusionment, the tragic discoveries, and the uncertainties of manhood lie just ahead. In the beautiful closing scene, fall has come, wind and rain whip the shore, the manager unhappily paces the empty corridors of his now unprofitable but far more charming hotel. The "pitiless and sensual virgins" have gone, and although Marcel sadly realizes that the "graceful oceanic mythology" with which he has surrounded them is illusory, he knows too that some part of it will cling forever to their image. Alone in his room, contemplating the tiny shafts of light that elude the closely drawn curtains, he hears again the shouts and laughter coming up from the deserted beach; Albertine will later say, "We looked to see if you'd be coming down, but your blinds were shut, even at concert time." And at "concert time," precisely at ten o'clock, the departed orchestra plays again, the violins blending with the wash of the waves, and the music seeming to come from beneath the sea.

Le Côté de Guermantes is laid chiefly in Paris, but includes a trip to Doncières, a fictitious garrison town at which Saint-Loup is in military service. The subject matter includes the infatuation of Marcel for the Duchesse de Guermantes, the reappearance of Albertine in his life, the unhappy love affair of Saint-Loup and Rachel, the ever stranger behavior of Monsieur de Charlus, and two important and lengthily described social functions: a reception at the home of Madame de Villeparisis and a dinner given by the Duc and Duchesse de Guermantes. Marcel, a little older now and excitedly pursuing his social ambitions among the aristocrats, can spare little time for the beauties of nature. Once, however, he is arrested in his feverish activity by the sight of a group of fruit trees in bloom, "guardians of the memories of the Golden Age, warrantors of the promise that reality is not what people think." His grandmother dies, and the demonic Charlus is in the ascendant.

And then comes the brief introductory episode of *Sodome et Gomorrhe,* with its "first appearance of the men-women, descendants of those of the inhabitants of Sodom that were spared by the fire from heaven." A chance episode reveals to Marcel the homosexuality upon which is based the hitherto incomprehensible behavior of Charlus. Abandoning at times the screen of Marcel and speaking as author, Proust strips away shams and directly exposes the vice of sodomy, but also makes a sincere and emotional plea for tolerance.

After this somewhat lurid introduction there is a brief respite, as we see, at the beginning of *Sodome et Gomorrhe II,* the moon and a star riding calmly in an evening sky above the obelisk of the Place de la Concorde. But almost immediately there arises the confused babble of many voices that is the dominant impression of this part. The social affairs of *Le Côté de Guermantes* are continued by a long account of a reception held by the Princesse de Guermantes, and Marcel's observations are enlightened by his new awareness of homosexuality, which he discovers to be widespread. At no one point does a shocking revelation stand out, as in the introduction to this section, but the continuously satiric tone, the impassive dissections of character, are increasingly depressing. We are among lost souls, grimacing, posturing, scheming creatures, deluded, vain, ceaselessly driven by their desires and their vices.

A second trip to Balbec follows. Marcel is alone in his room, and the tumult suddenly dies down. As he stoops to remove his shoe, he is overwhelmed, in a rush of tears, by an involuntary memory of his grandmother, who used to perform this service for him. But soon he resumes his social activities, this time chiefly at a villa rented by Madame Verdurin near Balbec, and the din breaks out again. Charlus, whose behavior, though no longer enigmatic, is still extraordinary, is now attached to the Verdurin circle, and overwhelmingly the dominant character. But at the end, the theme of Gomorrha—female homosexuality —begins to sound, as Marcel, who has been seeing much of Albertine and is tiring of her, becomes suspicious of her past and as a consequence newly attached to her present.

In *La Prisonnière* Marcel has withdrawn from the tumult with Albertine, whom he keeps secluded as much as possible in the apartment of his parents in Paris. At times he lies in bed in a revery, receiving indirect impressions of the weather outside, listening to sounds that float up from the streets or to the comings and goings of Albertine or Françoise within; at other times he tortures himself with fruitless speculations about Albertine's suspected homosexuality, and tries to spy upon her activities. He makes occasional sorties, particularly one to a musical entertainment organized by Charlus at the home of Madame Verdurin. The occasion gives rise to much reflection on music and its significance; it also spells the downfall of the proud Charlus. *La Prisonnière* closes with the sudden departure of Albertine.

In *Albertine disparue* the silence deepens, and for most of the book all that happens is what passes through the mind of Marcel. He had almost wished for the departure of Albertine, but now her absence is unendurable. Then comes the word that she is dead, and the long struggle between memory and oblivion begins. At first every sensation, every event, reminds him of her. A trip to Venice barely ruffles the surface of this deep inward life. He discovers that he has to live over in reverse order, mentally, the story of his love, and arrive back at the band of girls at Balbec. As the pain subsides, his jealousy still survives for a time, and prompts him to make retrospective investigations about Albertine's past through Aimé, the headwaiter at Balbec. Marcel's return from Venice is marked by his emergence from solitude, and by new information about the other characters, notably the marriage of Gilberte and Saint-Loup.

In *Le Temps retrouvé* we have further details about Gilberte and her husband, a chapter on Paris and French society during the war, and a final reception—the Matinée of the new Princesse de Guermantes, the former Madame Verdurin. Here a disillusioned and hopeless Marcel, after his long absence from society, sees again the people he had known as a child and young man, and finds them barely recognizable beneath the disguise of Time. He too has aged, less in appearance than in the slow desiccation of his heart. But suddenly he has a return of involuntary memory, and with it is inspired to a new conception of art and to his vocation as a writer. He is then ready to start writing the novel which we have just read, and we are back at the starting point, the present.

These events give a certain biographical structure to the novel, as well as suggesting obvious symmetries such as country and seashore, society and solitude, and the like. But as we look back on the novel other elements of design appear.

We find, first of all, that certain topics are recurring with a regularity that suggests method. There is, for example, the series of large dinners and receptions: we have first two dinners of

the bourgeois "clan" of Madame Verdurin; next an evening
musicale at Madame de Sainte-Euverte's, with many high-
ranking members of the nobility present; next a luncheon at
the Swann's, with Bergotte present (Swann at this time is building a new social life with Odette, and it is bourgeois); *Le Côté
de Guermantes* gives us social occasions at which the hostesses
are, as we might expect from the title, members of the Guermantes circle, the Marquise de Villeparisis and the Duchesse de
Guermantes; *Sodome et Gomorrhe II* opens with a long account
of an evening reception given by the first Princesse de Guermantes, and continues with the introduction of Marcel into the
Verdurin salon, now midway in its course from the bourgeoisie
to the aristocracy; in *La Prisonnière* comes the aristocratic
musicale arranged by Charlus for Madame Verdurin; and finally
the series (from which we have omitted family dinners with few
guests, and calls) closes with an afternoon reception of the second
Princesse de Guermantes, at which we see the same characters
that were at the reception of her predecessor, as they have become
after the lapse of many years.

A series of this sort might be dismissed as mere evidence that
the author was obsessed by social occasions; but the more we
examine the work the more indications of pattern appear. The
contact with mankind that the dinners and receptions represent
builds up an impression of uncertainty, confusion, and change;
but while this series punctuates the novel with its pessimism, a
second, that of the "privileged moments," marks the intervals of
the social occasions with compensatory optimism. The privileged moments, of which the madeleine incident is the first, are
solitary experiences of sudden and powerful emotion; usually
they are traceable to involuntary memory, but even when they
are not, the quality of emotion is characteristic and recognized
by Marcel as belonging to the madeleine series. A few incidents
of involuntary memory—for example, the hawthorn flowers in
A l'Ombre des jeunes filles en fleur (V, 215), a melody in *Le
Côté de Guermantes* (VI, 128), the burning twigs in *La Prison-*

nière (XI, 33)—for one reason or another are not quite characteristic; but nine incidents are unquestionable, clearly identified and related to each other by the author. They are, in order: the taste of the madeleine soaked in tea (I, 69); the sight of the steeples of Martinville (I, 258); the mouldy odor (III, 90, 93); the sight of three trees (IV, 161); the touch of a shoe button (VIII, 176); and four in rapid succession in *Le Temps retrouvé* II—the touch of the paving stones (p. 7), the sound of the spoon against a plate (p. 9), the touch of a starched napkin (p. 10), the sound of water in a pipe (pp. 17-18).

It is apparent that social occasions and privileged moments do not regularly alternate; the social occasions show most concentration toward the middle of the novel, and the privileged moments at the two ends. Clearly there is an incompatibility between these moments and a social life. The volumes concerned with Marcel's youth, before his appearance in society, contain four of the moments; the long stretch through *Le Côté de Guermantes, Sodome et Gomorrhe, La Prisonnière, Albertine disparue,* and the first part of *Le Temps retrouvé,* is marked by only one, and it, though clearly identified, differs from the others by its sadness; the explanation of the moments is revealed at the end when, in the midst of society Marcel has four successive experiences of the emotion he has heretofore known only in solitude.

We may note in passing that the encouragement offered by the privileged moments is reinforced by certain experiences of art (chiefly music and painting) and by the contemplation of nature, and that the relation between these various factors of stability in the midst of change is explained in *Le Temps retrouvé.*

Still further elements of design appear in the devices of first sketches *(premiers crayons)* of character, and of recurrence of situations. Some of the important characters are heard of before they are seen; next they drift in, casually and briefly, leave certain impressions, and disappear; later they come back more decisively, and their portrait is rounded out. Similarly with situations: Marcel's adolescent love for Gilberte is a first sketch for the more fully rounded and much longer account of his love for Albertine; the neurasthenic traits of Aunt Léonie prepare us for their recurrence in her nephew later; the scene of Mademoiselle Vinteuil and Léa in *Swann* is a foreshadowing of the later elaboration of the Gomorrha theme. Characteristic of all the recurrences is that the new situation is recognizably of the same type as the old, but has slight variations which justify a somewhat different development. The movement is not circular, but spiral.

An extension of the pattern of recurrences is to be found in a limited number of incidents and specimens of style which are clearly intended as parodies. In the "below stairs" scene at the beginning of *Le Côté de Guermantes* the servants parody their masters; in the same volume a group of waiters parody a meeting of the Academy (p. 151), and the "Marquise" of the comfort stations (p. 276 ff.), with her clientèle and her scale of prestige, shows up the absurd snobbery of the aristocrats in whose company we have just been. For stylistic parodies, we have an amusing *pastiche* by Albertine of the poetic manner of Marcel (XI, 176 ff.), and an extended one of the Goncourt *Journal* in *Le Temps retrouvé* (XV, 24 ff.).

With all its complexities of structure, *A la Recherche du temps perdu* is less intricately and symmetrically organized than Joyce's *Ulysses,* with which it may (but not very profitably) be compared. One must be on guard against reading into the diffuse text meanings that are not there. Nevertheless, enough has been pointed out to justify, partially at least, Proust's own insistence on this aspect of his work.

CHARACTERS

Repeatedly Proust protested that there were no keys to his novel. Perhaps the best description of this aspect of his character creations comes from *Le Temps retrouvé:*

The writer envies the painter, he would like to make sketches, take notes; he is lost if he does so. But when he writes, there is not a gesture of his characters, not a tic, not an intonation, that has not been inspired by his memory; there is not one fictitious name under which he could not set the names of sixty persons he has seen . . . it is the feeling for the general which, in the future writer, automatically selects what is general and can be put in a work of art. (XVI, 54-55)

The more carefully one studies the novel and looks into the character and manners of Proust's acquaintances, the more clear it becomes that for the great majority of his fictional characters there are no single valid keys. Partial keys and sources abound, by Proust's general admission above and, in some instances, by his specific identification. Charlus, as we have seen, seems to be founded on Montesquiou and Doasan; Françoise is Céleste Albaret, fused with a series of her predecessors, one of whom was named Françoise; Odette is Laure Hayman, plus Closmesnil and probably some others; the attractive side of Saint-Loup is traceable to Fénelon; the Duchesse de Guermantes physically resembles Comtesse de Chevigné, and conversationally Madame Straus. Proust is on record as denying the identification of Swann with Haas; he also went out of his way to admit it in *La Prisonnière*, where he unmistakably identifies a portrait of Haas by Tissot as being a picture of Swann. Swann has of course other originals, notably, for his artistic side, Ephrussi, the learned editor of the *Gazette des Beaux-Arts*.

Sources for non-personal creations are handled in a similar way. For Balbec and its Grand Hôtel and environs, he drew on his memories of many spots on the Norman coast, particularly on Cabourg, with its Grand Hôtel, and Trouville, with its Hôtel des Roches Noires. For the small local railway of Balbec he was thinking of the one passing through Thonon, on Lake Geneva. Combray, with its family home, is Illiers compounded with Auteuil; nevertheless he speaks of Combray in his original second volume as *champenois,* and apparently means literally in Champagne, for he later has it invaded by the Germans during the war. Doncières owes something to Versailles; the churches of Combray and of Balbec are fusions of various churches seen and descriptions by Ruskin. As for the "little phrase" of Vinteuil's sonata, Proust has mentioned thinking, at different times, of six different sources: a violin and piano sonata of Saint-Saëns, the Good Friday spell from *Parsifal*, Franck's violin and piano sonata, the prelude to *Lohengrin*, and "a ravishing piano piece by Fauré."

There are—to return to the characters—certain exceptions or special cases with regard to the rule of multiple sources. If Marcel's mother (and to a certain extent his grandmother) has any other source than Proust's mother (and possibly his grandmother), it has not been discovered. Marcel himself does not wholly coincide with Proust, but he certainly has no other source. He and Albertine, however, are special cases calling for more detailed examination later.

The point of departure for Proust's character portrayal is the idea that people are not what they seem. The explanation of his systematic reversals is that people judge one another on subjective, insufficient, and untrustworthy evidence, with the result that preliminary notions of a character are subject to modification by new evidence or by a change in the observer. The theoretic basis for the reversals and the beginning of its practical application are in *Swann:*

> But even in the most insignificant things in life we are not a materially constituted whole, identical for every one, to be consulted like a ledger or a will; our social personality is a creation of the thought of others. Even the simple act which we call "seeing a person we know" is partly an intellectual act. We fill in the physical appearance of the person we see with all the ideas we have about him and in the total picture these ideas have certainly the largest share. (I, 33)

The family of Marcel know Swann as the son of his broker father, who was a close friend of Marcel's grandfather. He is a courteous neighbor and a welcome guest. Although he has made an unfortunate marriage and they do not receive his wife,

Marcel's mother likes to draw him aside and make sympathetic allusions to his daughter. Of Swann the member of the Jockey Club, friend of the Prince of Wales and the Count of Paris, or of Swann the connoisseur of painting and music, they know nothing. Any hints they receive of his brilliant social connections or of his artistic competence are received with laughing incredulity.

The reader is aware from the outset that Swann is not as he seems to Marcel's family, so that there is no reversal in the revelation of his various sides. Nor is there one in the vast expansion of his personality which is accomplished in "Un Amour de Swann." The real surprise comes at the beginning of *A l'Ombre des jeunes filles en fleur*. Previously we have seen Swann very modest about his social position and very unhappy over his morbidly jealous passion for Odette, a passion which has ended in separation and final indifference; now we find him peacefully married to Odette and naïvely vain at the gradual extension of their exceedingly commonplace social relations:

. . . what had happened was that, to the "Swann junior" and to the Swann of the Jockey Club, the former friend of my parents had added a new personality (which was not to be the last), that of husband of Odette. (III, 7)

In this instance—perhaps because it is the first of the major reversals, perhaps too because it is an added passage—Proust explains with great care how the new personality really lay, unsuspected, beneath the old ones, awaiting only the right combination of circumstances to step forth. And if we look back, we can, in fact, see how Swann's excessive modesty was a form of conceit, and we can find instances, in the midst of his miserable jealousy, of a capacity for tranquil family life.

Other reversals in *A l'Ombre des jeunes filles en fleur* include Cottard, ludicrously literal-minded and stupid in *Swann*, but now revealed as a brilliant diagnostician and a famous doctor; and "Monsieur Biche," a somewhat pretentious and vulgar but otherwise negligible hanger-on of the Verdurin salon, who turns out to be the great painter Elstir. The case of Cottard is that of a man able in one field and limited in another: the simpleton of the salon was always potentially the great diagnostician—we have even been given a hint of the fact, but we have not believed it: "Don't speak to me about 'your masters,'" says Madame Verdurin to him; "you know ten times as much as he [Potain] does. . . . Anyhow, you don't kill your patients!" The great doctor of later on remains foolish in society, but, in the light of his reputation, his clumsy sallies are more favorably received. Elstir, at the period when he was known as M. Biche, was already a great painter, though at the beginning of his career; at its summit he is represented as having outgrown the follies of M. Biche.

The most carefully prepared and the longest delayed reversal is that of Charlus, who in the first part of *Sodome et Gomorrhe* is dramatically revealed as a homosexual, after numerous indications to the contrary. Other revelations of homosexuality— Saint-Loup, Legrandin, the Prince de Guermantes, Nissim Bernard, the Marquis de Cambremer, the Duc de Châtellerault, the Prince de Foix among the men; Albertine, Andrée, the sisters of Bloch, Léa, Rachel, Mademoiselle Vinteuil, even Gilberte and Odette among the women—become progressively less acceptable as true revelations of character; we feel rather that we are confronted by an obsession of the author.

Charlus, like several of the important characters, comes into the novel by gradual infiltration. He is first mentioned early in *Swann:* the family have just conducted Swann to the garden gate and said goodnight; as they return to the house, someone (probably Marcel's father) is heard to say of Swann, "I think he is having a lot of trouble with that wretched wife of his, who, as everybody in Combray knows, is living with a certain M. de Charlus. It's the talk of the town." Later, when they are on a walk near Tansonville, Swann's home, they meet a lady in white (Madame Swann) and a little behind her, staring at

Marcel with eyes that seem to be popping out of his head, is a man dressed in duck. When they have passed on, the grandfather says, "Poor Swann, what a part they are making him play: they have him go away so that she can be left alone with her Charlus, for it was he, I recognized him. And the little girl, mixed up in all that scandal!" When Charlus turns up in *A l'Ombre des jeunes filles en fleur* he again looks at Marcel in a strange way, and his behavior with the youth is more extraordinary still: it is at one moment attentive and friendly, at another shockingly brutal, at still another icily disdainful or angry. He deplores the effeminacy of the young men of the day and extols bodily strength and energetic action, but in talk his voice sometimes takes on the quality and intonations of that of a woman. His nephew speaks of him as something of a rake with women, but positively denies, to Marcel's astonishment, that he is or ever has been the lover of Madame Swann. Marcel's grandmother finds him charming. In spite of all counter-indications, the revelation of his complete homosexuality, when it comes, is seen to have been carefully prepared, not only by his strange looks, words, and behavior, but by a clear hint planted in "Un Amour de Swann," and probably passed over by the reader. Swann, the author tells us, was always glad to have Charlus with Odette: "Between M. de Charlus and her, Swann knew that nothing could happen."

The presentation of Charlus reveals the principal sources of the reader's information on a character. There is first of all hearsay, the opinion of one character on another; this may well be, and as often as not is, false. Observed behavior, interpreted in the light of hearsay, may also be misleading. Marcel, *the Marcel of the moment described,* is as liable to wrong judgment as anyone else, and his opinions are not to be trusted; but throughout the book there is a constant intervention of the Marcel of the present, wise with the accumulated experience of the whole book, whom we may perhaps consider the author omniscient; and this Marcel does not give us false clues. Such at least is the general rule, and a safe guide for the reader; trifling apparent exceptions are perhaps slips in method. There is, for example, the case of Jupien's niece. In *Swann* the grandmother comes home one day full of enthusiasm for a house (in which, in fact, the family later rents an apartment), and for a tailor and his daughter. Her words are not reported directly, and the reader can scarcely be blamed for taking the statement of the relationship between the tailor and the girl as trustworthy information from the author omniscient; in *Le Côté de Guermantes,* however, we learn that the girl is the tailor's niece, and that the relationship originally stated was a mistaken idea of the grandmother's. The difficulty is trifling, and generally, if one is attentive, it is a simple matter to distinguish the testimony of the author omniscient from that of Marcel, or of other fallible characters.

From the beginning of the novel to the end there is a constant mingling of direct and reliable analysis of character by the author with indirect and unreliable presentation through words and acts. In one interesting case, that of Rachel, the Marcel of the moment builds up one character and Saint-Loup a totally different one. We are absolutely convinced that Marcel is right and Saint-Loup wrong; but when the dramatic confrontation of the two Rachels takes place, the author, called in as umpire, takes refuge in a confession of incompetence to decide. Marcel, in *Swann,* has met Rachel in a brothel; because she is available for twenty francs he is indifferent to her. Later Saint-Loup talks much to him of his incomparable mistress, of her talent, her delicacy, her goodness; when Marcel meets her, he recognizes the Rachel of the brothel. There is no mistake of identity: the very same Rachel, who shortly before sold herself to anyone for twenty francs, is now jealously worshipped by Saint-Loup and receives from him a hundred thousand francs a year. We are clearly told that Rachel the paragon, known only to Saint-Loup, has been constructed out of his own infatuated imagination; we are told too that Saint-Loup gets a glimpse of the other Rachel, the trollop known to Marcel and his other friends:

He caught only a glimpse of this life, but in the midst of it was a Rachel quite other than the Rachel he knew, a Rachel like these two little "chickens," a twenty-franc Rachel. In short Rachel for a moment had become double for him, he had seen, at some distance from his Rachel, Rachel the little "chicken," the true Rachel, *on the supposition that Rachel the "chicken" was any more real than the other.* (VI, 145)

This last assumption—the italics are ours—startlingly opens up the possibility of its opposite: that Saint-Loup's Rachel is as real as the other; perhaps it would be better to say, no more unreal. Furthermore Rachel is an actress, and Saint-Loup, alone in believing in her superior character, is also alone in having faith in her talent; and in this respect Saint-Loup turns out to be right! Rachel in fact becomes a great actress, and at the end has taken the place of the incomparable Berma. The reader may well feel that he has been double-crossed; but if he has, it has been by the Marcel of the moment and other fallible observers, and not by the author, who has been careful not to commit himself.

When Marcel meets Gilberte and when he meets Albertine, he in both cases has an immediate first impression which is very quickly shown by subsequent experience to be grossly erroneous. We readily accept the correction as conforming to the experience of real life, and we are left for several volumes in the secure conviction of the error of the first impression. Then, suddenly, comes the suggestion that the first impression was right after all:

And suddenly I said to myself that the true Gilberte—the true Albertine—were perhaps the ones who had at the first moment declared themselves in a glance, one behind the hedge of pink hawthorn, the other upon the beach. (XIV, 208)

First impressions, according to Proust, are immediate and intuitive, subsequent ones are a reasoned product of the intelligence, and intuition is a better guide to character than reason. "Perhaps we live surrounded by electric, seismic signs, which we must interpret in good faith in order to know the truth about the characters of other people."

Despite these complexities and the confusions in which they may involve the unwary reader, most of Proust's characters are living and convincing, and some may lay claim to being great fictional creations.

Such eminence is reached in several ways. It may, first of all, be attained by complexity. We all recognize that a character who is "all of a piece," who is too simple, too consistent, does not give the illusion of reality. To be great on this score a character must be divided against himself, be convincingly inconsistent. Hamlet is the classic example, Stendhal's Julien Sorel a lesser one.

Secondly, there is the great character who exemplifies a major human passion, sometimes a virtue, but more often a vice which, through sheer immensity, attains to tragic dignity. Othello, Lear, and other Shakespearean examples at once suggest themselves; Balzac too furnishes such characters as Grandet, Goriot, and Vautrin.

A third class is the caricature, a character not literally true to life, but so incisively or amusingly exaggerated from real life that his characteristic poses, gestures, or words become part of an international heritage. Such are Don Quixote, Panurge, Uriah Heep, or Micawber.

In all of these categories Proust has a title to consideration.

By the original intention of the author and by the method of their presentation, Proust's characters are almost without exception very complex. They are not, of course, uniformly convincing, but few would dispute the masterly drawing and the authentic realism of such complex characters as Swann, Odette, Charlus or the Duchesse de Guermantes. Françoise may seem like a minor character because, as a servant, her rôle is limited, or because the total effect of her character is more amusing than vital; she is nevertheless important for the large amount of attention paid to her by the author throughout the book, and she is a splendid example of convincing inconsistency. In one of our first views of her she is receiving a New Year's gift from Marcel:

> No sooner had we arrived in my aunt's dark hall than we could see, under the flutings of a snowy bonnet, stiff and fragile as spun sugar, the concentric waves of a smile of anticipatory gratitude. It was Françoise, standing straight in the little hall door like the statue of a saint in its niche. When we had become somewhat accustomed to the religious darkness, we could make out in her face a disinterested love of humanity, a tender respect for the upper classes, exalted, in the noblest quarters of her heart, by the expectation of the gift. Mother pinched my arm vigorously and said in a firm voice, "Good-morning, Françoise." At this signal my fingers opened and let fall the coin, which found to receive it a hand that was embarrassed, but outstretched. (I, 80-81)

The "disinterested love of humanity" discernible on Françoise's face on New Year's Day was a ready emotion, frequently displayed. When soldiers passed the house and there was a general rush of the household to the garden to watch, she was there:

> "Poor children," said Françoise, barely arrived at the garden fence and already in tears; "poor boys that will be mowed down like grass; just at the thought of it I'm shocked," she added, putting her hand on her heart, at the spot where she had received this *shock*. (I, 130-31)

But the sentiment was general, and did not exclude indifference to the suffering of individuals. One night the kitchen maid whom Swann called the "Charité de Giotto" was seized with violent after-pains of childbirth. Hearing her groans, Marcel's mother awakened Françoise. "Just acting," said Françoise, "she's trying to play the lady." The mother sent Françoise into another room to get a medical book with a marker at the place containing directions for treatment of the sufferer. She went, but an hour later had not returned, and Marcel went to find her:

> I found Françoise, who, wanting to see what the marker was for, was reading the clinical description of the seizure and sobbing

violently over the abstract patient whom she did not know. At each painful symptom mentioned by the author of the treatise, she cried, "Oh, oh, Holy Virgin, is it possible that the good God can make a poor human being suffer like that? Oh, the poor woman!"

But as soon as I had called her and she was back at the bedside of the Charité de Giotto, her tears ceased at once to flow . . . and at the sight of the same sufferings the description of which had made her weep, she had nothing to offer but ill-humored mutterings, and even bitter sarcasm. (I, 179)

Her "tender respect for the upper classes" involved monarchist leanings and a veneration for the old nobility. Saint-Loup at first dazzled and charmed her, but when she found that he had Republican ideas, she was profoundly shocked; a Marquis, with Republican ideas?—it was inconceivable. For a time she had no use for Saint-Loup and was angry with Marcel for having him as a friend. After reflection, however, she decided that a Marquis with Republican ideas was an impossibility in Nature; if Saint-Loup made such professions it was only to ingratiate himself with the present régime:

From that day her coldness toward him and her irritation toward me came to an end. And when she spoke of Saint-Loup, she said: "He's a hypocrite," with a broad kind smile which made it clear that she again had as much respect for him as at the first, and that she had forgiven him. (V, 23)

These examples, and many others which might be given, reveal what makes Françoise such an intensely living character: her amusingly conflicting traits all give the impression of fidelity to one underlying character, which is Françoise herself.

The complexities of Gilberte contribute to the education of Marcel and are the subject of careful analysis. At first there is, for Marcel, just a vision of a vivid girl against a hawthorn hedge. She is the friend of Bergotte, inaccessible, and therefore intensely and romantically desirable. The vulgar gesture she makes (with, as he learns much later, a literal intention) he takes as proof of her scorn. Then comes the Gilberte of the Champs Elysées, a good playmate, who alternates with the ideal imagined by

Marcel between meetings and who—often painfully—corrects it. Still later she reveals new sides. Sometimes she is affectionate to Marcel, sometimes indifferent or hard; she adores her father, and yet seems totally insensitive to Swann's feeling for the anniversary of his father's death:

> . . . since the incident that had taken place on the anniversary of her grandfather's death, I wondered whether the character of Gilberte was not different from what I had supposed, whether this indifference to what people did, this good behavior, this calm, this constant gentle submission, did not on the contrary conceal very passionate desires, which from pride she didn't want seen, and which she revealed only when by chance they were opposed. (III, 196)

The characters, like the physical traits, of both her father and her mother appear in her:

> It is true that Gilberte was an only daughter, but there were at least two Gilbertes. The two natures of her father and her mother did not only mingle in her, they fought over her, and still this would be speaking inaccurately and would give the impression that a third Gilberte suffered at such times from being the prey of the two others. Now Gilberte was alternately one and then the other, and at a given moment no more than the one. (III, 191-92)

Still other Gilbertes are to appear, and at the end, although she has become strikingly like Odette, the Gilberte of the hawthorn hedge and the Champs Elysées is only a memory.

In the second category of great character portrayal, the example of a major passion, Proust's outstanding contribution is Charlus. To say that his is easily the best fictional portrait of a homosexual is certainly true, but no great praise; for the field is so far from popular that Proust has it, for practical purposes, to himself. We can go further, and claim that Charlus is great on any score. Choosing a character whose cardinal vice is peculiarly revolting to the great majority of readers, Proust has made of him such an extraordinary tragi-comic creation that the most fastidious reader cannot but be impressed.

Everything about him is colossal: his physical proportions, his vice, the social tyranny he exercises, his maniacal pride, his delusions of grandeur, his religiosity, his talents, his high position, and the thunder of his fall. With meticulous dress and painted face, the great body minces along with swinging hips; his eyes, prudishly lowered, will suddenly shoot forth at a passing porter or coachman a bold hard look, almost insane in its intensity but at the same time shrewdly appraising. He dominates any group he is in, forcing the conversation, pulverizing opposition, terrorizing those who are not sure of themselves (which is to say practically everyone), performing his social "executions" with incomparable skill. His insolence is calculated. He goes to the salon of Madame Verdurin, whom he scorns, for reasons of his own. "Listen, Charlus," says Madame Verdurin, who is beginning to get too familiar, "wouldn't there be some ruined old nobleman in your Faubourg who could be my porter?" "Yes, indeed," replies Charlus with a friendly smile, "but I don't advise it." "Why not?"—"I should be afraid for your sake that your smart visitors would stop at the lodge and go no farther."

In spite of his culture and erudition, his religious faith is sincere, naïve, and medieval:

For him, as for the sculptors of the XIIIth century, the Christian Church was, in the literal sense of the word, peopled with a crowd of perfectly real beings—Prophets, Apostles, Angels, holy personages of every sort, surrounding the Incarnate Word, His Mother and Her Spouse, the Eternal Father, all the Martyrs and Doctors of the Church, as they may be seen carved in high relief, thronging the porches or filling the naves of the cathedrals. Out of all these M. de Charlus had chosen as intercessory patrons the Archangels Michael, Gabriel, and Raphaël, with whom he had frequent conversations, so that they might convey his prayers to the Eternal Father before Whose Throne they stand. (X, 113-14)

In casual conversation Charlus mentions that he is thinking of staying on the Norman coast until the end of September. "The storms are fine then," puts in Madame Verdurin. "I wasn't thinking of that," continues Charlus. "I have recently been neglecting the Archangel St. Michael, my patron, and I should like to make it up to him by remaining until his day, the 29th of September, at the Abbaye of Mont Saint-Michel." This puts Madame Verdurin in something of a quandary, for at the moment anticlericalism is a part of the tone of her salon. "Does that sort of thing interest you so much?" she temporizes. "You are perhaps afflicted with intermittent deafness," replies Charlus insolently. "I have told you that St. Michael was one of my glorious patrons."

One of the best Charlus scenes is the one in which the Baron, temporarily deserted by Morel, tries to bring the violinist back by giving it out that he is about to fight a duel to quash a slander about their relations. The ruse is successful, for Morel dreads the threatened scandal and the consequent detriment to his career. When Morel returns, Charlus is nearly delirious with joy, but at the café where he has been he has meanwhile entered thoroughly into his part. Almost believing in the imaginary duel, he has identified himself with his illustrious ancestor the Constable of Guermantes and makes lunges and parries, with grave danger to the drinks on the table. "What an extraordinary thing you are going to see—the very descendant of the Constable in battle." Not once in a century could one have such an example of "ethnic revivification." What a chance for a painter! Elstir must come, a telegram must be sent to bring him. But grandly he allows Morel to persuade him not to fight.

In a little while they broke up and then M. de Charlus said to Morel: "I conclude from this whole business, which has ended better than you deserved, that you do not know how to behave and that at the end of your military service I shall myself bring you back to your father as did the Archangel Raphaël sent by God to the young Tobit." And the Baron began to smile with an air of grandeur and a joy which Morel, by no means pleased at the prospect of being thus brought home, did not seem to share. In the intoxication of comparing himself to the Archangel and Morel to the son of Tobit, M. de Charlus was no longer thinking of the purpose of his statement. . . . Drunk with love or self-esteem, the baron did not see, or pretended not to see, the grimace of the violinist left alone in the café, for he said to me with a proud smile: "Did you notice when I compared him to the son of Tobit how delirious with joy he was! That is because, being very intelligent, he at once understood that the Father with whom he was going to live thereafter was not his father after the flesh, who must be some horrible valet with moustaches, but his spiritual father, that is to say, Myself. What a triumph for him! How proudly he lifted his head! What joy he felt at having understood. I am sure he will be saying every day: 'O God who gave the Blessed Archangel Raphaël as *guide* to your servant Tobit on a long journey, grant us, your servants, always to be protected by him and furnished with his help.' I didn't even need," added the baron, fully persuaded that he would sit one day before the throne of God, "to tell him that I was the heavenly messenger, he understood by himself and was dumb with joy!" And M. de Charlus (whom, on the contrary, joy had not deprived of speech), heedless of passers-by, who turned, thinking him a madman, raised his hands and shouted with all his strength, "Alleluia!" (X, 159-60)

Charlus is not merely homosexual but sadistic, and the conflicts of the two aspects of his vice with each other and with his fantastic family pride involve him in continual difficulties. He is attracted by young Bloch, and suggests, to Marcel's horror, that it might be amusing if the young man could be persuaded to beat his father. At Marcel's suggestion that he present Bloch senior, Charlus cries out in consternation. "Present him to me? You have no sense of values!" He would deign to smile on the old man only on the condition that he let himself be beaten by his son; but an introduction was simply inconceivable. "I am not so easy to know as that." But he who is so careful that the honor of an introduction to him should not be granted to the unqualified, is driven to the pursuit of waiters, and rides in the interior of a public hack with its tipsy driver. And as we watch the humiliations he is forced to receive from the base-born and contemptible Morel, we come gradually to realize that this tyrant, this dynamo of self-will, is himself a victim, and pathetic. Madame Verdurin, always competent and utterly heartless, finding him and his connections useful to her salon, disregards his impertinences and affects ignorance of his vice; but when his usefulness is ended, she "executes" him more pitilessly than he has executed others. Charlus has organized for her a musical entertainment, featuring Morel and utilizing his great social prestige to invite the cream of society to the home of Madame Verdurin. But the aristocratic guests ignore the hostess and address their attention to Charlus, who accepts their attention as his right. Madame Verdurin, who can tolerate no rivalry in her salon, decides that the time has come to cast him off; she conveniently discovers his vice, and using it as an excuse she "rescues" Morel by setting him against the Baron. Triumphant at the success of the entertainment and without a suspicion of what has been going on, Charlus approaches to tell Morel that he is to have the Legion of Honor. "Leave me alone, I forbid you to approach me!" screams the hypocritical Morel. "I am not the first one you have tried to pervert!" Marcel, who is a witness to the scene and who, knowing what Madame Verdurin plans to do, is sorry for Charlus, now thinks gleefully that the moment has arrived for Charlus to pulverize both her and Morel. Nothing of the sort happens. The Baron is speechless, and looks questioningly, beseechingly, from one hostile face to another. Turning her back on him, Madame Verdurin goes elsewhere to spread her venom; Charlus would be deserted but for the Queen of Naples, who, loyal to the princely clan to which they both belong, slips her arm through his and, with a perfectly executed snub to Madame Verdurin, carries him off.

We now learn that the malice and the ferocity of Charlus are a sham. "The people whom he hated, he hated because he thought that they looked down upon him; had they been civil to him, instead of flying into a furious rage with them, he would have taken them to his bosom."

He appears no more in Madame Verdurin's salon, and the word spreads that he criminally assaulted a young musician and was thrown out. Too weary and unhappy to defend himself, the Baron is shortly laid low by a violent attack of pneumonia, and is for a time at death's door. His silence with regard to the

Verdurins is due to no failure of his usual loquacity, for he profoundly edifies the watchers at his sickbed by his words of Christian resignation, his quotations from Scripture, his flights of mystic eloquence. There is no question of penitence or fear; he is serenely confident of his worth. He begs the Archangel Gabriel to announce to him, as he did to the prophet, how long he must wait for the promised Messiah. "But he must not ask me, as he did Daniel, to wait seven weeks and sixty-two weeks, for I shall be dead before then." The awaited Messiah is Morel!

He recovers from his illness and leads for many years a life quite consistent with his past. His sadism becomes combined with masochism. At the end we see the formerly proud Charlus half-paralyzed, snowy haired, childish, bowing obsequiously to anyone who turns in his direction, cared for with a strange loyalty by Jupien.

Though there are comically exaggerated traits in Charlus, he is far too imposing a figure to be called a caricature; but there are many candidates in Proust's gallery for this final type of fictional distinction. Both the Verdurins, Cottard, the dowager Marquise de Cambremer, Legrandin, Bloch, and many others might be mentioned among the more important characters, and there are in addition many amusing silhouettes: waiters and bell-boys, an elevator man, a gardener's daughter, assorted domestic servants, and others. We can only refer to a few examples which prove to be revealing, not only of his methods, in caricature, but of the serious purpose behind them.

Here is Madame Verdurin, enthroned in her salon:

From this high post she took a spirited part in the conversation of the faithful and delighted in their "gags"; but since the accident to her jaw she had given up breaking out into actual laughter and performed instead a conventional pantomine which signified, without fatigue or risk to herself, that she was laughing till she cried. At the slightest word dropped by a member against a bore or against a former member gone over to the bores—and to the despair of M. Verdurin, who had long tried to keep up with his wife in amiability, but who, with his genuine laughter, got quickly out of breath and

had been outdistanced and beaten by this ruse of incessant and
fictitious hilarity—she uttered a little scream, closed entirely her
birdlike eyes which were beginning to film, and suddenly, as if she
had only just had time to hide an indecent spectacle or parry a
mortal attack, plunging her face in her hands which covered it entirely, she appeared to be trying to suppress, to extinguish a laugh
which, if she had given way to it, would have resulted in loss of
consciousness. So, dizzy with the gaiety of the faithful, drunk with
good fellowship, slander, and complicity, Mme Verdurin, like a bird
on its perch with a morsel dipped in wine, sobbed with amiability.
(I, 295-96)

Monsieur Verdurin finally discovers a technique to parallel his
wife's amiability:

Scarcely had he begun to make the movement of head and shoulders
of someone who bursts out laughing, before he began at once to
cough, as if, by laughing too hard, he had choked on the smoke of
his pipe. And keeping it always in the corner of his mouth, he could
prolong indefinitely the pretense of suffocation and hilarity. So that
he and Mme Verdurin, who, across from him . . . closed her eyes
before burying her face in her hands, had the air of two theatre masks
with different representations of gaiety. (II, 69)

And here are two ladies listening to music at a reception:

Mme de Franquetot [watched] anxiously, with frightened eyes,
as if the keys over which [the pianist] ran with agility had been a
series of trapezes from which he might have an eighty-meter fall, and
not without casting at her neighbor glances of astonishment and dis-
belief, which meant: "It is unbelievable, I would never have believed
a man capable of that"; Mme de Cambremer [listened] like a woman
who has received a fine musical education, beating time with her head
which had become the pendulum of a metronome whose sweep and
rapidity of oscillation from one shoulder to the other had become
such (with that sort of wildness and abandon in the glance characteristic of pain beyond control and excused by a "What can you
expect?") that she kept catching her diamond pendants in the trim-
mings of her gown, and was obliged to straighten the black grapes
she had in her hair—without, however, ceasing to accelerate the
tempo. (II, 160-61)

These passages are typical of a large number of others. What are we to make of them? Are they comic just by their incongruous elaboration and by their exaggeration? There is something more: in these cases and in hosts of others there is a constant implicit comparison of human behavior to the action of machines. The mechanism of the Guermantes bow and handshake; the flight of Saint-Loup's monocle before him, as, bending forward from the waist, he rushes into a drawing room; the Duc de Guermantes, a "statue of Jupiter cast in gold," "an inert mass of thirty million francs," maneuvered, without will of its own and by an inheritance of good breeding, into a standing position; Swann, when he is unhappy, mechanically passing his hand over his eyes and forehead, unconsciously repeating the gesture of his father before him: these are automatisms rather than rational behavior. A similarly mechanical effect is produced by the dissection of a glance or a laugh, the grotesque attribution of artificially assembled meanings to a single feature. Here, for example, is Ski laughing:

Ski assumed first a knowing air, then allowed to escape a single laugh like a first peal of bells, followed by a silence in which the knowing look seemed to be prudently examining the humor of what was being said, then a second bell of laughter broke loose, presently followed by a full angelus of hilarity. (XII, 116)

Legrandin reveals his snobbishness with a humble part of his anatomy:

Legrandin's face showed an extraordinary zeal and animation; he made a profound bow, with a secondary backward movement which brought his spine sharply up into a position behind its starting-point, a gesture which he must have learned from the husband of his sister Mme de Cambremer. This rapid recovery caused a sort of impetuous muscular wave to ripple over Legrandin's hind quarters, which I had not supposed to be so fleshy; I cannot say why, but this undulation of pure matter, this wholly carnal wave without the least hint of spirituality, lashed into fury by obsequious assiduity, awakened my mind suddenly to the possibility of a Legrandin quite different from the one we knew. (I, 181-82)

All this represents something much more than a technique of caricature, applicable to selected comic characters. If the physical mechanism is accentuated in some cases more than others, it is only an aspect of a general helplessness. The characters are all puppets, executing their pathetic gestures to the accompaniment of the author's sardonic laughter. They are "strong" or they are "weak," though not in conformity with appearances: " . . . in humanity the rule—which naturally involves some exceptions—is that the apparently hard people are the weak who have been rejected, and that the strong, caring little whether they are accepted or rejected, alone have that gentleness which the common herd takes for weakness." But "strong" and "weak" alike are the helpless instruments of forces which they do not understand, of whose very existence they seem sometimes unaware. They pursue their incomprehensible desires blindly, or in defiance of the faint counsels of intermittent reason, and they lie to themselves in self-justification. Swann does not really find Odette attractive, she is not his "type," and yet fall in love with her he does, because he must, because the time for his great passion has come. Studying her face carefully, he decides that she reminds him of Botticelli's daughter of Jethro and "he congratulated himself that the pleasure he felt in seeing Odette found a justification in his own esthetic culture." Everything about the Verdurin salon was obnoxious to him, yet because Odette went there he made himself believe that the "faithful" were splendid people; after his quarrel with Madame Verdurin, he convinced himself that he had long been trying to rescue Odette from that hotbed of malicious gossip.

In vain, experience teaches that the inevitable sequel to anticipation is disappointment, that desire is always frustrated, either because its object is withheld or because it is granted after the death of the desire: the characters pursue their will-o'-the-wisps just the same.

If they do not understand themselves, still less do they understand each other, as Marcel early learns: transported by the beauty of the world after the rain, he brandishes his umbrella almost in the face of a passing peasant, crying, "Beautiful weather, isn't it?"—only to be met with resentment and in comprehension. When he thinks Gilberte scorns him, she is really finding him very attractive; and when he imagines himself loved by some woman, the reverse is always true.

Communication between these beings has little to do with truth—if such a thing exists; instead it resolves itself into a complicated system of acting, intended to convey an impression favorable to the actor. Here are two brief examples, among scores:

> Coquettishly she embellished her smile . . . by giving to her glance, which was fixed on the abstract, a dreamy and gentle expression. (Princesse de Laumes)

> She extended her hand with a hesitant air intended to demonstrate the schooled reserve which she had to overcome and the spontaneous sympathy which successfully vanquished it. (Madame de Cambremer the younger)

Cruelty in some form and to some degree is almost universal, not even conventionally "good" people excepted: witness Marcel's great-aunt who delights in urging the grandfather to take some cognac, just for the spectacle of the grandmother's distress. The ferocity of Françoise in finishing off a chicken that is in no hurry to die reappears in Madame Verdurin when she gets rid of Swann and when later she "executes" Charlus; and in Rachel when she organizes a scandalous failure for a beginning actress. Witnesses to such scenes either join in with relish, or basely refrain from protest.

And yet, so mixed are these beings that kindness is as widespread as cruelty, and found in as unexpected places. Proust's startlingly optimistic statement that "it is not good sense which is 'the most widespread thing in the world,' it is kindness" is partially substantiated in the record. Rachel, who deliberately wrecks the career of an inoffensive fellow actress, and gouges millions from her hapless lover, shows flashes of genuine kindness; Jupien the procurer and pervert shows disinterested devotion to the fallen Charlus; even Madame Verdurin, consistently cruel and self-seeking hitherto, in *La Prisonnière* arranges with her husband to contribute, in the greatest secrecy, ten thousand francs a year to the support of Saniette, the former butt of their ridicule, the author adding:

. . . one should never feel resentment against men, never judge them, because of the recollection of an act of malice, for we do not know all the good that at other times they have sincerely willed and achieved; undoubtedly the evil pattern that we have once and for all observed will come back, but the soul is much richer than that, it has other patterns also which will return. (XII, 166-67)

For their kindness no more than for their cruelty are human beings responsible, and in the performance of a kind act they may be just as blind or ridiculous as at other times. Madame Cottard, for example, meeting Swann on an omnibus and taking occasion to pass on the pleasant things Odette has said of him, thus pouring balm on his wounds, makes her departure thus:

"Oh, mercy, there's the conductor stopping for me; here I've been gossiping along with you and almost went by the rue Bonaparte— would you be so kind as to tell me if my plume is straight?" And Mme Cottard withdrew her white-gloved hand from her muff and extended it to Swann; from it floated, filling the omnibus, a transfer coupon, a vision of fashionable life, and the odor of cleaning fluid. And Swann felt himself overflowing with affection for her . . . while from the platform he watched her with loving eyes, as she bravely threaded her way up the rue Bonaparte, her plume erect, lifting her skirt with one hand, with the other grasping her umbrella and her card case (held so that the monogram could be seen), and dangling her muff before her. (II, 227)

Even Marcel's grandmother, so honest, so sincere, so simple, the law of whose being is goodwill, devotion, and sacrifice, has her amiable absurdities—her passion for fresh air, for example:

. . . even when it was pouring rain, she could be seen in the drenched and empty garden, pushing back her gray, disheveled locks so that her forehead could better absorb the salubrity of the wind and the rain. She would say, "At last one can breathe!" and would rush along the soaking walks—much too symmetrically arranged for her taste . . .—with her jerky, enthusiastic little step, that was regulated by the various movements created in her soul by the intoxication of the storm, the power of hygiene, the stupidity of my upbringing, and the symmetry of gardens, rather than by any such desire, foreign to her nature, as avoiding mud splashes on her plum-colored skirt. (I, 22)

In the great dining room of the Balbec hotel the same passion causes her furtively to open a window; menus, newspapers, caps, and veils go flying, coiffures are disarranged, furious glances, to the distress of Marcel, are cast at her table, while she, "sustained by the heavenly breath, remains calm and smiling like Saint Blandine."

As the grandmother's life draws to a close, we suddenly realize that the great-hearted and occasionally amusing character we have come to know is a creation of the mind of Marcel. As he returns unannounced from Doncières he catches a glimpse of her as she is in his absence: "I saw, on the couch by the lamp—red-faced, heavy and vulgar, ill, vaguely scanning a book with wild eyes—a stricken old woman whom I did not know." This old woman is as illusioned and as helpless as the rest, no nearer than they to the truth about others, no more consciously self-directive in obeying the laws of her being. "If there was a person who, more than another, lived enclosed within his private universe, that person was my grandmother." And she, like all humanity, is subject to change and decay.

In Proust's puppet gallery it is not he, directly, who pulls the strings. He is the spectator, amused and sometimes moved to pity. The source of all the confused activity is a system of laws, which are the pessimistic intellectual themes. He did not invent them, he is trying to deduce them and discover them. Even before the horrible contortions of the depraved, he is sometimes stirred to a sense of the grave beauty of law in action.

MARCEL AND ALBERTINE

"Already in this first volume," Proust said in his interview for *Le Temps* in 1913, "you will see the character who tells the story, who says 'I' (and who is not myself) . . ."; on several occasions thereafter he approved critics who noted the distinction between author and narrator.

But the "I" of *A la Recherche du temps perdu* is a complex factor. There is the Marcel of the moment, who behaves, speaks, reacts, observes; there is the Marcel of the present, wise with experience, who describes the adventures of the earlier Marcel and comments on them; and finally, indisputably, there is the author himself who occasionally intervenes with his "I" and makes generalizations and deductions. It is not always easy to distinguish between the Marcel of the present and the author, although often the manner and the matter of the comment make it clear that Proust is not merely speaking for Marcel but for himself. But often in his correspondence he claims as his own the opinions expressed in the novel—opinions on art, on love, on friendship, on involuntary memory and the living past, on the lessons of experience in general; so that it is quite safe to assume that the generalizations of the novel are those of the author. If, in the rôle of commentator, author and narrator sometimes overlap, little is to be gained by trying to distinguish them. Marcel comments on fictitious situations and characters, and Proust makes observations applicable to real life; but their opinions are identical.

In personality, character, and general situation Marcel and Proust are much alike. Marcel is sensitive and delicate. His moral weakness is closely related to physical infirmity, for he has frequent attacks of suffocation. His mother and grandmother coddle him, but, realizing the importance of strengthening his character, frequently lecture him on the austere virtues and make vain attempts to develop in him courage and self-reliance. The result is that Marcel is at once dependent and conscientious, affectionately clinging, and remorseful over his weakness of will.

Although this basic character pattern is valid for the whole period through which we know Marcel, there is, as he grows older, a shift of emphasis in the distribution of characteristics, a shift that seems to follow a fairly consistent trend from sensibility to reason. Comparing the two extremes of his development, we can isolate two Marcels: the child, and the one referred to in *La Prisonnière* as "the other man I had become."

The extreme sensibility of the young Marcel is displayed toward both persons and things. He cannot face the terrors of a solitary night—for his conscientious mother has prescribed that he shall sleep alone—without the viaticum of the good-night kiss; and so intensely does he long for it that he dreads his mother's arrival in his bedroom, because that will set a definite time for her departure, and make it inevitable. The support which mother and grandmother offer to his weakness, coupled with his acute emotivity, make him an addict to the physical and moral caress, an addiction which he carries over into his relations to people outside the family. He cannot be content with casual friendships, but demands profound, exclusive, and lifelong devotions.

Toward the things with which he is habitually surrounded, particularly at night—walls and ceilings of a bedroom, furniture, a fireplace—he continues to feel, long into manhood, the physical devotion of the child for a favorite rag doll. He endows his surroundings with personal characteristics, considers them friendly or hostile in proportion to his habituation to them, imagines them capable of jealousy, or of revenge for neglect. On exceptional occasions he adapts himself quickly and happily to new surroundings, as when he visits Saint-Loup at Doncières. Standing at the door of Saint-Loup's room, he thinks he hears someone within:

But it was only the fire burning. It couldn't keep still, it kept displacing the logs, and very clumsily, too. I entered; it let one roll down and made another smoke. And even when it wasn't moving like vulgar people, it was always making sounds which, as soon as I saw the flame rising, revealed themselves as the sounds of fire, but which, if I had been on the other side of the wall, would have seemed to me to come from someone blowing his nose and walking. (VI, 67)

The halls of his hotel—a made-over palace—take on a sort of life and seem to inhabit the building rather than form a part of it; they wander around Marcel, coming, going, retracing their steps, without apparent objective, and hospitably offering him their company. The court is a "fair hermit," whom he is glad to have for a neighbor; another neighbor is the countryside, asleep when he arrives, but whose acquaintance he is happy to make the next morning. In his room is a little cabinet which, cornered and cut off from escape, stares sheepishly at him with a large blue eye.

Flowers and trees are his particular friends, of whom he asks questions and expects answers, and to whom he must say goodbye on departure.

These childlike and primitive attempts at making his surroundings participate in his personal life persist long after such habits ordinarily lose their hold. But in his later childhood, paralleling them, and coinciding with his dawning literary ambitions, comes the conviction that certain natural scenes, particularly trees and flowers, and roofs or steeples under the play of light and shade, or seen in perspective, have a secret message which they are trying to convey to him.

In intelligence Marcel is in his own eyes woefully deficient. In social relations he is continually displaying a disproportionate or untimely ardor, which, as experience regularly shows him, is "refrigerating" to its recipient. The most lofty reasoning leaves him unmoved, and he is only happy in idle reverie. He is totally devoid of capacity for detailed and methodical observation, and consequently, by the standards of the current naturalistic school of writers, of aptitude for literature. Sometimes he is naïve to the point of stupidity, as on the occasion when Charlus chooses to ignore that he has invited the boy and his grandmother to tea:

With a scruple for precision which I kept until I learned that one does not learn the truth about a man's intention by asking him, and that the risk of a misunderstanding which will probably pass unnoticed is less than that of a naïve insistence, I said: "But sir, you surely remember that you asked us to come this evening?" (IV, 220)

Such traits and such experiences convince Marcel that he is a "little imbecile." Gradually, however, growing understanding of himself and the accumulation of evidence that others hold his intelligence in high esteem, convince him that he is not congenitally and hopelessly stupid. In his way, he discovers, he is gifted, but his powers are particular and limited:

There was in me a person who knew how to observe more or less well, but he was an intermittent person, coming to life only when there was a manifestation of some general essence, common to several things: this was his food and his joy. Then this person watched and listened, but only to a certain depth, so that observation was profitless. Like a geometrician who, stripping things of their perceptible qualities, sees only their linear substratum, I missed what people said, because what interested me was not what they meant but the way they said it, in so far as that revealed their characters or their absurdities: or rather it was something which had always been the object of my search because it gave me a specific pleasure, and that was the point which one being had in common with another. (XV, 36-37)

But the most remarkable aspect of his intelligence is his power of self-analysis. He early learns to recognize his successive moods, which have such inner consistency and such a clear differentiation from each other that they amount to separate personalities; he becomes able to foresee their resurgence, discount their desires, and detach himself from their destinies. He discovers, once the painful self-depreciation of childhood is past, that his conversation can be diverting to others, and on his sorties into society he becomes his "alert and frivolous" self, chatters incessantly, delighted with the effect he is producing, but is incapable of observing or meditating. He displays an interest in correct behavior, and entertains social ambitions that are not devoid of snobbery. Once he is alone again he becomes what he considers a truer self, in meditation, memory, and feeling; it is this self that knows that experience is disappointing to anticipation, but rewarding when remembered.

He comes to realize that his ill health is largely neurotic: "By dint of thinking oneself sick one becomes sick, one gets thin, one has no longer the strength to get up. . . ." He knows that exercise, followed by the sleep of fatigue, would cure his troubles, but is unable to make himself follow such a régime.

Gradually there emerges "the other man," who shows, by comparison with the young Marcel, a marked increase in intelligence at the expense of sensibility and of the already weak will. The older Marcel knows himself all too well, and declines to rationalize his conduct to himself. With cynical awareness he coddles his neurotic body and is indulgent to the desires of his successive personalities. His behavior toward others becomes a series of complicated moves, performed with "detestable skill." He lies deliberately, to produce an effect, and believes nothing anyone tells him. Well understanding the feeling of vigor and joy which accompanies decision, he allows himself to become paralyzed in the face of any choice. He is resigned to the perversities of his conduct—to pursuing what he does not really want, to imagining he desires something because he cannot have it, to displaying affection toward one person because he loves another, whom he treats with coldness.

All in all, this "other man" is a disembodied intelligence, a sardonic observer of himself, no less than of others, disillusioned and dissociated almost to the point of madness. His desires are weak but irresistible, and his resigned subservience to their domination results from the habit he has acquired of getting along without will-power. We may surmise that all that keeps him sane and alive is an occasional experience of self-forgetfulness in the beauty of art. He is ripe for the psychic revolution which is accomplished in the final volume.

Marcel's sexual experiences, briefly described and almost hidden in dense paragraphs throughout the novel but more openly related in *La Prisonnière,* are in many respects in line with his character as we have seen it. Experience is preceded, as we might expect, by voluptuous and excessive imagination, in which simple sensuality combines with poetic aspiration. Walking in the woods near Roussainville, the adolescent boy conjures up in imagination a shapely peasant girl who is to be at once the instrument of his pleasure and the incarnation of the spirit of the place. Women seen in passing—a milkmaid at a railway stop, a fisher girl near Balbec, the band of "jeunes filles en fleur" before he has made their acquaintance—serve similar functions. His first experiment in solitary vice is accomplished in the face of a conviction that the result will be mortal, and in a small room—the only one where he is permitted to lock himself in—whose humble function contrasts with the beauty of the vines at the window and of its view toward Roussainville. He achieves sensation in a mock wrestling match with Gilberte on the Champs Elysées, feels some consequent remorse, and later believes himself to have been punished for the experience. What is stated to be his first complete adventure in physical love is an incident which has no visible connection with the rest of the novel; it occurs on Aunt Léonie's divan, and his partner is a "little cousin," who remains unnamed and is not elsewhere mentioned.

At Balbec Albertine comes to spend a night at the hotel and invites Marcel to come to her room after she has gone to bed. Marcel misunderstands her intentions—we can scarcely blame him—and casts himself upon her in the ecstatic conviction that he is about to realize his dreams; but Albertine repels him and rings for help. When later she proves more tractable, he wonders jealously whether he is indebted for her compliance to an intervening love, or whether the fact that on this occasion it is he who is prone and imprisoned and she who is up and able to leave at will is enough to calm her fears.

Like Swann before him he develops a taste for servant girls, and in the pursuit of his desires experiments with acting. At Balbec the results are negative:

> On each floor, on both sides of the communicating stairs, dark corridors spread out fanwise, in which, carrying a bolster, passed a chambermaid. I applied to my face, made vague by the dim light, the mask of my most passionate dreams, but read in the look which she turned upon me, the horror of my nothingness. (IV, 90-91)

At Doncières he is more successful. While he is being served by a maid in a private dining room, the lamp goes out, and with the help of transparent pretexts he makes effective use of the darkness. An unforeseen result of this adventure is that for some time his pleasure is conditioned to wainscoted private dining rooms.

His love for Albertine begins in his poetic group feeling for the whole band of adolescent girls at Balbec. Any one of them, given the right combination of circumstances, would have served as well as Albertine; in fact, after her death, he resuscitates the original feeling by physical half-relations with Andrée, formerly a member of the band. When he leaves Balbec, the group sentiment fades, but is quickly revived when he hears that Albertine is in Paris:

> It was enough for me to be told that she was in Paris and had called at the house for me to see her again like a rose beside the seashore. I do not really know whether it was desire for her or for Balbec that laid hold of me then; perhaps the desire for her was itself a lazy, weak, and incomplete form of possessing Balbec. . . . Besides, even materially, when she was no longer moving in my imagination before a sea horizon, but sitting still beside me, she often seemed to me a poor sort of rose, before which I would gladly have shut my eyes, so as not to see this or that defect of the petals and to believe that I was inhaling the breath of the shore. (VII, 41)

When this poor rose, whose principal merit is to excite a poetic memory, comes to see him, Marcel decides that he would like "to kiss the whole of the Balbec shore on the girl's two cheeks," with bizarre results:

In the brief passage of my lips toward her cheek, it was ten Albertines that I saw; this single girl, being like a goddess with several heads, that which I had seen, if I tried to approach it, gave place to another. At least so long as I had not touched it, I could still see that head, a faint fragrance came from it to me. But alas!—for in this matter of kissing our noses are as badly placed as our lips are ill adapted—all at once my eyes stopped seeing; next my nose was crushed and could catch no further fragrance, and, without thereby gaining any clearer idea of the taste of the rose of my desire, I learned, from these detestable signs, that I was at last in the act of kissing Albertine. (VII, 53-54)

After she has become his captive, Marcel is acutely jealous of her, but not without interruption. At times—and this is in line with his strong mother fixation—he tends to rest in Albertine, to find comfort in the support she gives him, and even, when receiving her caresses, to think consciously of his mother. He likes to spin out his dream undisturbed, while contemplating Albertine's face and figure, and to synchronize his sensations with his meditations. To any active reciprocity in his mistress, he prefers an indulgent complicity. Her physical presence is almost an encumbrance to love, and yet it has a certain utility: under proper conditions it can furnish the slight push that will set him afloat upon his dream. The solution of the difficulty is Albertine asleep; hence the extraordinary passage of "La regarder dormir," in *La Prisonnière*:

Stretched out at full length upon my bed, in an attitude so natural that no art could have designed it, she reminded me of a long blossoming stem that had been laid there, and so indeed she was: the faculty of dreaming which I possessed only in her absence I recovered at such moments in her presence, as though by falling asleep she had become a plant. In this way her sleep did to a certain extent make love possible; when I was alone, I could think of her, but I missed her, I did not possess her. When she was present, I spoke to her, but I was too far absent from myself to be able to think. When she was asleep, I no longer needed to talk to her, I knew that she was no longer looking at me, I had no longer any need to live upon my own outer surface.

By shutting her eyes, by losing consciousness, Albertine had stripped off, one after another, the different human characters with which she had deceived me ever since the day when I had first made her acquaintance. She was animated now only by the unconscious life of vegetation, of trees, a life more different from my own, more alien, and yet one that belonged more to me. . . . (XI, 92-93)

And so on—the whole exquisitely written passage should be read. Albertine is certainly at her best as a vegetable.

But as a character in a novel she fails to carry conviction. She is an enigma, such a bundle of contradictions that with the best will in the world we find it next to impossible to picture her physically or understand her morally. She is plump, rosy, energetic, and she is pale, thin, listless. Her eyes are blue and they are black. She is a sports girl who can scarcely sit still, and she is an intellectual and an esthete. She is simple, frank, affectionate, loyal, and she is profoundly deceitful, sly, and treacherous. She is vulgar and she has fundamental good taste. She comes from a family that is at the same time rich and poor, with and without much social standing.

Clearly the multiple model technique, which elsewhere resulted in brilliantly successful fictional portraits, has in this case gone astray—if Proust was trying to paint a portrait; but was he? One passage suggests that he was not: "These women [whom we love] are a product of our temperament, an image, a reversed projection, a 'negative' of our sensibility. . . . [A writer] should record in the character of the lover an indication of variation, which appears when he comes to new regions, new latitudes, of life. And perhaps he would be giving expression to still another truth if, when he drew characters for others in his book, he should refrain from giving any character to the woman loved."

Albertine is less the portrait of a woman than a device for describing the heart of her lover. She has, like other characters, models; but their, and her, external reality is blurred by its incorporation in the inner world of the narrator. As Proust puts it in another passage:

Even the beings who were dearest to the writer have, in the final analysis, done no more than pose for him as for a painter. Sometimes when an anguished passage has been left in rough draft, a new affection, a new suffering comes to us, allowing us to finish it, to fill it out. . . . Our passions sketch out our books and the intervals of rest between write them. When inspiration comes again, when we can resume work, the woman who posed for an emotion no longer makes us experience it. We must continue with a new model, and if this is a betrayal of the other, there is no great harm in the substitution, thanks to the likeness of our emotions, which causes a work of art to be at the same time a memory of our past loves and the vicissitudes of our present ones. This is one of the reasons for the futility of studies that try to guess of whom the author is talking. (XVI, 62, 65-66)

This passage is in itself almost a sufficient answer to the statement that Albertine "was" Agostinelli. He was an important model, but he was neither the first nor the last. There had been, and were yet to be, a succession of them, male and female—for Proust's Uranism did not exclude romantic attachments to the opposite sex *(amours de tête,* or as he called them to Gide, "spiritual loves"), among them Mademoiselle Benardahy, Comtesse de Chevigné, Laure Hayman, Louisa de Mornand (she especially), Princesse Soutzo, and many others who more or less briefly captured his imagination. Albertine is not a man, she is not a woman, she is the half-symbolic projection of the shifting fantasies of Marcel.

As for the relation between Proust and Marcel, their resemblance is so great that we can scarcely avoid taking them for one person. Most of Marcel's traits can be identified in Proust from sources outside the novel, and the few that cannot (such as his childlike personification of the objects by which he is surrounded) fit so naturally into his personality that they seem to be merely rounding out an authentic portrait. If, in spite of his warning, we sometimes confuse author and narrator, it is Proust who sets the example. In the passages we have just quoted he makes it quite clear that the author's loves have served as the model for Albertine, and that the emotions which he attributes to Marcel are his own. Furthermore, the book which he talks so much about in *Le Temps retrouvé,* the manuscripts of which are so patched and revised, is obviously both the book we are reading and the one Marcel is supposed to write when we leave him at the close; the distinction between Marcel and Proust breaks down in their common authorship of *A la Recherche du temps perdu.*

Yet there is some ground for Proust's plea for a distinction. Things happen to Marcel that did not happen to Proust; naturally, for Marcel moves through fictional places and events, and converses with composite fictional characters. Some of the events and situations which concern Marcel are Proust's authentic autobiography, and some are fiction; but is is very probable that there is a third category—events and situations which are transposed from the life of Proust.

Just as the situation of Marcel and Albertine in *La Prisonnière* and *Albertine disparue* is probably a transposition of that of Proust and Agostinelli from 1912 to 1914, so there is considerable likelihood that the episode of the band of adolescent girls—who seem distinctly boyish even to the unprejudiced reader—is the transposed version of Proust's experiences with the male youths whose antics and conversations aroused his affectionate amusement at Cabourg in 1909. Of the "jeunes filles en fleur" Montesquiou wrote Proust, "Will it not be curious to think that, to achieve the right of telling everything, under the innocent shield of a publisher who thought he was dealing with a rival of Berquin [author of insipid pastorals], and under the amused protection of a comrade attached to your cause, you have had the courage to jump over so many thorny hawthorns and girls in bud 'who became men in the jumping,' as reported by the ineffable Pliny."

Naturally Proust could not admit openly that he sometimes changed the sex of his originals in his transpositions, but, following his frequent custom, he planted a hint in his final volume: "The writer should not be offended if the invert attributes to his heroines a male face. Only this slight distortion permits the invert to give to what he reads its character of generality." The natural inference is that if the writer himself is an invert, he too may transpose, so as to give a "character of generality" to his heroes or heroines for the benefit of the heterosexual reader.

In the light of such transpositions the ostensible heterosexuality of Marcel is understandable and necessary. Moreover, the difference, in this respect, from Proust turns out to be trifling; the essential feature of their common nature is retreat from the disappointments of experience and recourse to fantasy.

SOCIETY

To some readers Proust seems unaware of social problems, or perhaps, shielded by his wealth, his illness, and his artistic preoccupations, exquisitely disdainful of such vulgar matters. It must be admitted that there are grounds for the impression. The great majority of his characters are wealthy idlers, with ample time for coddling their neuroses, elaborating their love affairs and attendant jealousies, gossiping, and trying in general to be as decadent as possible. Proust's lengthy and detailed descriptions of dinners and receptions of high society, and his occasionally precious style, accentuate the impression. Yet he was aware of how he must seem to others, and felt, occasionally, that his writing and his life should reveal more social consciousness; but his compunctions were transient. In a late passage of *Le Temps retrouvé* he said:

I felt that I need not encumber myself with the various literary theories which had for a time troubled me—notably those which criticism had developed at the time of the Dreyfus Affair and had resumed during the war [of 1914-1918], and which tended toward making the artist "come out of his ivory tower" and treat subjects that were not sentimental or frivolous, depict large proletarian movements. . . . (XVI, 28)

Snobbishness and the sense of caste are, however, accentuated in the novel, and if class conflict, or "labor" and "capital" in the

terms of the proletarian writer, are absent, the classes are nevertheless there. The majority of the principal characters belong
either to the aristocracy—Bourbon or Napoleonic—or to the
wealthy bourgeoisie. There is also the servant class—valets, maids,
concierges, butlers, major-domos, waiters, hotel staffs; the rest
of the proletariat is in the background, faintly rumbling like an
unexplored ocean and the subject of occasional nervous specula-
tion by the author. From time to time a specimen—a farmer, a
peasant girl, a milkmaid, a taxi-driver or cabby—is thrown up on
the beach, and is examined with the curiosity due to some strange
fish. And finally, there are the Jews—at once a class within a
class and a new category, overflowing the old boundaries.

No small part of the education of Marcel is concerned with the
dispersal of illusions and the formation of new ideas about the
aristocracy. In the bourgeois home of his early childhood the
aristocrats were, in the words of his great-aunt to Swann, "people
whom neither you nor I will ever know, and we can get along
without them, can't we?" Evidence that Swann was a friend of
the Marquise de Villeparisis had no effect on the aunt's opinion
of Swann, but instilled doubts as to the authenticity of the
Marquise's nobility. So for the child, too, inaccessibility was of
the very essence of aristocracy. The nobles were Names, and
with his readings of history and legend and his long hours of
reverie, the Names became vast complexes of centuries, great
events, castles, and feudal rights. Among the Names none was
richer than "Guermantes." In the family walks around Combray
they never pushed as far as the Château of the family:

> I knew that there lived the masters of the castle, the Duke and
> Duchess of Guermantes, I knew that they were real and truly living
> characters, but every time I thought of them, I pictured them some-
> times as in a tapestry, like the Countess of Guermantes in the "Cor-
> onation of Esther" in our church; sometimes in changing nuances like
> Gilbert the Bad in the stained-glass window, where he passed from
> cabbage green to plum blue, according as I stood in front of the font,
> or by our chairs; sometimes as wholly impalpable like the image of
> Geneviève of Brabant, ancestress of the Guermantes family, whom

the magic lantern paraded across the curtains of my bedroom or up to the ceiling:—in a word, always as if wrapped in the mystery of Merovingian times and bathed in the orange sunset light emanating from the word "antes." (I, 246-47)

One day in church he catches sight of a lady with a large nose, piercing blue eyes, and a small pimple, who in some respects bears a slight resemblance to the portrait of the Duchesse de Guermantes. The lady is seated in the chapel of Gilbert the Bad, over the Guermantes tombs; furthermore, the Duchess is expected in church that day, and it is on that very account that Marcel is present. Driven to the inevitable conclusion, he thinks to himself, "Is that all she is?" Gradually, as he gets used to the idea, he reclothes her with the glories of his imagination, and when the piercing blue eyes rest on him for a moment of apparent attention, he falls in love with her. Later, he sees her in a box at the opera, resplendent and unattainable, looking like the descendant of a goddess and a bird, and his infatuation is completed. To be received in her salon is his greatest ambition, and his adoration, uncomfortably apparent to the Duchess, is the greatest obstacle to its attainment. When he has sufficiently recovered from the adoration and when his desire to be received has lost its acuity, the ambition is realized. And so, through the Duchess and her circle, begins his education in the realities of the nobility.

One by one the old illusions drop away. Ancient castles, heirloom tapestries and portraits, sometimes even names and titles, turn out to be comparatively recent acquisitions of the family. Conversation between members of the noble families, which he has supposed to be at once Olympian and Parnassian, turns out to be merely flat. At the opera, when he saw the demi-gods pass a box of candy, he was quite sure that, even if the accompanying words were merely, "Will you have some candy?"—"Thank you, I'll have a cherry," the words and the gestures were mysterious rites, preludes to their real life. In the salons he was at first always awaiting the opening of the brilliant and high-bred conversation that never began.

As Marcel's imagination is overcome by experience, we are left in some confusion about the nobility, a confusion that reflects the contradictions of his own experience. If Aimé, the headwaiter of the Balbec hotel, "belongs to a race more ancient than that of the Prince [de Guermantes], and therefore more noble," the titles of the Duke and Duchess and of the Duke's brother Charlus are of unimpeachable antiquity—but their castles and heirlooms are not. If the conversation of the aristocratic salons is worse than mediocre, the Duchess is, on occasion, authentically witty—even though, too aware of her reputation for cleverness, she often works too hard at it, and fails. If as a class the nobles are incredibly vain and snobbish, they also bear as a class mark a gracious humility of deportment and a democratic way with commoners.

The most consistent and enduring characteristics of Proust's aristocrats of the old régime is a deeply ingrained inheritance of fine manners. The manners do not cut very deep: the Duc de Guermantes instinctively and unquestioningly rises to his feet to receive the farewells of a departing guest, of whatever social status, but does not hesitate to interrupt him brutally in the midst of a sentence. Their manners are a physical atavism, against which the personal tastes of the individual may rebel in vain. Of this Saint-Loup is an example:

> . . . my thought distinguished in Saint-Loup a being more general than himself, the "noble," which like an inner spirit moved his limbs, commanded his gestures and actions. At finding always in him this earlier, age-old aristocrat that Robert [de Saint-Loup] aspired precisely not to be, I experienced a keen joy, but of the intelligence, not of friendship. In the moral and physical agility that gave such grace to his good nature, in the social ease with which he offered his carriage to my grandmother and helped her in, in his nimbleness in leaping from his seat, when he was afraid I might be cold, to throw his own cloak over my shoulders, I felt not merely the hereditary suppleness

of the great hunters that for generations the ancestors of this young man (who aimed only at intellectuality) had been . . . but I felt especially in him the assurance, or the illusion, of these great noblemen of being "better than the others," thanks to which they had not been able to bequeath to Saint-Loup that desire of proving that one is "as good as the others. . . ." (IV, 188-89)

From the closing words of this passage we see that the easy, democratic way of the true noble is but an aspect of his sublime assurance; it is not gracious humility, as it seems, but pride.

This ease of manner, and the unshakable assurance from which it springs, distinguishes the nobleman of the *Ancien Régime* (the only "true" nobleman) from the Napoleonic aristocracy. A member of the old nobility takes the hand of a bourgeois, pats his shoulder, adjusts his coat, calls him *"mon cher,"* in his presence tips back in his chair and crosses his legs with a foot in one hand—because he is assured that his familiarity is flattering and that there is no possible doubt of his inherent racial superiority; a Baron of the Empire, less sure of himself and closer to the administrative or military achievements that are the source of his rank, stands on the authority of his title and assumes a majestic reserve not unlike that of a public official.

The sense of caste that separates the aristocrat from the bourgeois is operative also within the nobility. The gradations are numerous: at the top are the Duc and Duchesse de Guermantes and their brother Charlus; they consort with members of princely houses like their own, and confer sparingly the honor of their acquaintance. Their cousin the Prince de Guermantes and his wife, a German princess, have let down the bars a little too much in their receptions and have not quite the prestige of the Duke and Duchess. And so the hierarchy continues: a member of one circle scorns the one below and will stop at nothing to be admitted into the one above. The folly of playing the social game seriously is exposed when it becomes apparent how simply, given the right conditions, transition from one stratum to another is accomplished: the whole system—if system it can be called—is reduced to the absurd when the war hastens the normal social evolution, and the lady received by the Guermantes for the first time in 1914 stares through her lorgnon at the parvenue of 1916, with the remark, "It's all very sickening, what are we coming to?"

Before we have finished with the aristocrats, there is absolutely nothing left to justify their pretensions but a manner, and that manner, in the last analysis, is only a heritage of conceit.

For Marcel, himself a bourgeois, the bourgeoisie lacks the mystery and hence the charm of the aristocracy above and of the people below, but the distinctions within this class are no less varied than among the nobility. Money of course plays an important rôle, as does occupation, whether banking, magistracy, business, or government service. In the absence of titles, the bourgeois attach social prestige to a variety of trifles—an habitual pose, a detail of costume, a fancied resemblance to a well-known nobleman, the exact spelling of a name (Simonet with one "n," for example, has much better standing than the same name with two). As a class, however, and in spite of its large representation among the characters and deductions one can make therefrom for oneself, the bourgeoisie calls forth scant comment from Proust.

The servant class, on the other hand, excites in the author a constant curiosity, sometimes speculative, sometimes amused, sometimes—particularly in the added passages—irritated, but always somewhat superior. His attitude is that of the master of servants; they exist to serve him and his kind. In the performance of their duties they sometimes interest him by their unconscious imitation of scenes or poses in masterpieces of painting, by their speech, by their preservation of ancient modes of behavior and character; they sometimes disquiet him by their clairvoyance with regard to their masters and their ability to reflect in their behavior the master's shortcomings; they sometimes annoy him by their pretensions to an existence of their own, instead of performing their duties in constant, uniform, and uncomplaining devotion; and they divert him by their aping of the manners and the social distinctions of the upper classes. An amusing parody scene in the beginning of *Le Côté de Guermantes* shows the servants of Marcel's family awaiting the moment when the Duchess is to get into her carriage:

> It was usually shortly after our servants had finished celebrating that sort of solemn passover which no one must interrupt, called their luncheon, and during which they were so "taboo" that my father himself would not have taken the liberty to ring for them, knowing furthermore that no more notice would have been taken of the fifth ring than of the first, and that therefore his impropriety would have been a complete loss. . . .
>
> The last rites accomplished, Françoise, who was, as in the primitive church, at once the celebrant and one of the faithful, poured herself a last glass of wine, wiped from her lips a trace of reddened water or of coffee, folded her napkin, put it in its ring, thanked with a mournful glance "her" young footman, who, in his zealous attention, was saying, "Come, Madame, a few more grapes; they are *esquisite*,"— and went forthwith to the window, under the pretext that it was too hot "in this wretched kitchen." (VI, 16)

After a furtive and ostensibly indifferent glance has assured her that the Duchess has not yet come out, her attention is caught by some pigeons, which remind her of Combray:

> "Ah! Combray, Combray," she cried. (And the almost singing tone with which she delivered this invocation, as well as the Arlesian purity of her face, might have made one suspect that she came from the south, and that the homeland whose loss she deplored was a homeland by adoption only. . . .) "Ah! Combray, when shall I see you again, poor land! When shall I be able to pass the whole blessed day under your hawthorns and our dear lilacs, listening to the warblers and the Vivonne which makes a murmur like someone whispering, instead of hearing that wretched bell of our young master who never goes a half-hour without making me run the length of that devilish hall. And still he thinks I don't go quick enough, I'm supposed to hear before he rings, and if a body is a minute late, he flies into a terrible rage. Alas! poor Combray! perhaps I shall only see you again when I'm dead, when they throw me like a stone into the hole of the grave. Then I'll no longer be able to smell your beautiful white

hawthorn blossoms. But in the sleep of death, I think I shall still hear those three peals of the bell that have already been damnation to me in my lifetime." (VI, 17)

In general, the people, exclusive of the servant class, are for Proust merely another class like the aristocracy and the bourgeoisie, and have in several respects more kinship with the former than with the latter. Like the aristocracy they have preserved old modes of thought and speech, and are more indigenous, more of the old soil of France, than the bourgeoisie. Isolated specimens which he considers are either a focus for the projection of Marcel's poetic sensibilities, like the apparition of the milkmaid in the early dawn at a station on the way to the shore, or the fisher girl at Balbec, or the wholly imaginary peasant girl desired by Marcel to complete his impression of the woods of Roussainville; or they are picturesque objects of curiosity, like the chauffeur at Balbec, the barber at Doncières, the "marquise" of the public comfort stations, the vendor of sweets on the Champs Elysées. Like the bourgeois and the aristocrats, Proust conjectures, the people are snobs in their own way and have their own hierarchy of social prestige (electricians, he specifies in an addition, form a kind of knighthood in the proletariat).

To this attitude toward the people—now poetically imaginative, now curious in a superior sort of way—there are a few striking exceptions. In an added passage (which reflects his growing social consciousness and recalls scenes of the Revolution, with mobs muttering outside the palaces), Proust pictures a mass of the underprivileged—fishermen, with a sprinkling of the white-collar poor—crowding in the darkness outside the brilliantly lighted dining room of the Balbec hotel, watching, with sullen curiosity, the elaborate feeding of the strange fish behind their wall of glass. Now these strange fish in their brightly lighted aquarium are the world of Marcel, the world of those with money in their pockets and time on their hands. Normally it is among these people that he is at home; the unfamiliar species, a specimen of which he curiously examines from time to time, is outside. But in this passage the situation is reversed: in a sudden intuition he sees his world as the curiosity and the exception, and the crowd outside, by weight of numbers, as the norm. "It is a great social question whether the wall of glass will always protect the banquet of the marvelous creatures, or whether the obscure people greedily watching in the night will not come and pluck them out of their aquarium and devour them."

Similarly in the late chapter of *Le Temps retrouvé* in which he describes French society during the war, he savagely satirizes the futilities with which the wealthy and the socially elect concern themselves, and the spectacle of luxury which they offer to the soldier on leave:

At the dinner hour the restaurants were full, and if, passing in the street, I saw a poor soldier on leave, freed for six days from the continual risk of death and ready to return to the trenches, resting his eyes for a moment on these illuminated windows, I suffered as I did at the Balbec hotel when the fishermen watched us dine; but I suffered more because the misery of the soldier is greater than that of the poor, which it includes, and is still more touching because it is more resigned, more noble, and because it is with a philosophic and unresentful nod of the head that, ready to return to the war and confronted with the spectacle of slackers crowding to reserve their tables, he says, "Here, you wouldn't think there was a war." (XV, 60-61)

The Jewish race is depicted chiefly through Swann and through Bloch and his family. In Swann, the assimilated and socially accepted Jew, the better sides of his race appear: its vitality, its suppleness, its artistic sensitivity. At the height of his career, confronted by his social success and his healthy, prosperous appearance, one forgot his origin; his beaked nose was not, after all, so very different from that of a Guermantes. At the end, however, what with the progress of disease and the sufferings incident to the anti-Semitism stirred up by the Dreyfus Affair, he seems to be reclaimed by the physical type of the race he has all but denied, and his jutting nose and emaciated face make one think of an ancient Hebrew prophet.

Bloch and his relatives are tribal, unassimilated Jews. Although in them the author has concentrated every unpleasant characteristic that passes for "Jewish" with the most confirmed anti-Semite, they are such extreme caricatures that they are more amusing than odious, and they have, in accordance with the author's usual practice of combining good with bad, some redeeming traits. Albert Bloch's dominating characteristics are his monumental tactlessness and his unfailing bad taste. Arriving drenched at Marcel's home, he is asked, in some surprise, by Marcel's father whether it has been raining. "Sir," replies Bloch, whose erudition is, like himself, unassimilated, "I am absolutely incapable of telling you whether it has rained. I live so outside of physical contingencies that my senses do not take the trouble to notify me of them." When the grandmother says she is not feeling very well, he puts on a pantomime of stifling a sob and wiping away a tear. Arriving one day for dinner an hour and a half late and covered with mud, he disclaims any acquaintance with the use of such pernicious and stupidly bourgeois instruments as the watch and the umbrella. These incidents, while irritating, are not enough to exclude him from the house; but when he insinuates to Marcel that the virtuous great-aunt had a stormy youth, and was long and publicly a kept woman, the limit is reached, and Bloch comes no more.

At one moment he protests friendship with tearful eyes and quivering voice; at another, he circulates malicious gossip about his friend. Falsely and boastfully he names women who have granted him their favors. The crudest sort of a snob himself, he accuses Marcel of snobbery, and will take no denial. Introduced to an elderly lady whose name he does not catch, but whom he estimates as unimportant, he is curt and rude; learning that she bears the golden name of Rothschild, he exclaims, in her hearing, "If I had only known!" Apparently blind to the implications of his appearance and behavior, Bloch refers broad-mindedly on occasion to the slight traces left in him of his Jewish ancestry, and at Balbec, when Jews are crowding to the fashionable beach, reveals himself startlingly as anti-Semitic.

But this same Bloch has an encounter with a gentile in which he comes off the better of the two. He lends Morel, whose talent he admires, and who is in dire need of money, five thousand francs. At first Morel praises Bloch loudly, and arranges to repay him in monthly installments of a thousand francs, obtained from Charlus. The first month's repayment is made; at the second, finding other more attractive uses to which the money can be put, he begins to detest his creditor and to speak ill of him. Meanwhile Bloch has forgotten the exact sum loaned and speaks of the remainder of the debt to Morel as three thousand five hundred instead of four thousand; whereat Morel, indignant at such falsification, declares that he will not pay another centime, and that Bloch can consider himself lucky not to be dragged into court. Thenceforth, and with this incident as a source, Morel is fiercely anti-Semitic.

In the novel, as in history, the Dreyfus Affair makes strange companions-in-arms. The Bloch tribe rejoices fiercely over the anti-Semitism of a partisan of Dreyfus; the Duchesse de Guermantes, Swann's best friend in the aristocracy, avoids him during the Affair, and uses the famous case as an occasion for the display of her wit. Most of the nobility are anti-Dreyfus from a sense of caste, but there are exceptions. Saint-Loup's case is not surprising, considering the other respects in which he rebels against his clan; but we are genuinely astonished to find that the Prince and Princesse de Guermantes, unknown to each other, have been slipping away to the same priest to ask him to say masses for Dreyfus.

The position of Marcel is curious. Unlike the author, he has, so far as we know, no Jewish strain in him, and in *Le Côté de Guermantes,* among the aristocrats who are generally hostile to Dreyfus, he takes his tone from the society he is in. But deeply imbedded in this part, casual and easily overlooked, is the statement that he was a partisan of Dreyfus, and that when his father found it out, he would not speak to him for a week. As for the author himself, savage as is his caricature of the race in the persons of the Bloch tribe, he makes, à propos of disagreeable persons in a restaurant, a statement that may be taken to sum up his attitude:

They were unpleasant—the Jews principally, the non-assimilated Jews of course, there could be no question of the others—to people who cannot stand an appearance that is strange, bizarre (like that of Bloch for Albertine). Generally one recognized later that, if they had against them hair that was too long, nose and eyes too big, theatrical and jerky gestures, it was childish to judge them on such grounds; they had qualities of mind and heart, they wore well, and were people for whom one could have a deep affection. In the case of the Jews particularly there were few whose relatives did not have a generosity of heart, a breadth of mind, a sincerity, beside which the mother of Saint-Loup and the Duc de Guermantes cut a sorry figure with their barrenness, their superficial religiosity that objected only to open scandals, with their defense of a Christianity which led infallibly (by devious ways one would not expect from people claiming to value intelligence alone) to a colossally wealthy marriage. (VII, 91)

While Proust was writing his novel, and as the great tableau of French society grew and its details were filled in, he thought increasingly and hopefully of a possible comparison between his work and the *Memoirs* of Saint-Simon, which he had long admired. But the basis of such a comparison is lacking. Saint-Simon, for all his bias and inaccuracy, told anecdotes of real historical characters and painted a valuable picture of court life under Louis XIV; Proust, by the multiplicity of his models, created great fictional types, but renounced the right to be considered a memorialist. More justly he might have aspired to be compared to such skeptical philosophers and moralists as Montaigne, La Rochefoucauld, La Bruyère, and Vaugelas, whose penetrating, if pessimistic, understanding of human nature he rivals. Indeed, for many readers, this aspect of Proust's work is his clearest title to fame. Deeply as the shifting panorama of society and social change interested him, it was man as such that interested him more. His aristocrats, his bourgeois, his lackeys, his Jews, his artists, his courtesans, were representatives of classes and occupations, but even more they were men and women; for them, and for the multiple models that contributed to their creation, he felt pity and gratitude:

> ... I felt an infinite pity even for beings less dear [than his grandmother and Albertine], for those even to whom I was indifferent, for all the human destinies whose sufferings and absurdities I had tried to understand and put to use. All these beings, who had revealed truths to me and who were no more, seemed to me to have lived a life that had profited me alone; it was as if they had died for me. (XVI, 58)

In the face of such a conception of his work, the idea of a "proletarian" novel, or of any novel based on a social theory, seemed grotesque: "True art has nothing to do with all such proclamations; it is achieved in silence."

And to silence, indeed, we are at the end returned. The tumult and the activity, for all their illusion of reality, are but the figments of a dream; for "man," says this great subjectivist, "is the being who cannot get outside of himself, who knows others only in himself, and when he says the contrary, he lies."

INTELLECTUAL THEMES

To distinguish between the intellectual and emotional sides of Proust's nature, and their extension in his manners of writing, is at best a convenient starting point; and to insist, too much and too long, on the difference between them would be artificial. Nevertheless, when we come to his themes, we find that they are indisputably and intentionally of two distinct types, arrived at by wholly different processes. For Proust, truth is dual, material and transcendental. On the plane of normal human experience one can arrive, with the aid of observation and reason, at certain conclusions which are valid for that plane. On the level of mystic experience, which arises in emotion, and whose instrument is direct apprehension or intuition, a whole new field of truth is opened up, which supersedes, and to some extent contradicts, the conclusions of reason. And so, for want of better terms, we shall continue to use the distinctions originally applied to his temperament, and speak of intellectual themes and emotional, or intuitional, themes.

One of the basic subjects of the novel is the education of Marcel. He wants, insistently, to know what goes on, what it means, and what his function in life is. From this point of view the whole story is a demonstration that things are not what they seem. The lessons of his experience are contained in the intellectual themes, which are pessimistic, and teach a total determinism and the inexorable movement of time, with its fruits of instability, change, decay, and death. But here and there in this experience he has brief ecstatic moments which suggest that beneath the disappointing surface of appearances there is a deeper reality. These moments long remain incomprehensible to him, but at the end of the book he is overwhelmed by a renewal and concentration of them, and arrives at last at an understanding of that other reality at which they have previously hinted. The story of these moments is contained in the intuitional themes; they point to freedom and eternity. In *Le Temps retrouvé* an attempt is made to demonstrate the way of escape from the despair of one group of themes to the hope of the other.

A logical beginning for a consideration of the intellectual themes is Proust's conception of "reality." But first the word itself needs some clarification, for Proust, like most of us, uses it in various senses, and some of his apparently contradictory statements prove, when the word is defined in its context, to be perfectly compatible with each other. We can usefully distinguish three types of "reality." There is first the reality of the materialist and of the man in the street, the solidly existing world of things and organisms which we perceive inwardly by the reports of our senses, but which is really "out there." This we may distinguish as "material reality." A second type is intellectual, and amounts merely to what we mean by "the truth"; it is a body of facts concerning the outside world and ourselves, formulated by our minds, but thought of as having an existence independent of them. Finally there is the reality of the mystic and the Platonist, a hypothetical order, invisible and intangible, lying beyond (or above, or within) material reality, and more important, more "real" than it. This we shall call "transcendent reality."

A careful comparison of the various things Proust has to say about material reality points conclusively to what we may call his normal intellectual position, namely that material reality exists: "In spite of what may be referable to the various subjective points of view . . . the fact remains that there is a certain objective reality in all these beings. . . ." There are, apparently, qualities and relations inherent in external objects, as well as in the internal image: "every impression is double, one part being ensheathed in the object, the other being the prolongation of the first within ourselves." But external material reality is in itself unknowable; our acquaintance with it is at second hand, through the internal image, which, being subjective, varies with the observer and is liable to error.

We must emphasize that this point of view, which is only that of common sense, is Proust's *normal intellectual position*. Common sense sometimes wavers, but only in flashes. In one of these flashes, reality, both interior and exterior, vanishes; in another, he is on the verge of pure idealism: "Two or three times, for an instant, I had the idea that the world where this room and these bookcases were and in which Albertine occupied so unimportant a place, was perhaps an intellectual world, which was the only reality, and . . . that a small exercise of my will would suffice to attain this real world." Proust has two contradictory philosophies, one intellectual and one intuitional, and when his intellectual philosophy wavers, as in this instance, he is near, perhaps as near as he can get by intelligence alone, to the intuitional.

According to Proust's intellectual philosophy (which is our immediate concern), man has a strong desire to know external reality in itself, to learn the truth about what goes on "out there." Swann, watching Odette at a moment when she seems simple, loyal, and wholly his, wonders which is the "true" Odette, the one he now sees or the sly, deceitful one pictured by his jealous imagination, who has many other lovers and leads a life in which he has no part. But neither Swann nor any other man can ever be really sure, because our knowledge of external reality is limited to subjective internal images of it and to the no less subjective interpretations we put upon them. The conclusions we come to upon such grounds are continually contradicting one another; so Marcel, in the process, like Swann before him, of making discoveries about the woman he loves, declares: "My increase of knowledge about life . . . brought me for the time being to agnosticism. What can one affirm, when what one believed to be probable in the first place, was shown to be false in the second place, and in the third place was proved to be true?"

One cause of the confusions of both Swann and Marcel is their assumption that there is one true Odette, one true Albertine. As Marcel comes to realize through introspection, personalities are not single but multiple, not enduring but successive, not consistent but intermittent. At any given moment what we think of as a single personality is a group of them, each with a consistent inner organization and characteristic reactions, a group of which one is temporarily in the ascendant. They come successively into the dominant position through the impact of the environment without, and physiological and psychological rhythms within. For a limited time one of these personalities may tend to be in control more often than the others, thus giving a certain appearance of consistency to behavior; but all of them are subject to decay and death. Worn-out personalities are continually being shed, to be replaced by new ones. When one human being loves another, his love may implicate only one of his personalities, or two, or several. This variability in the number permeated by a love explains why what we think of as the same person can be loyal and devoted today, and deceitful and cold tomorrow: the personality of one day is not that of the next. When a loved one dies, we sometimes feel, according to Proust, little immediate sense of loss, because the personality that loved is for the time being submerged; at its reëmergence, perhaps, as in the case of Marcel and his grandmother, as much as a year later, profound grief is felt. But since all personalities die, the most dearly loved persons are eventually forgotten. "It is not they who died," says Proust, "but we."

The fact that our author of many personalities can observe their procession within himself would seem to postulate a permanent superpersonality to act as observer, a logical necessity parenthetically accepted by Proust at more than one point, as for example when he refers to "our permanent self which is prolonged throughout the duration of our life." Memory, however, the most obvious principle of unity, is granted in this connection only a dubious validity: "The memory of the most successive being establishes for him a sort of identity and makes him unwilling to repudiate promises which he recalls even if he did not countersign them." A more important contributor to the idea of unity of personality is the will: "The will . . . is the persevering and unchanging servant of our successive personalities; hidden in the shadow, disdained, tirelessly faithful, ceaselessly and without regard for the changes of the self, it works to supply that self with what it needs." More specifically it is the will to live which performs the unifying function.

These are but slight footholds in a flood of uncertainty and change; the permanent observer, or the memory, or the will, may carry over from one personality to the next, but they are quite incapable of modifying the succession, and they are of little assistance in the search for the truth about others. If multiplicity and intermittence were the only bars to knowledge, memory, aided by reason, might help, but there are other, and insuperable, obstacles. Not only is our interpretation of observations largely falsified by inapposite prejudices, but what people say (and this is one of the chief bases of our judgment) is the resultant of many more or less conflicting desires, the least of which is the desire to conform to objective fact. All men lie, and how should we blame them, if objective fact is unattainable in any case? People simply cannot know each other. As Marcel says, of himself and Albertine:

> So we were presenting to each other an appearance that was very different from reality [i.e., the truth]. And doubtless it is always so when two people confront each other, because each of them is ignorant of a part of what is in the other (and even what he knows he can only partly understand) and because each of them shows his least individual side, either because he doesn't understand himself and considers it negligible, or because insignificant and accidental advantages seem to him more important and more flattering. (XII, 195)

Since there is always a discrepancy between material reality and the internal image, between the "truth" and our conception of it at any given moment, it follows that disappointment and disillusionment are the common human lot. Particularly is this true of a pleasurable anticipation of experience, for desire both stimulates and falsifies the imagination; so that there is scarcely an exception to the rule that Marcel is disappointed in any experience or event from which he expects much satisfaction. A fleeting pleasure can sometimes be obtained from experience that is unexpected, or that has been pessimistically anticipated.

A succession of disappointments ought to teach one to discount them in advance, and to put less intensity into a desire that is sure to be frustrated; in Marcel we occasionally find attempts at this sort of worldly wisdom. But in Proust's idea a fundamental trait of human nature is to desire what one cannot have, so that the expectation of disappointment only serves to accentuate the desire. An obstacle serves as a dam, and builds up desire. Conversely, removal of the obstacle relieves the pressure; any object which is certainly and easily attainable seems undesirable. The final result is that desire bears no real relation to the quality of its object; it is a blind force, rising and falling in direct proportion to the degree of obstruction it meets. Happiness, conceived of as the satisfaction of desire, is therefore totally impossible, for a desire can be satisfied only at the cost of its own existence.

The supreme example of this blind and always frustrated outward push of the imprisoned soul is love, or that variety of it called romantic love—a shifting complex of poetic idealization, spiritual aspiration, and sexual desire. From the foregoing account of Proust's ideas it follows logically that such love is necessarily an illusion. It is an "aberration," "a feeling which, whatever its cause, is always erroneous," "created by falsehood"; it is an "evil spell" and an *"idée fixe";* it is "a disease of the heart," "the sacred sickness," and "a reciprocal torture." What one loves is an image, a projection of his desires, which bears little relation to the real person that is the ostensible object of his love. In man's heart love is always latent, organized according to the laws of his nature, awaiting its cue to come out and attach itself to some person. An inexperienced adolescent has a love story, which he has made up and learned by heart, and which, with boundless exuberance, he is ready to act out with any person of the opposite sex who gives him an opening. An older person, with a background of several love affairs, is on the lookout for familiar landmarks, and in any new affair tries to repeat the pattern of the old. And since the object always differs from the image and still more from the imaginary creature that symbolizes the lover's desire, disappointment in love is inevitable.

The choice of an object is not, however, a matter of chance; for every lover has his "type" [*genre*], and in the series of women he loves there is always, if not a physical resemblance, at least a community of "essence." Furthermore, "desire always goes out to what is the most opposite to ourselves, and forces us to love what will make us suffer." That man should attempt to complete

his nature by absorbing its opposite is a "law," one of the impersonal rules of the game that govern our behavior. But perhaps
too the selection, as an object of love, of the person best calculated
to cause us suffering is related to a subconscious recognition that
love *is* suffering, that the condition of its existence is its painful
non-fulfillment, and consequently that the person capable of
causing the most suffering will be the person most loved.

And yet "the most exclusive love for a person is always the
love of something else." Looking at the stars Marcel obeys the
ancient custom of lovers and wonders whether Madame de Guermantes is now looking at them too; but he continues: "It was
not in the firmament alone that I put the thought of Madame de
Guermantes. The breath of a gentle breeze would seem to bring
me a message from her, as in former times from Gilberte, across
the wheat fields of Méséglise; we do not change, we simply
insert in the feeling which we relate to a woman dormant elements which she awakens but which are foreign to her." When
he loved the group of adolescent girls at Balbec, they were to him
"a procession in silhouette against the sea. It was the sea that I
wanted to find, if I went to some town where they would be."
And again he says, "the mistresses whom I have loved the most
have never coincided with my love for them. This love was true,
because I subordinated everything to seeing them, to keeping
them for myself alone. . . . But it was rather that they had the
faculty of awakening and bringing to a climax this love, than
that they were its image. . . . Under the appearance of the
woman, it is to the invisible forces by which she is accessorily
accompanied that we address ourselves as to obscure divinities."

To arouse love—that is, to attach the inner dream to an external person—a hint of mystery is often enough, a suggestion that
the person has an existence into which we have not penetrated.
A real or imaginary obstacle—prestige, apparent superiority, a
reputation for inaccessibility, a disdainful manner—is an invitation. A moment of agitation, even irrelevant, prepares the
ground. Other contributing factors are the satisfied vanity of

believing oneself to be loved and the hope of receiving a declaration. If possible the incipient lover will rationalize the passion to which he wishes to yield into a virtue, making it a proof of generosity or altruism, or an indication of esthetic sensitivity.

For Proust, as for La Rochefoucauld, love is always unequally distributed between the lovers: there is one that loves and one that allows himself to be loved. At the outset, too great and too obvious a love effectively repels the beloved; later on, an increase in the love of one involves a proportionate decrease in that of the other. The only happiness possible is negative, a brief respite from suffering. The conduct of a lover is apt to follow a dual rhythm: declarations of tenderness and sympathy are automatically followed by an effort to conquer esteem by a display of domination and hardness. A young and timid lover often simulates coldness to the beloved and ardently woos one to whom he is indifferent.

Love may precede sexual desire; in its later stages it is accompanied, paralleled as it were, by physical possession, but without being greatly affected by it. What the lover aspires to is complete and permanent possession of the beloved; physical possession, while it may hold out some brief promise, is soon shown to be totally inadequate to the attainment of the ideal. Sexual relations may continue on an independent footing, as a sort of game in which the lovers act as each other's accomplices in the pursuit of individual sensations. Then love too goes its independent way, and its future is contingent upon the existence of further promise, mystery, or obstacles. Physical possession may, however, involve a real threat to love, and perhaps a farewell to it. So it seemed for a moment to Swann: "Perhaps moreover Swann was fixing upon the face of an Odette not yet possessed nor even kissed by him, an Odette whom he was seeing for the last time, the look with which, on a day of departure, one tries to carry away with him the whole of a landscape which is about to be left forever."

Left to itself, love soon dies a natural death. It is a rare person indeed who, having become accessible and known, yet retains sufficient mystery and promise to be an object of love. Hence the immense value of jealousy, which can prolong a love long after the initial impetus has died away, and revive one that is about to expire by the faintest suggestion of the existence of a rival. Fortunately for love, its multiple-personalitied objects are fertile in infidelities; any chance deficiencies are abundantly made up by the resourcefulness of the lovers, for whom a caress inevitably evokes another recipient, and a passing remark conjures up the shadowy horror of a double life. Jealousy may direct itself indifferently to the past, the present, or the future, or to all three. As in the case of the other sufferings of love, jealousy seems to correspond to some obscure need of the lover; it is as though some part of him welcomed and cultivated it, so that his love might survive.

In Proust's idea of love, habit plays a dual rôle. When it settles down upon lovers, as it must in any but the most passing affair, its effect is anesthetic—beneficent in so far as it brings the qualified happiness that results from the cessation of pain, but fatal to the continuance of love. The rupture of habit involved in the end of an affair, however, reverses its rôle; it then becomes, with its inseparable companion memory, the source of exquisite torture. Relief comes from oblivion, which appears in Proust as a positive force, invading progressively larger and larger areas of thinking, killing off one by one the personalities that loved and still suffer; until at last the ex-lover, drastically relieved and equipped with a new set of intact personalities, has a brief respite before succumbing to the next attack of love. In its healing surgery oblivion finds its greatest ally, as might be expected, in separation, an obvious remedy that anyone could apply if he would; the trouble is that lovers want to suffer.

Just as there is no villain without a redeeming trait, so the great disease of love is not an unmixed evil. Saint-Loup's detestable mistress, so justly deplored by his family, nevertheless "opened his mind to the invisible, put seriousness into his life, and delicacy into his heart." Even wholly sensual or perverted love is "unjustly decried," because it "forces a person to exhibit the least particles he may have of kindness, of self-renunciation, to such an extent that they shine out before the eyes of those around."

And why, one may well ask, if love is "unjustly decried," does Proust devote hundreds of pages to a minute destructive analysis of it? The answer is clear: the great target of his attack is *illusion* in love; if nine out of ten pages he devotes to the subject are pessimistic, it is because, in his opinion, an equivalent proportion of the human experience of love is based on illusion. Kindness, self-renunciation, delicacy, "the opening of the mind to the invisible" are also, as we have just seen, parts—if minor ones—of the experience. Proust recognizes too that there is such a thing as tranquil and trusting affection: Swann glimpses it in the midst of his unhappy passion, and achieves a slight measure of it after his marriage; even Marcel, in the prolonged neurotic self-torture of *La Prisonnière* and *Albertine disparue,* makes a passing acquaintance with the loving comradeship that results from a background of common experience and the daily sharing of a simple routine. Furthermore, the sufferings of love acquire significance from their very universality. "Something in us," notes Proust at one point, "tries to lead these individual feelings to a larger truth, that is, to attach them to a more general feeling, common to all humanity, with which individuals and the sufferings they cause are merely an opportunity of communication. To know that my suffering was a small part of the universal love added some pleasure to it."

What Proust is attempting is the dissociation of romantic love. The most disquieting feature of Marcel's love affairs is their bland mixture of sensuality and poetic idealism. Take the first vision of Gilberte against a bank of flowers, with her name being called by her mother in the background:

So there passed near me that name of Gilberte . . . uttered over the stocks and jasmines, pungent and cool as drops from the green watering can; impregnating and irradiating the zone of pure air through which it had passed—and which it isolated—with the mystery of the life of her whom the name designated to the happy beings who lived in her company. . . . (I, 205)

This blessed damozel has just made an indecent gesture which, if Marcel had understood it, would not have shocked him at all, because it corresponded precisely with his own desires. Similarly, later on, the view of Albertine asleep inspires Marcel simultaneously with profoundly poetic thoughts and a desire (which he gratifies) for indulging in a sort of nerveless auto-eroticism. It is all very well to dismiss such descriptions at the result of deplorable bad taste on the part of the author, or at best as revelations of the abnormal character of Marcel; the fact remains that many a reader suspects that "romantic love" *is* compounded of poetry and eroticism, only he prefers not to have the author say so. Or if he insists on bringing the matter up, let him register shame at the confession of his baseness. What shocks is not specific erotic detail, of which one can stand a great deal, but the suave manner, the apparent absence of any sense of incongruity. But does not this very matter-of-fact association of the poetic and the erotic produce a dissociative effect? Is it not intended to expose the illusion at the heart of romantic love?

For Proust, there is in such love an invitation to the self to an experience beyond its ordinary limitations; but in responding to it, man first, and most naturally, looks for satisfaction in the concrete and personal experiences with which he is familiar. Disappointment and confusion are the result, and beyond this stage of the illusions of love most men do not go; only a few, at the price of great pain, can arrive at some faint glimpse of a love dissociated from self-centered desire.

Less intense, less productive of suffering than love, but paralleling it in its disappointments and illusions, is friendship. Where love draws opposites to each other, friendship brings together the like-minded, who find each other easily and in large numbers. If one expects much from friendship, he is doomed to certain disappointment; for people make friends either from indolent amiability, in which case the relationship will not withstand a trivial test, or from reasons of gross opportunism or less obvious self-interest of some other sort, reasons which sooner or later will be unmasked. A peculiarity of friends in Proust's work is that while they are very officious in offers of unsolicited services, the moment they are asked to do something to which the asker seems to attach great importance, they become suspicious and evasive. Even Saint-Loup, the best example of a friend in the novel, behaves in this way when Marcel tries through him to be presented to the Duchesse de Guermantes.

Like love, friendship may concern a varying number of the multiple personalities in an individual; as in the case of love, the friend who is cold and distant today is not the friend who was effusive yesterday, but merely another personality in the same body. And like all human relationships, friendship is based on erroneous impressions, and is quite incapable of establishing true contact between individuals.

In his early adolescence Marcel dreams of an ideal new friendship with Gilberte; it is to break with all misunderstandings of the past and to take effect, like a treaty, on the first of the next January. He proposes the idea to her, but her enthusiasm is less than his, and partly on this account and partly because circumstances intervene, the new relationship makes no progress. At Balbec a little later he dreams of an ideal friendship with a young man, and he elects Saint-Loup, before he meets him, as the friend. In this case the friend comes more than half way, but Marcel soon discovers that Saint-Loup's society often palls, that he would rather think about friendship in solitude than practise it, and that Saint-Loup interests him more as a specimen than as a friend. And so, little by little, he outgrows his youthful idealization of a perfect human relationship.

The final result is that friendship in Proust turns out to be a snare and a temptation, a sheer waste of time. Particularly is this true for artists, who "have a duty to live for themselves; friendship is for them a dispensation from this duty, an abdication of self." "The artist who gives up an hour of work for an hour of talk with a friend knows that he is sacrificing a reality for something that does not exist." In *Le Temps retrouvé,* in answer to the complaint of friends that they never see him any more, he says that he is far more truly occupied with their interests in solitude than he ever has been in their company, exchanging the vain echo of words "for the sterile pleasure of a social contact that excludes all penetration." To withdraw from the commerce of friendship, says Proust, does not mean that one cares nothing for his fellow men; it is merely a recognition of the futility of a limited and particular human relationship, and of the superiority, for the attainment of truth, of solitude.

Another relative of love is homosexuality, a subject of very considerable importance in Proust. The title *Sodome et Gomorrhe* covers, in the current edition, three volumes and a part of a fourth, and as a subtitle two more; and the author at one time thought of using it for the whole novel. A large number of characters of both sexes turn out to be homosexuals, and the amount of exposition and commentary called forth by the theme is not much less than that given to normal love. The reason for its importance is not immediately evident from the text; Proust's theories, for which he explicitly disavows scientific pretensions, do not seem particularly original, and the subject does not appear indispensable to the plan of the whole work. But we must remember that he felt himself to be a pioneer in the field: few indeed before him had ventured to present homosexuals in fiction, and none on such a scale; and at the time that he wrote, the works of Freud and his followers were in all probability unknown to him, as they certainly were to the majority of the French and English reading public. The fact that the publication of *Sodome et Gomorrhe* so nearly coincided with the beginning of the Freudian vogue must be attributed to chance rather than to calculation.

The basis of homosexuality in Proust's treatment is psychological: following Ulrichs, he states that a homosexual has the "soul" of a woman in the body of a man, or vice versa. When a male homosexual desires a man, it is with his feminine nature, so that in the homosexual, as in the normal person, it is still the opposite sex which is sought after. Consequently Proust finds the term "homosexual" inaccurate (although he continues to use it occasionally), and prefers to it the word "invert."

Logically and theoretically a male invert hates effeminacy and inversion in others; his ideal is the strong and completely masculine male. He is thus involved in a dilemma, being driven by his abnormality to seek out precisely those who will have nothing to do with his advances; and his experiences must be a series of compromises, subterfuges, and deliberate self-delusions. But the confusion is not in experience alone; it lies in the very basis of his inversion, for soul and body react upon one another. The most extreme male invert, who detests effeminacy in others, nevertheless betrays in his voice, his gestures, sometimes even in the way his hair grows or in the cast of his features, his woman's nature; but when this woman's nature urges him toward a male, he may display an aggressive and dominant behavior dictated by his physiologically masculine sex. From the unequal distribution among homosexuals of these conflicting elements arise the immense variety and complexity of their "race"—from this, and from a benevolent disposition of Nature, which provides that every individual vagary of desire shall somewhere find its complement. There are the gregarious and aggressive and there are the timid and solitary—the "medusas" or jellyfish, who wait until, inevitably, they are sought out; there are those who are comradely with women, or even, in their way, love them, and there are those who hate them; those who are drawn to the young and those who are drawn to the mature.

The vice may be hereditary, as in the Guermantes family, where a fixed proportion of the male descendants are its victims; and cases that lack specific ancestral antecedents are also hereditary in their way, since a predisposition to the vice is the result of some combination in the moral or physical inheritance, and all homosexuality goes back to an original individual and racial hermaphroditism. A man may not discover his abnormality, whether specifically or generally inherited, until half his life is past, but when he does, much that has been strange and painful in his experience becomes clear. To speak of homosexuality as a vice, Proust insists, is only a manner of speaking, and to condemn it is unjust; for a homosexual, like a heterosexual, merely obeys the laws of his nature, for which he is not personally responsible. The behavior of Charlus and Jupien, at their meeting, is not grotesque to the watching Marcel; it is a performance of an ancient ritual, in which the actors unconsciously play rôles that seem to have been carefully rehearsed. Marcel feels also that there must be natural law at the back of it all. His efforts to discover analogies in the vegetable and animal kingdoms are not very successful, but the impression persists that back of the grave spontaneity of the evolutions which he witnesses there must lie some general plan and purpose.

The theme of Gomorrha (as Proust, following Vigny, calls female inversion), roughly parallels that of Sodom. This vice springs from the same duality of nature and has the same antecedents. In Charlus a woman's nature shines through the gross masculine body; in Mademoiselle Vinteuil a shy and delicate girl is horrified by the behavior of an imperious and cruel male companion in the same body. In both these cases sadism complicates the abnormality; with Charlus masochism is added to the sadism as a late development, with Mademoiselle Vinteuil the two exist together from the start. Female inverts, like male, have an extraordinary flair for recognizing each other.

There are, however, striking differences in Proust's treatment of the two types of inversion. Where the male invert may not discover his real nature until late, but when he does, remains true to it, the female may be early and profoundly inverted, but later, without actually changing her nature, may yet transcend and spiritualize the vice, as happens in the case of Mademoiselle Vinteuil and Léa. Furthermore, there seem to be among the women many cases of indulgence in homosexual practices without participation in the homosexual nature; Odette and Gilberte are examples. These false inverts have a depraved curiosity, and are truly vicious; for neither the normal nor the inverted can be blamed for following the law of their natures. Proust, like Krafft-Ebing, believes that vice begins for the homosexual in the pursuit of the opposite sex, for the heterosexual in that of his own.

The chief use of the Gomorrha theme is as a subject of deep and painful jealousy for Marcel; in itself it is less discussed and apparently less well understood by the author than the theme of Sodom. The introductory discussion of homosexuality in Part I of *Sodome et Gomorrhe* is presumably applicable, at least in part, to both aspects of the vice; but it is precipitated by the Jupien-Charlus conjunction and supported by male analogies and examples. A serious and eloquent plea for social tolerance and comprehension is made in this section, but in the succeeding pictures of the behavior of male inverts the tragic element is nearly always accompanied and often covered by the comic. Female inversion is provided with no separate introduction, and its protagonists are never comic—they are a subject of too much pain to the narrator.

From a general view of Proust's whole treatment of homosexuality, his purpose and the reason for the great importance he attaches to the subject become apparent. His purpose is to reveal the illusions upon which desire is based, and the importance of homosexuality is that, better than heterosexuality, it accentuates the grotesque disparity between the emotion and its ostensible object. Homosexual love, Proust insists, precisely parallels normal love in all its psychological phases; if the pitiful blindness of Saint-Loup in idealizing Rachel is striking, how much more so it is to see a tailor romantically sighing for a stout elderly man. And lest we should miss the point of his demonstration, he makes it explicit in *Le Temps retrouvé*:

Had not my encounters with M. de Charlus . . . better than my love for Mme de Guermantes or for Albertine, better than the love of

Saint-Loup for Rachel, shown me that the subject is a matter of indifference and that anything can be put into it by the mind?—a truth which the phenomenon of homosexuality, so little understood and so futilely blamed, makes even more clear than that of love, instructive though that is. . . . (XVI, 69)

The only constant elements in humanity's pursuit of illusions are a ceaseless blind desire and its invariable disappointment in the world of material reality.

The rôle of heredity in homosexuality is in Proust only an aspect of a larger theme, that of repetition. Just as the multiple personalities of an individual are, when viewed separately, intermittent, so in society forms, types, ideas, and patterns of conduct are constantly recurring. Through heredity a man is obliged to repeat the gestures of his various ancestors, imitate their vices, commit the same mistakes; if any variation from ancestral type is allowed, it is only through the operation of forces no less implacable and equally beyond the individual's control. Even outside the domain of heredity, "all things in life which have once existed tend to be re-created," and the result is perceptible through the perspective afforded by art and literature. Théodore, a young scamp of Combray, unconsciously displays, when he helps Françoise turn Aunt Léonie in bed, the naïve zeal of the cherubs surrounding the Virgin in a medieval bas-relief of Saint-André-des-Champs, "as though those carved faces of stone, naked and gray like trees in winter, were, like them, asleep only, held in reserve and waiting to flower again in countless plebeian faces, reverend and sly like the face of Théodore, and glowing with the redness of ripe apples." So the kitchen maid takes on the symbolic appearance of Giotto's "Charity"; so Odette at moments becomes the daughter of Jethro in Botticelli's "Life of Moses." The recurrence of situations, which, as we have seen, is a part of the plan of Proust's novel, is a further example of his law of repetition.

The subjects of time, of the subconscious, and of their relation to each other, are obviously of great importance in *A la*

Recherche du temps perdu. Receiving frequent brief comment, everywhere implicit, written into the fabric of Marcel's experiences and into the very style of the narration, time and the subconscious yet differ from the other intellectual themes in that they are less openly and less continuously expounded. They are as disquieting to the reader as they seem to be to Marcel; one is left with the conviction that they are very important, but profoundly inaccessible to the conscious intelligence. They contradict normal experience. Not until reason is reinforced by an emotional illumination does Marcel arrive at a more satisfactory conception of their place in his philosophy. Mysteries they then remain, but congruous, no longer paradoxical.

Meanwhile, purely intellectual observations about time and the subconscious accumulate, and although many of them are familiar or obvious, they have importance in that they furnish the raw material upon which the illumined intelligence of Marcel is later to work.

A considerable number of Proust's comments and examples tend to establish a distinction between the measurement of time, conceived of as external, and the inner experience of its passage; in other words, between chronometric and psychological time. Marcel early comes to realize that time seems to pass slowly or quickly in accordance with the nature of his other experiences. More or less painful emotions, such as anxiety, physical or moral suffering, and expectation, prolong psychological time; happiness, activities that result from habit, and deep absorption in thought (his own, or that of an author he is reading) shorten it, or even seem to eliminate entirely a block of the time that a clock measures. Sleep and dreams seem to have a time system of their own; a dream that seems long can be compressed into a moment of chronometric time. The return of waking consciousness involves some confusion as adjustment is made between two differing time scales, but some part of the mind seems nevertheless to have recorded the passage of chronometric time during the interval of sleep: "one seems then to be absent from time for several

hours; but the forces which have accumulated during that time
without being expended measure it by their quantity as exactly
as the weights of a clock or the shifting sands of an hourglass."

But Proust reconsiders his idea of separate time schemes for
sleeping and waking: "I said that there are two times; perhaps
there is only one, not that that of the waking man is valid for
the sleeper, but perhaps because the other life, the one in which
one is asleep, is not subject to the category of time." On the brink
of sleep reason and the will become paralyzed, and it is the
unprotected sensibility that makes the plunge into the visceral
depths of the subconscious, there to become subjected, with a
sensitive immediacy unknown to the waking state, to the organic
rhythms and dislocations of the body. It is an ancient and a
primitive world, this world of sleep; in it, by the glow of a half-
consciousness, are unveiled

the return to youth, the recapture of past years and forgotten feelings,
disincarnation, the transmigration of souls, the evocation of the dead,
the illusions of madness, the return to the most elemental kingdoms of
nature (for it is said that we often see animals in a dream, but one
forgets that in it we are ourselves animals, deprived of that reason
which projects on things the clear light of certainty) . . . all those
mysteries which we imagine we do not know and into which we are
initiated almost every night, as we are into the other great mystery
of annihilation and resurrection. (V, 77-78)

The subconscious is a storehouse of the whole of experience.
But to explore it in sleep is of little value, for the sleeping consciousness is deprived of the use both of will and of reason.
Without the will it is at the mercy of the body; without the continuous clarity of reason, it brings to the contemplation of the
accumulations of experience in the subconscious only "a vision
that is doubtful and at every moment obliterated by forgetfulness,
the preceding reality vanishing before the one which succeeds it,
like a magic lantern projection before the following one, when
the plate has been changed."

The waking consciousness, with will and reason at its disposition, meets other obstacles to the exploration of the subconscious. It is accustomed to ignore the quality of experience as a whole, and to abstract from it only that small part which is useful. Borne on an unending stream of time, experience pours into the subconscious, only a small trickle being diverted through the reasoning waking consciousness. The trickle is available to the voluntary memory; the rest is buried.

Probably it is the existence of our body, like a vase in which our spirituality is enclosed, which leads us to suppose that all our inner wealth, our past joys, all our sorrows, are perpetually in our possession. . . . If they remain in us, it is, most of the time, in an unknown domain where they are of no use to us.

To say that nothing is forgotten is of small help to Marcel in his intellectual search, for "what is a memory that one does not remember?" The most that such a statement can do is to lead him to speculate as to what else, besides lost records of individual experience, may lie in the subconscious:

Since I do not know a whole block of the memories which lie behind me, since they are invisible to me and I lack the power to recall them, who is to say that in this mass of memories there are not some that reach back far beyond my personal life? If I can have in me and around me so many memories that I do not remember, . . . this forgetfulness may apply to a life I lived in the body of another man, even on another planet. The same forgetfulness obliterates all. But then what is the meaning of that immortality of the soul whose reality the Norwegian philosopher affirmed? The person I shall be after death will have no more reason to remember the man I have been since my birth than the latter has to remember what I was before it. (X, 39)

But the past which is inaccessible to the voluntary memory may occasionally be fragmentarily restored by spontaneous and accidental experiences. One type of such experiences is furnished by the organic memory, the faculty by which incidents, feelings, and habits from the past, forgotten or never fully realized by the conscious mind, are recovered from the subconscious through attitudes of the body associated with them.

More important is the involuntary memory, which, set in operation by a chance sensation, may recover a whole segment of the past, equipped with its full qualitative value which consciousness, in the past, had failed to register. But involuntary memory operates rarely and briefly, and it poses new problems. When Marcel touches a button of his shoe and becomes again, through this accidental reëxperience of a past sensation, the boy who loved his grandmother, now dead, and when he realizes that in this resurgence of a past personality he has a far more intense experience of his love for her than when she was alive, he wonders where reality is, in the present or in the past. And what about his grandmother? In the past she was to him an inner experience, and so she is now; but then she was alive, and now she is—where? Reality, Marcel realizes, is somehow missed by intelligent consciousness when it is brought to him on the stream of time, and yet in some way intelligent consciousness must be brought to bear upon it. "This reality does not exist for us so long as it has not been re-created by our thought (otherwise men who have taken part in a gigantic battle would all be epic poets)."

It is the existence of the subconscious and of means of access to it through memory, whether organic, voluntary, or involuntary, that makes the inner experience of the passage of time so different from the abstract conception of it as something external, and introduces such difficulties into any attempt to measure inner time. Any given moment of consciousness is a blend of present perception and past experience, whether remembered or not. "We do not recall our memories of the past thirty years, but we are wholly steeped in them. . . ." This thoroughly Bergsonian sentence occurs in a passage in which the "Norwegian philosopher" (nowhere given a name) expounds Bergson at La Raspelière, and which acknowledges Proust's debt to the philosopher of time. Even without the specific allusion, it would be clear that Proust's ideas on psychological time add up to something very close to Bergsonian "duration," that non-measurable, purely qualitative experience in which the present is being continuously added to the past, without obliterating it.

The net result of Marcel's intellectual speculations about time and the subconscious is confusion and discouragement. The useless burden of the past which he carries within him destroys his freedom. As a child it is a shock to him to realize, as he suddenly does from a chance remark of his father's, that his idea of a new life upon which he can enter "tomorrow" and in which everything will be different from the unsatisfactory past, is impossible, because tomorrow is made from yesterday, and cannot greatly differ from it. Furthermore, time, whether measurable or not, fast moving or slow moving, continuing to exist after the passage of the moment or dropping continually and permanently into oblivion—time does move for the individual, who bears in his body the marks of its passage, and who ages and dies as the clock runs down. "In spite of everything that can be said about survival after the destruction of the brain, I notice that to each deterioration of the brain corresponds a fragment of death." And Marcel is not a mere observer of the passage of time for others; in his body and in his multiple personalities he is subject to its laws. His problem is to determine whether there is, as he profoundly hopes and as logic seems to postulate, a permanent self that can be detached from time, and thus escape time's consequences—illusion, uncertainty, relativity, change, decay, and death.

TRANSCENDENT REALITY

Efforts of the unaided intelligence have brought Marcel occasional fleeting glimpses of eternity beyond time, and stability beyond change. But not until intuitional and emotional factors have supported and illuminated his reason does he arrive at a revelation of transcendent reality—"that reality far from which we live, and from which we become more and more separated as the conventional knowledge which we have substituted for it grows in density and impermeability, that reality which we risk not knowing before we die, and which is simply our life, true life, life at last discovered and enlightened, consequently the only life that is really lived, the life which, in a sense, dwells at every instant in all men, and not in the artist alone."

The factors which combine with intelligence to bring Marcel to the discovery of this reality are contemplation, art, and involuntary memory, and each of the three calls for special attention.

The practice of contemplation began for Marcel in early childhood and was continued, with diminished frequency, into manhood. Its occasion and purpose are explained in the Combray chapter:

. . . all at once a roof, a reflection of sunlight on a stone, the odor of a road, arrested me by a special pleasure they gave me, and also because they seemed to be hiding, beyond what I could see, something which they were inviting me to come and take, and which despite my efforts I did not succeed in discovering. As I felt that this was to be found in them, I stayed there, motionless, watching, inhaling, trying to send my thought beyond the image or the odor. (I, 256)

Back at home he thought of other matters, but he had added to his collection of images which were by then dead, but under which had lurked "a reality which I had sensed, but which I had lacked the will power to succeed in discovering."

Once, however, on a drive with Dr. Percepied he had an experience of this nature with a more successful conclusion:

At a turn of the road I suddenly experienced that special pleasure that resembled no other, at seeing the two spires of Martinville, upon which the setting sun was shining, and which, from the movement of our carriage and the winding of the road, seemed to be continually changing their position, and then the spire of Vieuxvicq, which, separated from them by a hill and a valley and situated on a higher plateau in the distance, seemed nevertheless quite close to them. (I, 258)

Resisting the temptation to take the easier way and let the image of the spires, with their message undelivered, join his collection of unfulfilled promises, Marcel continued to contemplate and to search, until at last the surfaces of the spires seemed to break open like a kind of bark, revealing a little of what they had hidden. At once there took form in his mind a thought, and the thought brought forth words. He asked Dr. Percepied for a pencil and paper and began to set them down. When he had finished he began to sing at the top of his voice, with the satisfaction of a hen that has just laid an egg.

The thought that had come to him was that the moving spires were first like three golden pivots in the sky, then like three flowers painted on the sky, and finally and definitively that they were the three virgins of a legend, abandoned in a lonely place at nightfall, and timidly seeking their way in the gathering darkness. With this result Marcel seemed quite satisfied: the spires had delivered their secret. What the secret really meant and why the joy he felt was something more than the satisfaction of having found and set down words that on previous occasions had eluded him, he was to discover later.

The success of this experience made it unique in the recorded series of moments of contemplation. In vain he asked his questions of the hawthorn blossoms—"the feeling which they awakened in me remained dark and vague, trying in vain to detach itself, to come and fasten itself upon their flowers." Later, in the course of a drive near Balbec, he experienced the distinctive emotion at the sight of three trees, but here there was added to it a feeling of familiarity. Where had he seen them before? It could not have been, he decided, in any landscape of his past experience. Was he having a hallucination, or obscurely remembering a dream? He could not tell, and was never to know. But he had the clear impression that the trees were stretching out their arms to him, begging him to read them aright. Before the intensity of his emotion Balbec and the surrounding country became an illusion, Madame de Villeparisis a fictional character, and all that had happened in his life since the last such experience a matter of no importance. Here was true reality, here was the promise of his true life. But he could not reach it, nor, despite the successful turn of the experience at Martinville, would he ever have understood the true significance of contemplation without the assistance of art and of involuntary memory.

No reader of *A la Recherche du temps perdu* can fail to be struck, before he is far advanced in the novel, by the great importance which art is assuming. It is, as Marcel comes to realize near the end, "the most real of all things, the most austere school of life, and the true Last Judgment." Generalizations on art abound, some of the most frequently recurring being that the great artist always leaves his absolutely individual mark upon his work; that this mark is the fruit of an inner activity, the external materials which he uses being relatively unimportant; that he has the right, even the duty, to be solitary, since the work must be engendered in silence and meditation; and that the great work of art is, because of its originality, at first necessarily misunderstood by the majority, and if it comes to be appreciated by succeeding generations, it is because it has created its own posterity, by gradual changes it has effected in the public taste.

Five specific arts are represented in the novel, each with an exponent: dramatic art with the actress Berma, the sculpture and architecture of cathedrals expounded by Elstir, painting with Elstir again, music with Vinteuil, and literature with Bergotte. The theatre serves as Marcel's introduction to art. At first his great expectations of the acting of Berma in *Phèdre* (there is at one point a hint that the author is thinking of Sarah Bernhardt in the same play) are disappointed. Later he comes to a true appreciation of her art, but his interest in the theatre has meanwhile been superseded by one in painting. Elstir's comments on cathedrals are echoes of Ruskin in *The Bible of Amiens,* and make no important contribution to the general theory of art which concerns us. Literature, of course, is of great importance; but since its exponent Bergotte, who was partly founded, as two clues inform us, on Anatole France, becomes increasingly, in later parts of the novel, a mask for the author himself, and since Proust's final ideas on literature are a part of his conclusion, the subject calls for no separate consideration at this point. But painting and music make important contributions which must be examined.

Elstir, whose name seems a partial anagram of that of Whistler, but whose work and whose theories most resemble those of Claude Monet, is, like Monet, an impressionist, and believes in the importance of the innocent eye. As Proust puts it:

The names which designate things always correspond to a notion of the intelligence, which is foreign to our true impressions, and which forces us to eliminate from them all that is not related to this notion. Sometimes at my window in the Balbec hotel . . . I had chanced, by an effect of sunlight, to take a darker part of the sea for a distant coast, or to look with joy on a blue fluid zone, without knowing whether it belonged to the sea or to the sky. Very quickly my intelligence restored between the elements the separation which my impression had abolished. . . . But of those rare moments when one sees nature as it is, poetically, the work of Elstir was made. (V, 98-99)

Elstir's painting is metaphoric in that it may represent the sea as indistinguishable from the sky, or a part of the sea as a distant coast. But the painting is poetic only as Nature is poetic; it is based upon a true impression caught by the innocent eye in the fleeting moment before the intelligence has asserted its habitual sway and argued it out of existence.

An analogous procedure is followed by Elstir in portraiture, although here the "true" impression is not a fleeting effect of light and shade, but a vision of the ideal behind deceptive appearances. The painting has conformity to the artist's individual mode of vision, and bears no necessary relation to the past or present appearance or character of the sitter:

Artistic genius acts like those extremely high temperatures which have the power of dissociating atoms and regrouping them according to an absolutely contrary order, corresponding to another type. All that false harmony which a woman has imposed upon her features and over whose persistence she watches daily, in her mirror, before going out . . . this harmony the penetrating glance of the great painter destroys in a second, and in its place he makes a regrouping of the characteristics of the woman, in such a way as to satisfy a certain feminine and pictorial ideal which he bears within him. (V, 133-34)

In a landscape and in a human face the painter sees a reality that escapes the eye of an ordinary person, whose vision has been dulled by the superimposition of conventional intellectual interpretations; and the resulting painting, particularly in the case of a portrait, reveals the mark of the artist's inner and absolutely individual artistic activity.

Meditating, under the influence of Vinteuil's septuor, on the function of music, Marcel notes:

I wondered whether music were not the single example of what—but for the invention of language, the formation of words, the analysis of ideas—might have been the communication of souls. It is like a possibility that has no sequel; humanity set out on other roads, on that of spoken and written language. But this return to the unanalyzed [by means of the music he had just heard] was so intoxicating that, on coming out of this paradise, contact with more or less intelligent beings seemed to me of extraordinary insignificance. (XII, 76)

These ideas are reached as a result of one of those recurrent situations which, as we have observed, is one of the features of the novel's structure. Swann is represented to be (at about the time of Marcel's birth) a man of natural artistic sensitivity who, in the fever of an active social life, has been losing, not merely this sensitivity, but his very belief in the validity of beauty. In this state he hears for the first time the sonata of Vinteuil. At first he feels only a superficial esthetic enjoyment; but then a little phrase occurs, which stirs, deep within him, the memory of something long forgotten. When the phrase recurs, the impression is clarified and intensified:

Swann found in himself, in the memory of the phrase he had heard . . . the presence of one of those invisible realities in which he had ceased to believe, and to which, as if the music had had a sort of elective influence on the moral aridity from which he was suffering, he felt again the desire and almost the strength to devote his life. (I, 303)

He does not know, and is prevented from learning, the name of the composer, so that he is unable to get to the bottom of his impression by hearing the music repeated, and with the passage of time he forgets. Then, unexpectedly, he hears the sonata again, and again the elusive emotion arises. This time he learns the name of the composer, and henceforth can hear the music as often as he chooses. But by now he is beginning to be in love with Odette. He associates the little phrase with the delightful emotions of dawning love, and it becomes for the lovers the "national anthem" of their affair. For the rest of his life the phrase remains precious, but only because it resuscitates a happy moment of the past. Its further implications are forgotten, and Swann has missed his chance.

Many years later Marcel, who has often heard the sonata with keen pleasure but no unique emotion, hears the septuor of Vinteuil, and is swept by the same emotion as Swann before him. He too has been leading an excessively social life, he too is in love. Like Swann he associates the emotion with his love, but, his affair being further advanced than that of Swann, he is able to view it with more detachment, and to make the dissociation which is the price of deeper understanding. He realizes, not merely that the music does not stand for the love, but that the music and the love have beauty because they both point the way to a reality beyond. For Marcel the septuor contained "the strange call which I should never cease to hear, like the promise and the proof that there existed something else, attainable by art no doubt, than the emptiness which I had found in all pleasures and in love itself." And under the influence of the same impression he states: "It is not possible that a piece of sculpture, a work of music, which give an emotion which one feels to be higher, purer, more true, should not correspond to a certain spiritual reality. It must surely symbolize one, in order to give this impression of depth and of truth."

He still insists on the individual touch of the artist, that "unique accent to which rise the great singers that original musicians are, to which, in spite of themselves, they return, and which is a proof of the irreducibly individual existence of the soul. . . . This song, different from those of other singers, similar to all his own, where had Vinteuil learned it, heard it? Every artist seems then to be a native of an unknown country, which he himself has forgotten, and which is different from the one from which will come, setting sail for the earth, another great artist."

But now at last appears the reason for his insistence on the individual touch of the artist. Marcel has been ineffectually searching, with his reason, for a point of stability in the midst of change, for some proof that he has a permanent self not subject to the succession of his multiple personalities; and art, it seems, promises just such proof. For the artist, whatever his subject, remains identical with himself and "proves the fixity of the constituent elements of his soul." Despite all change, there is a residuum that qualitatively differentiates a personality. We all feel it, says Proust, without being able to put it into words. But art, "the art of a Vinteuil, like that of an Elstir, makes it appear, exteriorizing in the colors of the spectrum the intimate composition of those worlds which we call individuals, and which, without art, we should never know."

But freed from the immediate influence of the music Marcel begins again to doubt. Perhaps the apparently inspired character of great music is only a matter of technical skill. Perhaps the elusive quality of the mood which it induces would vanish before more adequate analysis. In this doubt he remains for the time being, but further evidence and a fuller revelation are to come from involuntary memory.

At the time of the madeleine incident, the first example and the prototype of the "privileged moments," Marcel, we recall, was content to establish, without inquiring the reason, that his profound and unique emotion was caused by a memory of the past. At the same point in the novel the conditions and the quality of the emotion are faithfully described. It comes at a moment when the intelligence lies relatively fallow; fatigue, apathy, and discouragement are favorable to its appearance. Its coming is sudden, and carries no indication of its source. It fills Marcel with "a precious essence; or rather this essence was not in me, it was me. I had ceased to feel myself mediocre, contingent, mortal." The state brings with it "no logical proof, only its clearly evident felicity, its reality before which other realities disappeared." Successive "privileged moments," although less fully described, are clearly identified as having the exact quality of emotion as the one experienced in the madeleine incident.

But when we come to the last four of the series, those described in the second volume of *Le Temps retrouvé,* we find a reinforcement of the original conditions and a greater intensity in the experience. At this time many years have passed without a "privileged moment." He is much older, much more deeply and generally discouraged than on the first occasion. With the usual suddenness he is seized by the old emotion, and the memory back of it shows the old reluctance to disclose itself. But scarcely has the identification been made when a new involuntary memory appears, and another, and another, until there are four "privileged moments" standing side by side, all identified with their corresponding memories, but all clamoring for a more complete explanation of their intensely moving character. These new involuntary memories have brought with them more intense identifying sensations than any in the past series: an impression of deep blue and powerful light precede the memory of Venice; a sensation of heat and the odor of smoke in a forest prepare the way for the memory of the stop on the railway journey; the touch of the starched napkin again brings a vision of blue, but this time "pure and saline," and shortly to be identified with Balbec; and the sound of water in a pipe, by its suggestion of the whistles of pleasure boats, again evokes Balbec and the whole panorama of the seashore. The incidents so recalled, Marcel discovers, are not merely remembered, as happens when the mind is voluntarily turned to the past, but resuscitated, lived through again. Furthermore, experience as reproduced by the involuntary memory is far more beautiful and intense than the original, which may, as in the case of the railway stop, have been a moment of *ennui* and discouragement. Why, Marcel asks himself; and under the powerful impetus of his new experiences he finds the answer to the question which he had deferred at the time of the madeleine incident: "the least word said, the most insignificant gesture made, at a period of our lives, was surrounded by, and carried upon it the reflection of, things which had no logical connection with it and which were separated from it by the intelligence, which could not make use of them for rational ends. . . ." And in this answer is contained the explanation of why such incidents of contemplation as the observation of the spires of Martinville and of the three trees on the road near Balbec were felt to have, despite their absence of a source in memory, the precise quality of expereince as the madeleine incident: in both involuntary memory and contemplation he was seeing into the true essence of the objects observed, and not merely considering the cold abstraction which the intelligence makes from perception. In rare moments of contemplation one can partially evade the officiousness of the intelligence and see into the hidden reality; in involuntary memory the same end is more effectively achieved by the aid of oblivion, which has blotted out the intellectual abstraction and allowed the pure essence of the moment, never before fully realized but none the less noted and stored away in the subconscious, to rise unimpeded into consciousness. As to the comparative "reality" of the intellectual abstraction of experience and of the perception of essences, Marcel does not hesitate: truth is in the essence, truth is poetry. Why? Because of the evidence of joy; the intelligence finds Dead Sea fruit of despair and uncertainty, but the perception of essences brings certainty and happiness.

It brings something more: it leads to a feeling of immortality, of escape from time. In contemplation and in music Marcel has experienced this feeling, but, being unable to justify it, has begun to doubt. In involuntary memory he finds the justification and the explanation: if a moment of the past can be re-lived, not merely remembered, re-lived with such intensity that it seriously threatens the reality of the present, then there is a coexistence of the past and the present, and consequently escape from time. The true essence is unchanging; the past moment coexists with the present because in both an identical essence is perceived. "In truth, the person within me who was at that moment enjoying this impression enjoyed in it the qualities it possessed which were common to both an earlier day and the present moment, qualities which were independent of all considerations of time; and this person came into play only when, by this process of identifying the past within the present, he could find himself in the only environment in which he could live and enjoy the essence of things, that is to say, entirely outside of time." "One minute freed from the order of time has re-created in us for perceiving it a being freed from the order of time."

It is the function of art to reveal the timeless essence. A man with a gift for painting, music, or literature, can turn contemplation to account, and record, for others to see or to hear, his perception of identity behind illusory disparities. This perception, whatever may be the medium in which he works, is externalized as a metaphor, which is not a mere embellishment of literature, but art itself. It is by the metaphor that Elstir and Vinteuil, quite as much as Bergotte, translate the product of their contemplation. And when the young Marcel, without fully understanding what he was doing, discovered and recorded the "essential" relation between the spires of Martinville and the three virgins of the legend, his joy was the result, not of having finished a piece of writing nor of having devised a pretty figure of speech, but of having penetrated for a moment to the domain of art.

But this Martinville incident is troublesome. However successful the metaphor, would not its absence be still more effective? Do not the three trees of Balbec, with their undelivered message, have more of what Proust himself calls "the poetry of the incomprehensible"? The metaphor seems inadequate to its implications. How can the spires of Martinville, which exist externally in material reality, have a true and significant relation of essence to purely imaginary characters in a legend? If they have, is not the transcendent reality in which the relation exists, itself imaginary?

Another objection to Proust's philosophy suggests itself. If transcendent reality is not a figment of the imagination, but immortal and unchanging truth, as he says, how can it be based on the evidence of such eminently fallible, changing, and mortal instruments as the human senses? To this objection Proust has a reply:

Whether it were a question of impressions like those given me by the spires of Martinville or of reminiscences like that of the paving stones or the taste of the madeleine, I had to try to interpret the sensations as the signs of so many laws and ideas, by trying to think, that is, by bringing out into the light of day what I had felt, and converting it into a spiritual equivalent. (XVI, 24)

The senses are fallible, but they are only intermediaries. Their testimony must be checked and analyzed by the intelligence, and its "spiritual equivalent" discovered. In other words transcendent reality is ideal, not material, and Marcel is being led by both reason and emotional intuition to the position of the pure philosophic Idealist. The conclusion does not escape him:

I understood furthermore that the slightest episodes of my past life had contributed to the lesson of idealism from which I was to profit today. . . . Only gross and erroneous perception places everything in the object, whereas everything is in the mind. (XVI, 69, 72)

From this point of view the relation of the spires of Martinville to the virgins of the legend is less puzzling, for if the spires no less than the virgins are creatures of the mind and have no reality except in it, then the essential relation established by Marcel is more nearly comprehensible.

Marcel's new-found philosophy has not, however, disposed of the problem of time. If involuntary memory evokes the immortal man, it is only for "one minute." In the time-defying struggles of the present with the past, it is the past which is the more beautiful, because more "essential," but it is the present which always emerges victorious. Never so clearly as after the final revelations of involuntary memory has Time—which Proust now spells with a capital "T"—seemed to Marcel so imposing, and never so clearly has he seen it incorporated in the creatures who now surround him at the reception of the Princesse de Guermantes—"a Punch and Judy show of puppets, bathing in the immaterial light of the years, exteriorizing Time." And the outer ravages of Time are but the symbol of the burden of the past within, as Marcel knows from his own experience; for deep within him is still ringing the little bell which, in his childhood, marked the departure of Swann and the beginning of the deterioration of his health and his will.

Time is still the implacable master of human destinies, but the tragedy of its implications have a character of universality which Marcel finds inspiring for his book: "Throughout the whole duration of Time, great tidal waves dredge up from the depths of the ages the same angers, the same sorrows, the same courage, the same eccentricities, across superimposed generations . . . like shadows on a succession of screens."

Time must win and Marcel must die, but from defeat comes victory. For the shadow of that death is necessary to the creation of his work, and by means of that death he will escape from time.

STYLE

Prerequisite to the enjoyment of Proust is a preference for the overtones of experience to experience itself. Proust writes for introverts. If the reader wants action and events, he is sure to be disappointed, for all he will get will be the careful exploration of an inner world.

For the most part, this exploration is pursued in the sentence that is the most characteristically Proustian—long, sinuous, suspensive, parenthetical, insistently returning to the point of digression, and often ending on a postscript. Its rhythm is the result of following, in his own phrase, "the meanderings of his thought." He began to use this type of sentence, in a less developed form, as early as 1895, when he wrote "La Fin de la jalousie." By the time he had finished with Ruskin, it was his settled manner, and to a certain extent he deplored it. In 1905 he wrote to Dreyfus that he had not dared to send him the preface to *Sesame and Lilies* because "I thought that you who can say so much in half a line would be exasperated by sentences that run to a hundred. Ah, how I should like to be able to write like Madame Straus! But I am forced to weave these long strands as I spin them, and if I shortened my sentences they would be little pieces of sentences, and not sentences at all. So I am like a silk worm, whose temperatures, incidentally, I inhabit."

As this passage suggests, his addiction to the long and complicated sentence was partly a matter of temperament, the result of a combination of scrupulousness and indecisiveness. He was always afraid of letting some morsel of the truth evade him; in authorship as in life he was forever weighing off against each other motives, opinions, courses of conduct, values; first a bit on one side, then a bit on the other; coming to a hesitant decision, seeing some new point, and changing his mind.

But partly, too, his way of writing was based on theory—a theory that was developed after the manner, but which is nevertheless a legitimate partial explanation of why he found himself obliged to write as he did. He was trying, not only to describe reality (in all three senses), but to imitate it, in all its complexities of past and present, its relationships, its analogies.

Complexity, therefore, Proust accepted as inseparable from

his intention, but deliberate obscurity was never a part of his program. In statements from "Contre l'obscurité" in 1896 to letters in 1921, he is unequivocal in his insistence upon grammatical correctness and precision both of thought and of form. While fully aware of the resources of rhythms and of verbal overtones and associations, he never intentionally sacrifices literal immediate meaning to psychological impact. Genuine obscurity, when it does occur, is a shortcoming, and instead of trying to make stylistic subtleties of his errors, enthusiasts would do well to adopt his own attitude, well expressed in a letter of June 17, 1921, to Paul Souday:

Several times, alas! (and already in the distant time of *Du Côté de chez Swann*) you have reproached me with the sentence about the "hat"; the one of mine that you quote (in absolute conformity with the text of *Guermantes II*) is, I admit, absolutely incomprehensible. But if already I correct my proofs very badly, when a book like this comes out printed directly from my indecipherable draft, my publishers may kindly do their best with the printing but it remains terribly incorrect.

I do not try to excuse myself in this way for the thoroughly justified criticism of making my sentences too long, too sinuously attached to the meanderings of my thought. I laughed heartily at your "It is limpid." But I found you too indulgent when you claimed that at the third reading it became clear, because for my part I don't understand it at all.

Nor did he make the slightest attempt to write in the "stream of consciousness" manner. For him the subconscious offered inspiration, but he did not take its suggestions down like dictation; he rationalized them, planned them, arranged them. For writers who, like Péguy, with superstitious veneration for the unknown being within, conscientiously wrote down his stammerings and repetitions, he had only contempt; and he had no interest in recording the whimsicalities of free association.

Yet the first impression made by his style is that it is loose and tortuous, and it is something of a surprise to find that, at the turn of the critical tide in his favor after the war, he began to be spoken of as "a new classicist." The critics may have been thinking chiefly of his classic analyses of human nature; but in his style too, beneath its deceptive surface, there lies a firm classical substratum of precision, balance, and antithesis.

One notices it most readily in phrases and shorter sentences, for example in the handling of adjectives in such a way as to give a neat, antithetical, and often humorous effect: "a delicious, hostile, and scandalized armchair," "the scornful, disheveled, and furious tourists," "a cordial and contagious attack of coughing." It is present in longer, but still relatively simple, units such as the following:

On one side of her bed were a large yellow commode in lemon wood, and a table, at once a pharmacy and an altar, where, above a statue of the Virgin and a bottle of Vichy, there were prayer books and prescriptions, all that she needed to follow in bed the services and her health régime, so that she should miss neither the time for pepsin nor that of Vespers. (I, 79-80)

And it can still be traced in the complicated passages:

So M. de Bréauté began to lick his chops and to sniff with eager nostrils, his appetite whetted not only by the good dinner he was sure to have, but by the nature of the gathering which my presence could not fail to make interesting and which would furnish him with a piquant subject of conversation at the lunch of the Duc de Chartres. He had not yet made up his mind whether I was the one on whom the cancer serum had just been tried or the author of the next curtain raiser at the Théâtre Français, just put into rehearsal, but as a great intellectual, as a great fancier of travel tales, he never stopped bringing out before me bows, signs of complicity, smiles filtered through his monocle; whether in the erroneous impression that a man of worth would have more esteem for him if he succeeded in inculcating the illusion that for him, Comte de Bréauté-Consalvi, the privileges of thought were not less worthy of respect than those of birth; or simply because of the need and the difficulty of expressing his satisfaction, in his ignorance of what sort of language he should use to address me, in short as if he had found himself in the presence of one of the "men of nature" of an unknown land where his raft had touched, and with whom, in hope of profit, he would try, while curiously observing their customs and without interrupting their demonstrations of friendship and without uttering, like them, loud cries, to exchange glass beads for ostrich eggs and spices. (VII, 110-11)

Here the precision in choice of words and the balanced structure of his sentence are almost concealed as a result of his anxiety to track down the exact quality of Monsieur de Bréauté's expression and movements. And so it is with most of Proust's complex manner. There is little to be gained, so far as pure style is concerned, in distinguishing between "intellectual" and "emotional" writing. There is a distinction in the sources of inspiration, but when it comes to setting it down, Proust first intellectualizes and then arranges to suit his purpose, and the result is the same peculiarly Proustian rhythm.

But his style is not, even when he is developing an idea, strictly analytical. With him analysis, of which he is a master, precedes composition, but is not fully carried over into it. He declines to tick off his points, like one who sets out to count to ten and does so. His points are not dispatched and forgotten. Instead, they are kept in suspension, they overlap, they recur; he is bent on getting as much of his idea as he can into our minds at once, and keeping it there.

Proust accentuated his early and natural tendency toward this sort of writing by theories developed while he was writing his novel, particularly by his doctrine of essences. In a much-quoted passage of *Le Temps retrouvé,* which has been called the key to his style, he said:

What we call reality is a certain relationship between those sensations and those memories which surround us simultaneously—a relationship suppressed by simple cinematographic vision, which departs from truth by its very effort to limit itself to it—a unique relationship which the writer should find in order to bind together forever in his sentence its two different terms. In a description he can place one after the other the objects of the place described indefinitely, truth will only begin when the writer takes two different objects, establishes their relationship (analogous in the world of art to the law of causation in the world of science), and confines them by the inevitable chains of a beautiful style; or else when, as in life, by isolating a quality common to two sensations, he releases their essence by bringing them together in a metaphor, to free them from the contingencies of time. . . . (XVI, 39-40)

It is the business of the writer, according to Proust, to portray reality, and reality is not attained simply by looking at objects in succession; it lies rather in a relation, established by sensations, between a moment of the present and a moment of the past; it also lies in the relation, perceived in contemplation, between two objects viewed simultaneously, or of which one is viewed and the other voluntarily recalled. The principle by which such relationships exist is the essence.

What Proust wants to do in his writing is to lay things side by side—a moment of the present beside a moment of the past, one object seen beside another with which it has a relation of essence. This laying side by side is what he means by a metaphor, a procedure more extended and more important than the verbal device to which we usually apply the term.

Proustian discontinuity is usually intended as one of these large-scale metaphors. It is not the accidental result of haphazard additions during the war years, but is present as a basic feature of the narrative method of *Swann,* as well as of the successive volumes. The metaphoric (or occasionally symbolic) intention of discontinuity becomes clear enough simply by attentive reading of the text. But there is one instance in *Swann* where the process becomes still clearer if we compare the text of the novel with an article which appeared in the *Figaro* on March 21, 1912, and of which Proust wrote to Lauris that it was an extract from his book which he had "arranged" for newspaper publication.

The article, entitled "Epine rose, Epine blanche," is a description of hawthorn blossoms. When we compare it with the version in *Swann,* we find that, except for two short introductory paragraphs necessitated by its detachment from context, the whole of the article appears in the novel and in its original order, but broken up by interpolations varying in length from half a sentence to thirty-one pages. Two of the more important of these digressions concern Mademoiselle Vinteuil and Gilberte Swann.

It is immediately clear that the dispersal of the material about the hawthorn blossoms injects their atmosphere into the current of Marcel's life more effectively than would the insertion of a solid block of description. The abrupt juxtaposition of the blossoms first with Mademoiselle Vinteuil and then with Gilberte is at first disconcerting, but if we look carefully at the points of interpolation we see readily enough what Proust is doing. In the case of Mademoiselle Vinteuil he is establishing a relation of essence between the delicate, feminine side of her dual nature and the blossoms, which seem to him like shy young girls. The case of Gilberte is somewhat different. Her sudden appearance interrupts Marcel in his contemplation of a pink blossom that stands out against the white ones. It is the first time that he has seen her, and her reddish hair against the bank of white establishes a permanent association. The blossoms become her floral leitmotif. His first love for a flower had been for hawthorn blossoms; now his first love for a woman was for Gilberte.

But in addition to these large organisms of style Proust insists on the importance of the unicellular image. As he wrote before the war to Louis de Robert, in praise of Francis Jammes:

Even if he did not know how to put his sensations in order, or write a book, even a story, even a paragraph, even a sentence, it would still be true that the cell itself, the atom, that is, the epithet and the image, are with him of a depth and an exactness which no one else attains. In the bottom of our hearts we indeed feel that things are like that, but we haven't the strength to push down to this extreme depth where lies the truth, the real universe, our authentic impression.

What Proust admires in Jammes is the ideal which he has set himself, and which is valid, not only at the time of *Swann,* but in 1921, when he wrote Vettard that he would have none of rhetoric, of decoration, of forced images, for the expression of his "profound and authentic impressions."

Two examples will illustrate what Proust tries to do with his images. The first concerns the adolescent girls at Balbec:

... I saw advancing five or six young girls, as different in appearance and manners from all the people to whom one was accustomed at Balbec as might have been a flock of seagulls, arrived from nowhere and executing gravely on the beach—the laggards fluttering to catch up with the others—a promenade whose purpose is as obscure to the bathers (whom they ignore) as it is clear in the minds of the birds. (V, 35)

In the second example a group of flowering shrubs offer Marcel a moment of rest and encouragement in depression:

About these shrubs which I had seen in the garden and taken for foreign gods, had I not been mistaken like Magdalen when, in another garden, on a day whose anniversary was soon to come, she saw a human form and "thought it was the gardener"? Guardians of the memories of the Golden Age, warranters of the promise that reality is not what one thinks, that the splendor of poetry and the marvelous light of innocence can shine out and can be the reward which we try to merit, these great white creatures wonderfully stooping over the shade propitious to rest, to angling, to reading, were they not rather angels? (VI, 144)

The poetic effectiveness of these images—the adolescent girls as a flock of seagulls, the trees as angels by the Sepulcher—is due to the fact that beneath the superficial unlikeness of the objects compared is a symbolic likeness, which does not occur to the reader unaided as in the banal simile, but which, once pointed out, strikes him as consistent and true. The idea behind physically disparate phenomena is shown to be the same: in other words, Proust has, to use his own terms, successfully established a relation of essence.

Sometimes images, individually effective, appear in such rapid succession that they jostle and neutralize each other. Such instances may well be the result of insufficient revision, as is surely the case on the last page of *Le Temps retrouvé,* where aged archbishops, a trembling leaf, a narrow summit, living stilts, and church spires, all in one sentence, leave the reader in some confusion. But there are other examples which seem to suffer from the opposite defect, that of being too much worked over. These are in Proust's ornate manner, in which he shows a tendency to saccharine, inconsistent, and too numerous images, to coy personification, and to elaborate mythological metaphors. Examples are: a scene in the Place de la Concorde in *Sodome et Gomorrhe* (VIII, 7-8: pink nougat obelisk turning into a jewel; moon like a peeled and slightly damaged quarter of orange, then gold, then an oriental symbol, then an irresistible weapon; poor little star huddled beside her bolder friend the moon); asparagus in *Swann* (I, 176); fruit in *Jeunes Filles* (IV, 136); apostrophe to the hawthorn blossoms in *Jeunes Filles* (V, 215-16); the box at the Opera in *Guermantes* (VI, 36 ff.); the Ladies of the Telephone in *Guermantes* (VI, 119-20). The list might be extended to include parts of otherwise beautiful passages in *Swann* and *La Prisonnière,* which read like elaborately synesthetic program notes.

We are safe in assuming that this preciosity belongs to Proust's earlier writing. Of the passages to which we have made direct reference, five can definitely be identified as having been written by 1913 (and the Ladies of the Telephone by 1907), and only one, the description of the Place de la Concorde in *Sodome et Gomorrhe,* cannot positively be so dated, although it sounds like early Proust. Further evidence that he outgrew his preciosity is the objectivity with which, through Albertine, he parodies himself in *La Prisonnière* (XI, 176-77). Through more than a page Albertine elaborates a eulogy of ice cream, in the manner, only slightly exaggerated, of Marcel describing asparagus, fruit, or the moon; listening, he both recognizes his own touch and finds it "a little too well said." For his parody Proust has seized upon the basic fault of his precious style: disproportion between the object described and the elaborate image.

In a work so extensive, and written over so long a period, it is not to be expected that imagery should be uniformly successful.

But in the perspective of the whole work the faults appear only as trifling exceptions to the general rule of "profound, authentic impressions," and no rhetoric.

The adherence to deeply felt images does not, however, prevent Proust from occasionally using deliberate stylistic devices such as the refrain. One example is the amusing passage in *Swann* (I, 161-63) with its recurrent "it is Saturday." Another instance is the long rhythmic passage describing the tortured efforts of Marcel's mind to escape the pain of Albertine's death: the mournful refrain "but she was dead" tolls through it with the regularity and insistence of a passing bell.

Many fine passages make conspicuous use of musical effect of one sort or another. One of the best (again from *Albertine disparue*) constitutes a sort of waiting music—waiting for time to pass and the pain to grow less:

Que le jour est lent à mourir par ces soirs démesurés de l'été. Un pâle fantôme de la maison d'en face continuait indéfiniment à aquareller sur le ciel sa blancheur persistante. Enfin il faisait nuit dans l'appartement, je me cognais aux meubles de l'antichambre, mais dans la porte de l'escalier, au milieu du noir que je croyais total, la partie vitrée était translucide et bleue, d'un bleu de fleur, d'un bleu d'aile d'insecte, d'un bleu qui m'eût semblé beau si je n'avais senti qu'il était un dernier reflet, coupant comme un acier, un coup suprême que dans sa cruauté infatigable me portait encore le jour. (XIII, 105)

(How slow the day is to die on these endless summer evenings. A pale ghost of the house across the way continued to wash into the sky its persistent white. At last it was night in the apartment, I bumped against the furniture of the reception room, but in the stair door, in the midst of the darkness which I thought was complete, the glass was translucid and blue, with the blue of a flower, the blue of an insect's wing, a blue that would have seemed to me beautiful if I had not felt that it was a last reflection, sharp as steel, a last blow dealt me by the tireless cruelty of the day.)

It is noteworthy that deep feeling seemed to have a simplifying effect upon Proust's style. The rhythm and thought remain Proustian, but under the stress of emotion he has shortened phrases and sentences, eliminated parenthetical modifiers, and repeated key words, thereby achieving both logical clarity and poetic refrain. This telling style is used throughout more than half of *Albertine disparue* (the part written at a stretch in 1915) and appears in occasional other passages of the novel, notably in *La Prisonnière*.

Another, but more intellectual, application of music to style occurs in certain patterns of recurrence. The little phrase of Vinteuil's sonata, the painting of Vermeer, the "privileged moments," personal mannerisms or peculiarities of dress, themes like those of oblivion, Gomorrha, the subjectivity of love—these and other recurring materials are woven intricately into the composition in a way that suggests the Wagnerian leitmotif.

The most important effect of painting on Proust's style is not allusions to painters and paintings, which abound, not even artistic analogies and comparisons, but something deeper, more thoroughly assimilated: it is a whole point of view in description. Proust seems to have adopted from the impressionist painters their principle of the "innocent eye"; he tries to divest himself of intellectual preconceptions and to present objects as seen, and in the order of seeing.

The quality of vision was the aspect of his style upon which he laid the most stress, and this quality extends far beyond the limits of mere description, and detaches itself from theories. It is not just essences, metaphorical discontinuities, images, epithets; it is a whole way of seeing, a highly individual slant on the world and on experience.

This quality is probably at the root of the fascination Proust exerts on those who are susceptible to him. When, to the accompaniment of sardonic laughter, he describes the antics of marionettes in the lurid glow of Sodom and Gomorrha, he manages to see and to record what is mechanical, foreordained, helpless, and pathetic in their behavior. When he invites us to leave "the lust of the flesh and the lust of the eyes," and to contemplate the true reality, "life at last discovered and enlightened," he catches the inevitable comparison which best evokes the real behind the illusory, the eternal behind the temporal. And both worlds, the Cities of the Plain and the Earthly Paradise, are seen in the perspective of time. They have become a part of his inner world, the secure treasure of the living past, which he touches and turns and holds up for our inspection.

THE MEANING OF PROUST

ALTHOUGH there has always been a great diversity of opinion about the value of Proust's work, it is possible to distinguish since his death successive trends, alternately favorable and unfavorable. His popularity began with *A l'Ombre des jeunes filles en fleur,* and continued to grow (though always with strongly dissenting opinions) through *Le Côté de Guermantes* and *Sodome et Gomorrhe* to *La Prisonnière* in 1923, the latter installment having arrived in time to check a regression that threatened after *Sodome et Gomorrhe.* There followed a gap in publication, during which the enthusiasm of such interpreters as Crémieux, Pierre-Quint, and Jacques Rivière battled to maintain Proust's reputation. *Albertine disparue,* in 1926, gave them little help; it seemed, on the contrary, to play into the hands of the opposition. But the publication of *Le Temps retrouvé* a year later caused a new turn of the tide in Proust's favor, and appeared to justify his apologists.

On the whole the nineteen-twenties marked the high point of Proust's prestige. The difficulty and complexity of his work, and comparisons made between him and Bergson, Einstein, and Freud, combined to make him a shibboleth among the intelligentsia. He was a fad with literary and esthetic snobs, and in wider circles his name was mentioned with a respect that was unhampered by sound knowledge. Obviously mere complexity is no valid criterion of worth, and the comparison with Bergson, although true enough in some respects, has been greatly overemphasized. The bracketing of Proust with Einstein was chiefly done by people who knew nothing of Einstein and little of Proust. It was enough that some critics (beginning with Camille

Vettard, who really did have some preliminary qualifications for speaking of Einstein) had mentioned the two together for the word to be busily repeated among the bright young moderns. Whether or not there was any useful connection between a principle of astro-physics and a reputed point of view on truth and morals, did not matter; the magic word "relativity" was enough—"everything was relative."

Another magic word, "the subconscious," connected Proust and Freud, although here—Freud being much more accessible to the layman than Einstein—the comparison had a better chance of validity. Freud dealt with the subconscious, the unconscious, and the id; Proust dealt, it was generally said, with the subconscious, although his word was really *l'inconscient,* the unconscious. But there is nothing Freudian in Proust's point of view or terminology, and not the slightest indication that he was personally acquainted with Freud's work. The grounds on which he referred, in his Bois interview and subsequently, to his work being "a series of novels of the unconscious" were the phenomena of forgetting and remembering. We note, he claimed (and here he crossed Bergson's path), what our reasoning minds consider to have possible future or present utility. Such items may drop out of our mind, but can be recalled by an effort of the voluntary memory, or occasionally by accident through the organic memory. But we *unconsciously* note a host of other items which we can scarcely speak of forgetting because they never occupied the focus of attention, but which may rise to the surface, intact and powerful, through the involuntary memory. In these ideas there is no hint of repressions, the id, the censor, moral tumors, or their cure by analysis; nor does sex play any rôle.

Of course there are numerous small ways in which Proust touches on Freud's domain. Something like the id is evoked by Proust's allusions to "visceral depths" and "primitive existences" to which one descends in sleep; human conduct is of course subconsciously motivated; various associational elements in memory and thinking are observed. And finally, but quite unconsciously, Proust presented in the character of Marcel (and himself) a beautiful Freudian case, complete with mother fixation, father rivalry, fantasy, perversion, neurosis, dreams, repressions—practically everything the most confirmed Freudian could ask for. But he was merely giving a personal history; he had no idea of writing a Freudian novel.

Although Proust's ideas on homosexuality were derived from Ulrichs and Krafft-Ebing, as well as from introspection and observation, the fact that he treated the subject at all was enough to associate him with the Freudian interest in sex in all its manifestations. Proust expected *Sodome* and *La Prisonnière* to call forth moral condemnation of his work and ostracism of his person; instead, they added a new cause for his popularity. *Sodome et Gomorrhe II* did indeed lead some critics to say that Proust's powers were declining, but the grounds for the criticism were the monotony of his pessimistic dissections and the absence of signs of clear direction in his plan rather than scandal at his treatment of homosexuality. The calmness with which his *Sodome* was received made Proust wonder whether readers really understood what he was saying. As a matter of fact, his immunity was due, not merely to the beginning Freudian vogue, but to the whole spirit of the times. The "war to end war" had been followed by disillusionment, bitterness, and cynicism, and with the loss of belief western civilization was faced anew, after forty years, with an outbreak of decadence. Relativisim, futility, and hopelessness were the order of the day among the young intellectuals, and license of speech and behavior followed as a matter of course. Homosexuality came into the open; to have been shocked at Proust's *Sodome* would have been scandalously unmodern.

To these attitudes Freudianism made its contribution by the analytic approach to sexual problems. Life had ceased to be a moral battle; it was rather a game, whose purpose was to placate the id, to circumvent repressions, and thus to assure to the conscious self—not happiness, for that would have been absurd, but enough open-eyed sanity to carry on with. Pessimistic determinism now wore the mantle of Freud, as earlier it had assumed that of Darwin.

Abundant support for these ideas could be found in the pages of Proust, where the puppet-like behavior of human beings, the vanity of hope, the illusions of friendship and love, the tyranny of habit, and the degeneration of society were all satisfyingly modern. That the positive, the hopeful content of Proust should have been ignored, despite the protests of some better informed admirers, is entirely natural. In Proust's demonstration the description of the disease is many times longer than the analysis of the cure. Artistically the disproportion is justified, because it corresponds to experience; but for the reader who dips, it invites misconception. The long delay in publishing *Le Temps retrouvé* is a further excuse for misinterpretation; not until 1927 was Proust's argument explicit and complete.

His prestige of the twenties had unsound foundations, and when the new decadence was succeeded by the inevitable new moral earnestness, it went into a long decline. True, Proust was now much better understood, as several well-informed and intelligent studies testified; but to offset this advantage to his reputation came new attacks on his character and personality. How could so evil a tree, it was argued, bring forth good fruit? Proust was a decadent, a weak-willed homosexual neurotic; it was high time he and all he stood for were forgotten. The publication, in 1930, of the first volume of his collected correspondence, the letters to Montesquiou, showed his obsequiousness in its most unpleasant light, and aided in the depreciation. Then came Professor Feuillerat's attempt to demonstrate that Proust's poetic mysticism was an early phase of his thought, disavowed by the skeptical and pessimistic Proust that came into being during the war. Feuillerat professed a guarded respect for the later Proust, and one was left with the impression that if there was anything of worth in him it was to be found in his later phase; the rest was mere naïve nonsense, an infirmity of childhood which he had thrown off like the measles.

The net result was that by the late thirties implacable opponents of Proust took heart; clearly he was on his way out, and some even declared that he was already dead.

"Forever dead? Who shall say?" Proust's words about the death and possible survival of Bergotte are applicable to the fate of his own work, which shows a disconcerting tendency to return to life. No sooner has the dust of the supposedly ultimate battle settled, than new readers, indifferent to his annihilation, discover him and sing his praises. A new world war has made the society Proust described seem more remote than ever; and yet during it, as in the first war, and before the days of his unwholesome notoriety, he acquired admirers.

It is time to drop attack and defense and, without evasion or concealment, but also without idolatry, to take Proust for what he is. The continued vitality of his work shows that he cannot be shrugged off as a mere abnormal phenomenon, of passing historical interest; but his weaknesses as a man and as an artist are written into his work, and must also be recognized.

The immense length of *A la Recherche du temps perdu* is not justified by the maintenance of a uniform standard of excellence. Parts of it are masterly; other parts, merely dull. There are confusions, irrelevances, inadvertent repetitions; and the frequent complexity of the style imposes on the reader a burden of attention not always warranted by the effect produced.

As a realistic panorama of society the novel is far inferior in scope to Balzac's *Comédie humaine,* to which it is occasionally compared. Proust's limited world is largely made up of decaying aristocrats, wealthy bourgeois, and servants. Within these limits he has given us some unforgettable portraits, but they remain fictional creations; living, indeed, with a monstrous vitality of their own, but seldom convincing us that they are representative. It is impossible to believe that people are, literally, such as Proust represents them—at least in any large numbers; in particular we cannot accept his estimate of the prevalence of homosexuality. And his hordes of characters remain aggregations of individuals; one does not feel them to constitute a society.

As a psychologist Proust must unquestionably be ranked very high, and yet even here he is one-sided. He is inclined to attribute to everyone his own peculiarities, weaknesses, and limitations. There is more in love, for example, or in friendship, than he seems prepared to admit.

The only way to take Proust is on his own terms. The mere fact that he wrote a very long novel containing a large number of characters is insufficient reason for judging him on the same standards as one would judge Balzac. His characters, his viewpoint, and his psychology are of a very special kind; within the limits of his domain he is supreme.

The singularity of Proust's viewpoint, and of much of his power, results in large part from the combination in him of the poet and the analyst. Poetry, obviously, is much more than a matter of rhythm; it is a way of seeing. And Proust saw like a poet. He was not content with surface resemblances and disparities; he always struggled to get at the "profound, authentic impression," and to relate it to something else. It was in this relating to something else, this effort to classify and to explain, that the analyst in him came into play.

But a part of Proust's special savor comes also from his invalidism and neuroticism. His world is that of the man in bed, seen at one remove, and this fact is his strength and his weakness. Imagination and memory play larger rôles than in the case of a more normal writer. He remembers and he imagines slights, deceptions, tricks; he projects his idiosyncrasies beyond his cork-lined walls and fastens them on to others. But from his claustration, too, he drew his extraordinary acuity of vision and the rich quality of his memory. "Never," he wrote, long before he could realize how fully the statement was to apply to himself, "was Noah able to see the world so well as from the Ark."

His great achievement as a psychologist is his description of himself. No one, not even Stendhal, has told himself so fully; and no one has probed more patiently and more exhaustively into the dark corners of the neurotic personality. To do this, it was not enough to be himself the neurotic introvert; he needed, and he had, a remarkable power of detachment and a strong analytic talent. The result is that from his own highly special psychology he was able to extract general truth.

But social panorama, character creation, style, psychology— all these aspects of Proust's individuality acquire significance only in relation to his basic philosophy, his report on experience. Here what Proust has to say sifts down to this: there are two worlds, one the world of time, where necessity, illusion, suffering, change, decay, and death are the law; the other the world of eternity, where there is freedom, beauty, and peace. Normal experience is in the world of time, but glimpses of the other world may be given in moments of contemplation or through accidents of involuntary memory. It is the function of art to develop these insights and to use them for the illumination of life in the world of time.

That there is a relation between this message and the ideas of other writers seems clear enough. Like Schopenhauer, whom he read and admired, Proust believed that in the world of ordinary experience illusion was inescapable, desire insatiable and always frustrated, and happiness impossible; like him he asserted the possibility of rising above ordinary experience in contemplation; like him he believed that the function of art was not to describe superficial appearances but to penetrate to the world of Platonic Idea. Unlike Schopenhauer, who believed that this superior insight was attainable only in proportion to the surrender of individuality, Proust clung to a faith in an irreducible minimum of personality in artist or seer.

Proust's sense of the continuing past has often and with some justice been compared to Bergson's idea of duration. There is also a resemblance to be noted between Bergsonian intuition—

instinctive apprehension and reason fused into a higher instrument of knowing—and Proust's moments of contemplation. Yet here Bergson is nearer to Schopenhauer's fusion of will and idea than he is to Proust, in whom emotional apprehension and reason appear rather to play successive and complementary rôles.

It is also evident that contemplation, whether in Proust or Schopenhauer, is psychologically much the same experience as the one described under the same name by mystics of various times and places. But the very word "mysticism" has the unfortunate effect of awakening obstinate ready-made attitudes of hostility or of veneration. To the favorably disposed the mystic is one who has risen above ordinary humanity and seen into immortal Reality; to the hostile, he is a self-deluded hysteric. We are not concerned (nor was Proust) with the experiences of supermen or of a lunatic fringe; we simply want to know whether there is a faculty, latent in all and developed in some, whereby may be apprehended a transcendent Reality which, as Proust puts it, "is simply our life, true life . . . the life which, in a sense, dwells at every instant in all men, and not in the artist alone." There is, as we have seen, strong evidence that Proust had experiences of involuntary memory and of contemplation, and that the philosophy expounded in his novel was not to him mere literary capital, but a personal view of the world and a way of life. What we need is evidence outside of speculative philosophies which Proust read and which colored his thinking, independent evidence tending to show that resemblances between Proust and this or that other writer are due, not to borrowings or "influences," but to the fact that they are talking about the same thing.

Involuntary memory—the resurgence of the past through the repetition of a sensation—is a fairly common experience, though few have had it with the intensity of Proust. Somewhat less common, but still familiar, is the sudden feeling that around us, at this place and in this moment, there is something real, beautiful, important, and permanent, if we could but shake off preoccupation with our personal concerns, open our eyes, and see it. But we can go farther than such vague appeals to the possible experience of the reader.

It happens that there exists a document so situated in time that the possibility of literary influence is virtually excluded. *With the Door Open,* by the Danish novelist J. Anker Larsen, was first published in 1926, after the death of Proust, whose ideas were consequently unaffected by it, and before the publication of *Le Temps retrouvé,* so that Larsen was in the highest degree unlikely to have had a clear idea of Proust's philosophy.[1] Furthermore, *With the Door Open* is not a novel, but a simple and patently honest autobiographical record. Describing the first of a series of what he calls "lightning flashes," Larsen says:

One winter's day I was taking a walk in the Geels forest. . . . My usual sense of ego had gone to sleep like a little child in its crib. I only just remember how the frozen leaves crunched under my big, heavy boots. Otherwise my consciousness was not very active, but as I looked up to get my bearings, I became quite confused in regard to place and time, for I beheld before me a small wood path, so fresh, pure and fairylike that it must have been a path in the Garden of Paradise. There could be no doubt about it, my own joy at the sight of it belonged likewise to Paradise. That lasted perhaps a second— measured by the temporal clock. I went on standing there with my gaze fixed on the footpath—and now it was merely the one which led to the house in which I lived. . . . But in my memory still shone the image of the path in the Garden of Paradise, accompanied by the feeling that it was familiar. And now I remembered it quite distinctly. It was the one that lies in a small wood near a village school on the island of Langeland. But it is not worth the trouble to journey thither to find it; it certainly looks commonplace, unalluring and insignificant. . . . Until now I had completely forgotten that the path existed. It had never figured among the home scenes which used to visit me; it had been stored away far below the "threshold of consciousness." . . . I stood still, swayed by two feelings which it would be hard to conceive of as being present simultaneously: by a profound

[1] In a letter of Dec. 31, 1947, Mr. Larsen confirms this supposition, writing: "You are right, when I wrote that little book I knew absolutely nothing of Proust, who certainly could not know of my existence."

happiness which declared itself as indestructible, and a verdict upon my whole life as being fundamentally misdirected.

Of a later experience of the same sort he records:

I walked and walked, until I found myself standing in front of a dyke by the wood. As I glanced at it, there was a flash of lightning. . . . It was a dyke by one of the fields belonging to the estate where I was born. I actually saw it. That is to say, at that moment I did not distinguish between this dyke and the old one, between my present ego and the one of the past. The two phenomena were *simultaneous and one.* . . . Suddenly a change occurred. I saw another dyke by another field at home—with the same feeling of present experience. . . .

Now it was quite evident that this dyke resembled the others just as much as any other dyke. . . . No, the similarity did not lie outside of myself, in what I was looking at, but within myself, in the manner of my perception. I had succeeded in seeing this dyke *honestly and straightforwardly* with the eyes which were my birthright. The profound joy of reality filled me; my own inner condition opened out, and became one with all the homogeneous conditions. It was not a question of remembrance, but of a state of being. I did not miss the old dykes, for they were present.

Larsen's "lightning flashes" were accompanied by a joy so intense that he could not remain indifferent to it; but as soon as the joy passed into conscious enjoyment, the moment ended. Gradually he learned to rest in the moment, to be content with being, without self-conscious feeling. The result was that he became able to a certain extent to control the experience. He could look upon a road in the usual way, and then see it freed from space and time. "If I looked at the Holte road . . . it *opened* itself out, and I *saw within it* the road to Rudköbing." Finally he reached what he calls his first "meeting with Eternity," an experience that seems to be a heightening and prolonging of the "lightning flash," but without the image from the past. He confesses himself unable adequately to describe it, but his few halting words are enough to identify it as full mystic experience. He concludes, "That was my first actual meeting with Reality; because such is the real life: a Now which *is* and a Now which *happens.* There is no beginning and no end. I cannot say anything more about this Now. I sat in my garden, but there was no place in the world where I was not."

It is scarcely necessary to enlarge on the extraordinary likeness between the experiences of the Danish author and those of Proust: the resurgence of the past with such vividness that it competes with the present; the sense of freedom, joy, and escape from time; the idea that in contemplation an object "opens," and reveals its true nature; the feeling that life as lived at other times than such moments is futile and meaningless; the description of transcendent Reality as the true life and the eternal Now. Proust and Larsen are talking about the same experience.

But clearly Larsen carried it farther than Proust, who did not get beyond the unpredictable and uncontrolled "flash." Yet for literary purposes the advantage is not wholly with Larsen. Such a novel as his *Philosopher's Stone* is at once too esoteric and too explicit: the sense of the other world is so strong that this one loses its reality. Larsen lacks the colossal humor, the horror, the subtle analysis of Proust's relentless probing into ordinary human experience. *A la Recherche du temps perdu* has neither the serenity of assured spiritual achievement nor the unrelieved pessimism of the cynical materialist; what it does give is a somber panorama of time lit by flashes of eternity.

The mood of exaltation which prevails at the end of the novel came to Proust in mid-career, and was but the most conspicuous peak in a long series of ups and downs. His conflicts remained unresolved to the end, and he could subscribe to the words of St. Paul: "For the good that I would I do not: but the evil which I would not, that I do. . . . O wretched man that I am, who shall deliver me from the body of this death?"

Basically his difficulties sprang from his temperament. The sensitivity of his emotional side gave him insights and aspirations which the weakness of his active nature prevented him from realizing, while the acuity of his intelligence precluded the narcotic of self-deception. He had a tendency to asthma and to homosexuality; he rationalized both, but was unable to avoid the conviction that both were in a sense his own fault. He was not responsible for the original respiratory sensitivity, but he believed that with a steady adherence to a sound régime of diet, exercise, work, and rest, and with a little self-control, a little willingness to face discomfort without recourse to drugs, he could conquer asthma. This effort he could not make, and his incessant lamentations about his health were his excuse, to himself as much as to his correspondents, for his failure. Similarly with homosexuality: he was not to blame for the predisposition, but he felt that he should and could conquer his inclination. He did not, and from "Avant la nuit" in 1893 to *Sodome et Gomorrhe* in 1921, he rationalized homosexuality, without ceasing to consider it a vice and without convincing himself by his own arguments.

His life was a series of disappointed hopes and new beginnings. In his childhood he was not seriously worried; life stretched before him intact, and the next first of January could mark the beginning of his "true life." But the beginnings kept failing and calling for new ones, and even as late as February 1915 he was able to write to Madame Scheikévitch, "The experience of the past has not discouraged me from hoping for a future which does not resemble it." But hope deferred could not live forever, and three years later he wrote to the same correspondent that he no longer believed in new beginnings: "like you I know that characters continue." In the melancholy conviction that habit was now wholly his master, he watched himself behave as from the outside—without indulgence, but without the capacity to interfere.

The hope which he had lost for himself he put increasingly into his work. If he had failed as a man, he could at least find consolation in his art. "Perhaps," he wrote, "it is only in really vicious lives that the moral problem can be posed in the full force of its anxiety. And to this problem the artist gives a solution, not on the plane of his individual life, but of what is for him his true life, a solution that is general, literary. . . . Often artists use their own vices to arrive at a concepiton of the moral rule for all."

As for his personal life, its only solution lay in death—"death which comes to the aid of destinies that find difficulty in fulfillment." And beyond death, perhaps, lay the world which he had glimpsed but could not grasp—"a world wholly different from this one, which we leave in order to be born on this earth, before perhaps returning to the other to live once more beneath the sway of those laws which we have obeyed because we bore their precepts in our hearts." It was the presentiment of these laws, of this other world, that he found in involuntary memory, in art, and in contemplation.

APPENDICES

SOURCES

References without title, below and in the text, are to the 16-volume Nouvelle Revue Française edition of *A la Recherche du temps perdu* (1919-1927), in accordance with the following table:

I: Du Côté de chez Swann, I.
II: " " " " " II.
III: A l'Ombre des jeunes filles en fleur, I.
IV: " " " " " " " II.
V: " " " " " " " III.
VI: Le Côté de Guermantes, I.
VII: " " " " II, Sodome et Gomorrhe I.
VIII: Sodome et Gomorrhe (II), I.
IX: " " " " II.
X: " " " " III.
XI: La Prisonnière, I.
XII: " " II.
XIII: Albertine disparue, I.
XIV: " " II.
XV: Le Temps retrouvé, I.
XVI: " " " II.

Abbreviations used for other writings of Proust:

C: Chroniques.
CG: Correspondance générale de Marcel Proust, 6 v.
PJ: Les Plaisirs et les Jours, N.R.F. 1924 (text identical with 1st edition).
PM: Pastiches et Mélanges.

Other references are to author and short title.

All translations from the French in this book are by the author.

I. *The Climate of Ideas*

Page 2: "Complete natures being rare . . .": XIV, 97.
Page 3: Incident of "zut! zut!": I, 224.
Page 5: Auguste Comte on positivism: *Cours de philosophie positive*, 1re leçon.
Page 6: Taine on vice and virtue: Introduction to *Histoire de la littérature anglaise*, section III.

Page 6: Théodule Ribot on the will: *Maladies de la volonté*, 11th ed., p. 179.

Page 8: "Take the Self . . .": Barrès, "Examen des trois romans idéologiques," in *Sous l'Œil des barbares*, nouvelle éd., 1892, p. 41.

"Soyons ardents . . .": Barrès, *Un Homme libre*, préface, p. xxiii.

Paul Bourget on the two young men: Preface to *Le Disciple.*

Page 9: Poe's "Imp of the Perverse" was published in 1845. Baudelaire's "Le Mauvais Vitrier" first appeared in *Petits Poèmes en prose* (later called *Le Spleen de Paris*) in 1869, in *Œuvres complètes*, IV.

"It is a kind of energy . . .": from "Le Mauvais Vitrier."

Page 10: "Aux objets répugnants . . .": Preface "Au lecteur," *Les Fleurs du Mal.*

Page 15: For the case of *Le Disciple,* see Taine, *Vie et Correspondance*, IV, 287-93; France, *La Vie littéraire*, III, 54-78; Brunetière, *Nouvelles Questions de critique*, pp. 330-36; Feuillerat, *Paul Bourget*, pp. 135-150.

Paul Desjardins, *Le Devoir présent*, p. 3.

II. The Child

Page 20: Portraits of Proust and his parents are reproduced in Abraham, *Proust.* The incident of the New Year's present is told by Proust in a letter to Lucien Daudet, *Autour*, p. 97; recollections of Robert Proust in *Hommage*, p. 17.

Page 21: ". . . a roof, a reflection . . .": I, 256.

Page 22: Letter to Comtesse de Noailles, CG II, 49-50.

Page 23: Details about family life at Illiers are based on Proust's preface to *Sesame and Lilies* ("Journées de lectures," PM, pp. 225-72).

Page 24: On the Jewish side of Proust, see *Crémieux*, "Proust et les Juifs," a chapter of his *Du côté de Marcel Proust.*

Page 25: "barometric personage": XI, 13-14.

"I ought to have been happy . . .": I, 60.

"It was from that evening . . .": XVI, 258.

Page 26: "the fraternal stranger . . .": PJ, p. 36.

Page 27: The story of Mlle Benardahy and Princesse Radziwill can be pieced together from "Rayon de soleil sur le balcon," C, 100-05; photographic reproduction of dedication to Lacretelle, front of Gabory, *Essai sur Marcel Proust;* CG IV, 119; CG V, 41-42 and 190-91; PJ, 185-86.

Page 28: Photographic reproduction of page in souvenir album in Abraham, *Proust,* pl. VIII.

Page 29: Correspondence with Dreyfus: GC IV, 173-74, 176, 179.

Page 30: "to distinguish between . . .": I, 263.
"As for the pleasure . . .": V, 148.
"Note: the sadness . . .": quoted by Martino, *Le Naturalisme français,* p. 160.

Page 31: Lavallée on Proust and Gaucher, CG IV, 3.
"What we have in common . . .": CG IV, 172.

III. *Activity*

Page 33: The bodies of these peasants "had remained . . .": PJ, 216. Among many accounts of the young Proust in salons may be mentioned Blanche, *Mes Modèles,* and Clermont-Tonnerre, *Robert de Montesquiou et Marcel Proust.* For the "hopeless little imbecile," XI, 273.

Page 34: "I owe in large part . . .": Billy, *Marcel Proust,* p. 23. For relations of Gaston and Proust, CG IV, 130-39.

Page 35: For Proust's travels, PM, p. 256, note 1; Billy, *Marcel Proust,* pp. 95, 111; CG I, 58-59; cf. also *A la Recherche,* VI, 230.

Page 36: "Believe that I feel . . .": CG I, 6.

Page 37: "I am too much moved . . .": CG I, 7-8.
". . . since two of your friends . . .": CG I, 8-9.

Page 38: "Flattery is often . . .": PJ, p. 82.
"All these bows . . .": PM, pp. 261-62. See also Vigneron, "Marcel Proust et Robert de Montesquiou."

Page 39: "the traveling salesman of my wit": CG I, 20-21.
Delafosse letters: CG I, 50-53, 35-36. Cf. *A la Recherche,* VI, 238.

Page 41: "He immediately indicated . . .": Bibesco, *Au Bal,* p. 160.
"Just imagine, I have learned . . .": Bibesco, *Au Bal,* p. 166.
"great silent democracy": C, p. 165.

Page 42: "her laugh impresses me . . ." PJ, pp. 74-75. See also Billy, *Marcel Proust,* pp. 78-79; Dreyfus, *Souvenirs,* p. 92; Bibesco, *Au Bal,* p. 46.

Pages 43- "At last I have found . . .": Billy, *Marcel Proust,* pp.
44: 40-41; "I received . . .": p. 42; "You wouldn't believe . . .": p. 43; "There is nothing . . .": p. 103.

Page 44: "We dreamed then . . .": PJ, pp. 12-13.
"It is sweet . . ."; PJ, p. 199.
". . . don't go supposing . . .": *Autour,* p. 178.

Page 45: "platonic passion . . . absorbing liaison . . .": CG IV,
180.
For Laure Hayman, *Lettres et vers,* p. 14, note byGeorges
Andrieux; CG V, 212-14; CG I, 112; Dreyfus, *Souvenirs,*
pp. 43-46.

Page 46: "Odette de Crécy . . .": CG V, 220-23.
"Dear friend . . .": CG V, 209-10.

Page 47: "Fair sweet and cruel . . .": CG V, 211.
"I am all the happier . . .": CG VI, 4-5.
"I am unlucky . . .": CG VI, 3-4.

Page 48: "My dear little Madame . . .": CG VI, 5.
"But you haven't . . ." CG VI, 11.

Page 49: Studious activities: Billy, *Marcel Proust,* pp. 23-24; C,
pp. 133-36.
"Give me, if you will . . .": Billy, *Marcel Proust,* p. 44;
"I scarcely dare . . .": p. 103.
"I am a hard worker . . .": CG VI, 7.

Page 50: Studies, examinations, letters to Billy: Billy, *Marcel
Proust,* pp. 41, 51, 54; CG IV, 184; CG VI, 7, 195.
Notary's practice: Pierre-Quint, *Marcel Proust,* p. 33.
For *Revue Lilas,* Dreyfus, *Souvenirs,* pp. 56-66.

Page 51: For *Le Banquet,* Gregh in *Hommage,* pp. 35-37; Dreyfus, *Souvenirs,* pp. 66-113.

IV. *Proust in 1896*

Page 52: "this year a collection": Billy, *Marcel Proust,* p. 52.
Letter to Lavallée: CG IV, 9.

Page 53: *Journal des Débats:* 1 Jan. 1925. See Alden, *Proust and
his French Critics,* pp. 159-202.

Page 54: Letter to Maurras: Guichard, *Sept Etudes,* p. 327.
Page 55: Imitation of Anatole France: PJ, p. 26.
Page 62: "If I have succeeded . . ." CG IV, 17.
Page 63: "From excess of dreaming . . .": C, p. 134.
"one and infinite . . .": C, p. 176.

Page 66: On "Mystères," de Messières in *Romanic Review,* XXXIII, 113-31, and XXXV, 232-37.

Page 68: Incident related by Reynaldo Hahn: *Hommage,* pp. 33-34.

Page 69: "I have been working . . .": *Lettres à une amie,* no. ii.
"This same Reynaldo . . .": CG VI, 14.
". . . in proportion as Christmas . . .": *Lettres à une amie,* no. i.

Page 70: "What we have not had to decipher . . .": XVI, 27.
"Our lives have been . . .": CG V, 89-90.

Page 71: "when my will is too sick": CG VI, 5.

Page 72: Gide's *Journal: Œuvres complètes,* X, 514-16.
"race over which . . .": VII, 267.

Page 73: "For no one knows . . .": VII, 274.

Page 74: Letter too startling to quote: CG VI, 27-28.
"The young man whom . . .": VII, 273.
"Do you remember how . . .": *La Revue Blanche,* V (Dec., 1893), 383-84. Vigneron in *Genèse de Swann* first called attention to the significance of this article.

Page 75: "Most people withdraw . . .": *La Revue Blanche, loc. cit.,* p. 384.

Page 78: "The sweetest perhaps . . .": C, p. 125.
"Let us not trust . . .": CG IV, 183.
"spontaneous gushing . . .": CG I, 5.
"To a generation concerned . . .": C, p. 78.

Page 79: "Three years ago . . .": CG I, 24-25.

Page 80: Gide's *Journal: Œuvres complètes,* X, 534.

V. *The Religion of Art*

Page 82: For the Mazarine episode, see "Proust à la Mazarine," in *Lettres à la NRF.*

Page 83: Dinner for Anatole France: CG I, 129-30.
Proust's duel: Alden, *Marcel Proust and his French Critics,* pp. 4, 159-60; CG I, 128; CG III, 86; C, pp. 73-74; XI, 110-11.

Page 84: "Oh! my little Louisa . . .": CG V, 174.

Page 85: "Thereupon L. de M. . . .": *Hommage,* p. 57.
"Finally and above all . . .": Robert, *De Loti à Proust,* pp. 176-77.
"For if our ideas . . .": CG I, 101.
Proust in Dreyfus affair: CG II, 152-53; CG III, 19, 71;

CG VI, 16-17, 47-50, 75-79; Robert, *De Loti à Proust,* p. 161.

Page 86: Earnest letter to Lauris: *Revue de Paris,* XLV (15 June 1938), 756-61.

Page 87: "with a politeness covering indignation . . .": VII, 271. For Proust and the Bibescos, see Princesse Bibesco, *Au Bal.*

Page 88: "But my little Lucien . . .": *Autour,* p. 29. "found, read and liked . . .": CG V, 129-30.

Page 89: *Queen of the Air:* CG IV, 21. "about Ruskin and some cathedrals": *Lettres à une amie,* no. ii; translating Ruskin, no. iii. "Thousands of the faithful . . .": C, p. 145. "Ill comprehending . . .": PM, pp. 145-46.

Page 90: For Venice trip, see *Lettres à une amie,* preface by Marie Riefstahl (née Nordlinger), p. ix. Health: *Lettres à une amie,* no. iii; PM, p. 194; CG V, 197, 165; CG IV, 24-25.

Page 91: "Whistler is right . . .": *Lettres à une amie,* no. xxxiii. "Beauty cannot fruitfully . . .": PM, p. 154.

Page 92: "I have not the courage . . .": CG II, 48-51.

Page 93: "If, in the course . . .": PM, pp. 107-08. note.

Page 94: "He even climbed . . .": *Hommage,* p. 41. Cf. Billy, *Marcel Proust,* pp. 121-22.

Page 95: "The universe took on . . .": PM, pp. 193-94; "There is no better way . . .": pp. 195-96. "It is known that . . .": PM, pp. 251-53 (footnote mentioning Ribot omitted).

Page 97: "I go out . . .": CG IV, 196-97. Cf. also Vigneron, "Marcel Proust et Robert de Montesquiou." "All that I am doing . . .": Bibesco, *Au Bal,* pp. 40-41.

Page 98: "that I still wonder . . .": Bibesco, *Au Bal,* pp. 74-75; cf. VI, 120-22.

Page 99: "My life has now . . .": CG I, 162-63.

Page 100: "What a confused . . .": *Revue de Paris,* XLV (15 June, 1938), 771. For Proust in Sollier's institution: Robert de Billy, *Marcel Proust,* pp. 159-64; CG VI, 42-44; CG V, 195-96. Health and moves: CG IV, 203; CG VI, 50-59, 62-73. Vigneron in "Genèse de Swann" first put together the story of Agostinelli. See also, for the summer of 1907,

CG VI, 85-90; Clermont-Tonnerre, *Robert de Montes-quiou et Marcel Proust,* pp. 102-04; Billy, *Marcel Proust,* pp. 212-13; "Journées en automobile," PM, pp. 91-99 (reprint of "Impressions de route en automobile").

VI. *Writing the Novel*

Page 103: "Trees, I thought . . .": XV, 221.
"Being unable . . .": PM, p. 197.

Page 104: Dinner for Calmette: CG VI, 82-85.
Article on homosexuality: CG IV, 233-34; Vigneron, *Genèse de Swann.*

Pages 104- Letter to Lauris: *Revue de Paris,* XLV (15 June 1938),
105: 764-65; to Dreyfus, CG IV, 237: to Montesquiou, CG I, 227; to Princesse Bibesco, CG V, 139.

Page 105: Letter to Lauris, *Revue de Paris, loc. cit.,* p. 767; to Montesquiou, CG I, 224: to Dreyfus, CG IV, 241; to Madame Straus, CG VI, 116 (cf. also CG III, 72 and Crémieux, *Du Côté de Marcel Proust,* p. 159).
At Cabourg, 1909: CG II, 67-69; *Revue de Paris, loc. cit.,* p. 766; CG V, 203-04.

Page 108: "Furthermore by continuing . . .": CG IV, 255.
"Nothing is more foreign . . .": CG V, 141-42.
"What you say about . . .": CG VI, 135-36.

Page 109: Letter to Blum: *Comment parut,* pp. 44-45.

Page 110: "My corrections up to now . . .": CG IV, 58.
"Often writers in whose hearts . . .": XVI, 52.

Page 111: "Across from the sensitive child . . .": XI, 147.

Page 112: The return and death of Agostinelli: Vigneron, "Genèse de Swann"; CG VI, 166-69, 241-47; CG IV, 61-62, 68, 91-92; CG V, 228, 230-31, 41; *Comment parut,* 50-51, 122, 172-73; CG I, 270.

Page 115: "If you haven't yet . . .": CG V, 233; further letters to Madame Scheikévitch, CG V, 234-41, 254, 260, 265.

Page 118: "I am incapable . . ." CG I, 270.

Page 119: Proust's opinion of *Albertine disparue: Lettres à la NRF,* p. 153.
"I bless illness . . .": CG V, 232.

Page 120: To Lucien Daudet, war attitude: *Autour,* pp. 102-07.
Letters about death of Gaston de Caillavet: CG IV, 130-39.
Letter to Maugny: CG V, 91-92.

Page 121: "images arising from an impression . . .": CG III, 109, 111.

Page 122: "Since it has not been known . . .": *Comment parut,* pp. 173-74.

Page 123: "At the moment it is . . .": *Autour,* pp. 190-91.
"I had guessed it all . . .": CG V, 248.
"At the time when I believed . . .": XV, 106.

Page 124: "I write you this . . .": CG V, 253-54.
"Alas, a day comes . . .": C, 125-26.
"I thought of you much . . .": CG VI, 185.

Page 125: "I have in myself . . ." CG V, 118.
"The parents who suffer . . .": CG V, 97-98.
"It is sufficiently within . . .": PM, pp. 69-70.

Page 126: On secretaries: Blanche, *Mes Modèles,* pp. 136-37; CG IV, 75; CG III, 202, 205, 18, 27.
"My health . . .": CG VI, 220; "an unhappy love affair . . ." CG V, 57.

Page 127: "We have thought too much . . .": CG VI, 212; "Yet for my part . . ." p. 222.
"I do not like people . . .": Blanche, *De David à Degas,* preface by Proust, p. viii, note.
"Frankreich über alles": CG IV, 278-79.

Page 128: For growth of Proust's reputation, Alden, *Marcel Proust and his French Critics,* chaps. III and IV.

Page 129: "For if after that . . .": *Comment parut,* pp. 36-37.
"This idea of death . . .": XVI, 253-54.

Page 130: "What you took for . . .": CG I, 206.
"Architectonic line": CG III, 300; cf. also CG III, 72.
"as for style . . .": CG III, 195.
Sodome et Gomorrhe the worst: CG V, 133.

Page 131: "Alas! I have known . . .": CG IV, 155-56.
For visit to exhibition, CG IV, 85-88, 90; CG V, 264.

Page 132: "At the first steps . . .": XI, 254-55.

Page 133: "Day before yesterday . . .": CG III, 262.
"True literature reveals . . .": CG III, 313.

Pages 133-134: Account of last illness and death based on story of Céleste, reported by Madame Scheikévitch, *Souvenirs d'un temps disparu,* pp. 163 ff.; last letter, *Lettres à la NRF,* p. 273; "They buried him . . .": XI, 256.

VII. *A la Recherche du temps perdu*

References to longer quotations from the novel are indicated in the text; but the analysis of Proust's thought involves such a very large number of minute allusions that to give references for them all is impracticable. Many of them can be tracked down with the aid of Celly, *Répertoire des thèmes,* or Daudet, *Répertoire des personnages;* others can be traced by continuity to longer passages whose location is indicated; for the rest, the reader must trust to the good faith of the author, or to his own knowledge of Proust.

Page 140: "Not once does one . . .": CG IV, 260.

"Novelists who count . . .": C, p. 106.

Page 150: Proust's keys for the "little phrase": *Hommage,* p. 190.

Page 229: "I thought that you . . .": CG IV, 201.

Page 230: "Several times, alas! . . .": CG III, 93-94.

Page 233: Version of hawthorn description in *Swann:* I, 163-210.

Page 234: "Even if he did not know . . .": Robert, *Comment débuta,* p. 40.

VIII. *The Meaning of Proust*

Page 240: For trends in Proust's reputation, see Alden, *Marcel Proust and his French Critics.*

Pages 248-249: *With the Door Open* . . . by J. Anker Larsen, tr. by E. and P. von Gaisberg. N. Y., The Macmillan Co., 1931 (foreword 1926). Pp. 29, 30, 31, 37, 38, 39, 73.

Page 251: "The experience of the past . . .": CG V, 231.

"Perhaps it is only in really vicious . . ."; III, 181-82.

Page 252: "a world wholly different . . .": XI, 256.

CORRESPONDENCE

Correspondance générale de Marcel Proust. 1930-36. 6v.

Barrès, Maurice.
Mes Cahiers, vol. IX. Plon, 1935. (Contains letters)

Chauvière, Claude.
Colette. 1931. (Contains letters)

Daudet, Lucien.
Autour de soixante lettres. 1929.

Défense de Marcel Proust. Bulletin Marcel Proust I. 1930. (Contains letters)

Lauris, Georges de.
"Marcel Proust d'après une correspondance et des souvenirs." *Revue de Paris,* XLV (15 June 1938), 753-76.

Lettres à la NRF. Bibliographie proustienne, par G. da Silva Ramos. *Proust à la Mazarine.* 4ᵉ éd. Gallimard [1932].

Lettres à une amie [Marie Nordlinger]. Manchester [England], Edition du Calame, 1942.

"Lettres à Maurice Duplay." *La Revue nouvelle,* XLVIII (June, 1929), 1-13.

"Letters to Natalie Clifford Barney." *Dublin Magazine,* January-March, 1931, VI, 5-13.

Pierre-Quint, Léon.
Comment parut Du Côté de chez Swann [letters to Blum, Grasset, Brun]. Kra [1926].

Pierre-Quint, Léon.
Quelques lettres . . . précédées de remarques sur les derniers mois de sa vie. Flammarion [1928].

Robert, Louis de.
Comment débuta Marcel Proust. Gallimard, 1925.

Miscellaneous:

Mercure de France, 1 Aug. 1926, p. 760.
Modern Language Notes, Dec., 1932, 522-24.
La Nuova Antologia, 16 March 1935, pp. 319-20.
Nouvelle Revue Française, 1 Nov. 1928, "Lettres à André Gide."
Revue d'histoire littéraire de la France:
   Fragments in: April-June, 1926, p. 330.
            April-June, 1930, pp. 305-06.
            January-March, 1932, p. 159.
            January-March, 1933, p. 159.
   Record of autographs in *Chroniques:* XLII (1935), 465.
                        XLIV (1937), 291-92.
La Semaine litteraire de Genève, 6 Jan. 1923. "Une Lettre de Marcel Proust."

See also below under:

Bibesco, Billy, Cattaui, Clermont-Tonnerre, Crémieux, Guichard, *Hommage,* Pierre-Quint, Pouquet, Robert.

IMPORTANT WORKS
ON PROUST

Abraham, Pierre.

Proust, Recherches sur la création intellectuelle. Rieder, 1930.
Contains interesting plates and a chronological list of Proust's publications.

Alden, Douglas, W.

Marcel Proust and his French Critics. Los Angeles, Lymanhouse [1940]. Valuable account of critical reaction to Proust, with important chronological bibliography.

Andrieux, Georges.

Lettres et vers [de Proust] à Mesdames Laure Hayman et Louisa de Mornand. Preface and notes. 1928. The letters have been reprinted in CG V.

Bédé, J.-A.

"Marcel Proust, Problèmes récents." *Le Flambeau,* March, 1936, pp. 311-24; April, 1936, pp. 439-52.
Reply to Feuillerat's book.

Bibesco, Princesse [G. V].

Au Bal avec Marcel Proust. Gallimard [1928].
Important letters to Antoine and Emmanuel Bibesco.

Billy, Robert de.

Marcel Proust, Lettres et Conversations. Editions des Portiques [1930].

Blanche, Jacques-Emile.

Mes Modèles . . . 6ᵉ éd. Stock, 1929.

Blondel, C. A. A.

La Psychographie de Marcel Proust. Vrin, 1932.
Contains material on Bergson and Freud.

Cattaui, Georges.

L'Amitié de Proust . . . 6ᵉ éd. Gallimard [1935].
Contains letters.

Celly, Raoul.

Répertoire des thèmes de Marcel Proust. 6ᵉ éd. Gallimard [1935].
Very useful.

Chernowitz, Maurice E.

Proust and Painting. N. Y., 1945 (Columbia Thesis).
Important and interesting study.

Clermont-Tonnerre, Elizabeth, Duchesse de.

Robert de Montesquiou et Marcel Proust. Flammarion [1925].
Contains letters from Proust and from Montesquiou.

Cochet, Marie-Anne.

L'Ame proustienne . . . Brussels, Collignon, 1929.
A powerful, but over-symmetrical analysis of Proust on the lines of
vice, remorse, and redemption through art.

Crémieux, Benjamin.

Vingtième Siècle. Gallimard, 1924.

Crémieux, Benjamin.

Du Côté de Marcel Proust, suivi de lettres inédites de Marcel
Proust à Benjamin Crémieux. Ed. Lemarget, 1929.

Curtius, E. R.

Marcel Proust, traduit de l'allemand par Armand Pierhal. La
Revue Nouvelle, 1928.

Dandieu, Armand.

Marcel Proust, sa révélation psychologique. Firmin-Didot, 1930.
An important study, the first to bring out the importance of the
metaphor and of the "privileged moments" in Proust.

Daudet, Charles.

Répertoire des personnages de "A la Recherche du temps perdu."
Gallimard, 1928.
Moderately useful.

Dreyfus, Robert.

Souvenirs sur Marcel Proust. Grasset, 1926.
One of the most valuable sources on the youth of Proust. The letters have since been published more fully in CG IV.

Du Bos, Charles.

Approximations I. Plon, 1922.

Ellis, Havelock.

From Rousseau to Proust. Boston, Houghton Mifflin, 1935.
Chapter on Proust contains interesting material on asthma.

Feuillerat, Albert.

Comment Marcel Proust a composé son roman. New Haven, Yale University Press, 1934.
Despite certain excessive conclusions, this work remains of great importance. Valuable appendix showing additions to original second volume.

Fiser, Emeric.

L'Esthétique de Marcel Proust. Rédier, 1933.

Guichard, Léon.

Sept Etudes sur Marcel Proust. Cairo [Egypt], Institut Français [1942].
Contains two letters.

Hier, Florence.

La Musique dans l'œuvre de Marcel Proust. N. Y., Columbia University [1933].

Hommage à Marcel Proust. Gallimard, 1927.
Contains letters.

Jäckel, Kurt.

Bergson und Proust. Breslau, Priebatsch, 1934.

Kolb, Philip.

"A Lost Article by Proust." *Modern Language Notes,* LIII (1938), 107-09.

Massis, Henri.

Le Drame de Marcel Proust. Grasset [1937].
Based on book of Marie-Anne Cochet (above) and adding little to it, it nevertheless attracted more attention.

Messières, René de.

"Un Document probable sur le premier état de la pensée de Proust: Mystères, per Fernand Gregh." *Romanic Review,* April 1942, 113-31.
The first to call attention to "Mystères." But see also Mme Gabriel Czoniczer, *Romanic Review* for October 1944, pp. 232-37, with reply by M. de Messières.

O'Brien, Justin.

"La Mémoire involontaire avant Marcel Proust." *Revue de littérature comparée,* January 1939.

Pierhal, Armand.

"Sur la Composition wagnérienne de l'oeuvre de Proust." *Bibliothèque universelle et Revue de Genève,* June 1929.

Pierre-Quint, Léon.

Comment travaillait Proust. Bibliographie. Variantes. Lettres de Proust. Aux Editions des Cahiers libres, 1928.

Pierre-Quint, Léon.

Marcel Proust, sa vie, son œuvre. Nouvelle éd. Ed. du Sagittaire [1935].

Pouquet, Jeanne Maurice.

Le Salon de Madame de Caillavet. Hachette, 1926.
Contains letters to Anatole France and others.

Rivière, Jacques.

Quelques Progrès dans l'étude du cœur humain. Librairie de France, 1926.

Robert, Louis de.

De Loti à Proust. Flammarion [1928].
Contains letters.

Sachs, Maurice.
"Historiette." *Nouvelle Revue Française,* L (1938), 863-64.
Scandal about Proust's homosexuality.

Santayana, George.
"Proust on Essences." *Life and Letters Today,* II (1929), 455-59.

Scheikévitch, Madame Marie.
Souvenirs d'un temps disparu. Plon [1935].

Vettard, Camille.
"Proust et Einstein." *Nouvelle Revue Française,* 1 Aug. 1922.

Vigneron, Robert.
"Marcel Proust et Robert de Montesquiou." *Modern Philology,* XXXIX (November 1941), 159-95.
Important for letter dates.

Vigneron, Robert.
"Genèse de Swann." *Revue d'histoire de la philosophie* (Lille), 15 Jan. 1937, pp. 67-115.
First documented account of Agostinelli, with letter dates.

Vigneron, Robert.
"Genesis of Swann." *Partisan Review,* Nov.-Dec. 1941.
Condensed and undocumented English version of preceding.

Wilson, Edmund.
Axel's Castle. N. Y., Scribner, 1931.
The chapter on Proust contains the first discussion of the biographical significance of "La Confession d'une jeune fille."

INDEX

Abraham, Pierre, 256, 257, 266
Agostinelli, Alfred, 101-02, 112-18, 119, 180, 181, 260, 261, 270
Agostinelli, Anna, 112, 113, 114, 118
Agostinelli, Emile, 113
Albaret, 112, 113, 133
Albaret, Céleste, 112, 113, 126, 133, 134, 149, 262
Albertine disparue, 71, 116-17, 118-19, 121-22, 133, 135, 145, 147, 181, 204, 237, 238, 240, 255, 261
Alden, D. W., 258, 259, 262, 263, 266
A l'Ombre des jeunes filles en fleur, 54, 107, 115, 118, 121, 127, 128, 137, 138, 141-43, 146, 151, 153, 236, 240, 255
"Amitié," 44
Andrieux, Georges, 258, 266
Aretino, 131
Arman de Caillavet, Gaston, 34, 35, 43, 51, 120, 257, 261
Arman de Caillavet, Mme, 34, 43, 53, 83, 269
Arman de Caillavet, Mme Gaston, 35, 120, 269
Arvers, Colonel, 33
Aubernon, Mme, 40
Aubert, Edgar, 44, 52, 79
"Avant la nuit," 74-75, 79, 251

Baignères, Jacques, 33, 50
Baignères, Mme Arthur, 34
Baignères, Paul, 33, 49, 50
Balzac, Guez de, 55

Balzac, Honoré de, 1, 156, 244, 245
Barbey d'Aurevilly, J., 13
Barbusse, Henri, 51
Barney, Natalie Clifford, 264
Barrès, 8, 9, 15, 256, 264
Baudelaire, 9, 13, 14, 31, 256
Bédé, J.-A., 266
Beethoven, 88
Benardahy, Mlle, 27, 28, 180, 256
Béraud, 83
Bergson, 1, 16, 18, 63, 78, 100, 215, 240, 241, 246-47, 266
Bernardin de Saint-Pierre, 55
Bernhardt, Sarah, 219
Berry, Walter, 126
Bibesco, Antoine, 41, 87, 88, 94, 97, 266
Bibesco, Emmanuel, 87, 88, 94, 123, 266
Bibesco, Princesse Marthe, 41, 104, 108, 257, 260, 266
Bible of Amiens, The (Proust translation), 90, 92, 93, 103
Billy, Robert de, 34, 43, 49, 50, 52, 92, 94, 100, 257, 258, 260, 261, 266
Bize, Dr., 133
Bizet, Jacques, 29, 33, 51, 54, 69, 100
Blanche, J. E., 40, 121, 257, 262, 266
Blanche of Castille, 42
Blondel, C. A. A., 266
Blum, Léon, 51, 54
Blum, René, 109, 112, 129, 261, 264

Bois, E. J., 241
Borda, Gustave de, 83
Botticelli, 211
Bourget, Paul, 8, 9, 13, 15, 45, 256
Boutroux, Emile, 16
Boylesve, René, 131
Brancovan, Constantin de, 87, 93
Brancovan, Princesse de, 35, 87
Briand, 86, 94
Browne, Sir Thomas, 62
Brun, Louis, 264
Brunetière, 8, 256
Bunyan, 93
Byron, 93

Caillavet, de, *see* Arman de Caillavet
Calmette, 104, 261
Caraman-Chimay, Princesse de, 35, 87
Carlyle, 79, 93
Castellane, Marquis de, 83
Cattaui, Georges, 267
Céleste, *see* Albaret
Celly, Raoul, 263, 267
Chateaubriand, 104
Chauvière, Claude, 264
Chernowitz, M. E., 267
Chevigné, Comtesse de, 42, 149, 180
Chopin, 53
Chroniques, 51, 255, 259, 263
Clermont-Tonnerre, Duc de, 86, 267
Clermont-Tonnerre, Duchesse de, 86, 257, 261
Closmesnil, 45, 46, 149
Cochet, Marie-Anne, 267, 269
Colonne, 88
Comte, Auguste, 5, 255
"Confession d'une jeune fille, La," 53, 65, 71, 72, 75-77, 79, 270
"Contre l'obscurité," 51, 65, 66, 230

Côté de Guermantes, Le, 42, 46, 98, 106, 107, 121, 132, 135, 138, 143, 146, 147, 148, 154, 188, 192, 230, 236, 240, 255
Crémieux, Benjamin, 256, 261, 267
Croce, 9
Curtius, E. R., 133, 267
Cuyp, 53
Czoniczer, Mme Gabriel, 269

Dada, 14
Dandieu, Armand, 267
D'Annunzio, 9
Darlu, 31
Darwin, 6-7, 243
Daudet, Alphonse, 30, 44, 256
Daudet, Charles, 263, 267
Daudet, Léon, 30, 44
Daudet, Lucien, 44, 88, 120, 123, 260, 261, 264
Delafosse, Léon, 39-40, 257
Desjardins, Paul, 15, 16, 78, 256
Doasan, Baron, 40, 149
Dostoievski, 120
Dreyfus Affair, 24, 85-87, 140, 182, 190, 192-93, 259
Dreyfus, Robert, 29, 45, 50, 51, 78, 96, 97, 100, 104, 105, 108, 140, 229, 257, 258, 261, 268
Du Bos, Charles, 268
Du Côté de chez Swann, 30, 45, 46, 106, 107, 108, 110, 112, 115, 128, 135, 136-42, 148, 150, 151, 152, 154, 230, 233, 234, 236, 237, 255, 259, 260, 261, 263, 264, 270
Duplay, Maurice, 264
Duval, Paul, 83

Einstein, 1, 128, 240-41, 270
Eliot, George, 31, 69, 93
Ellis, Havelock, 268
Emerson, 79
Ephrussi, 149

"Epine rose, Epine blanche," 233-34

"Etranger, L'," 55, 57, 71

Fasquelle, 106
Fauré, 150
Fénelon, *see* Salignac de la Mothe-Fénelon, Salignac-Fénelon
"Fête chez Montesquiou à Neuilly," 104
Feuillerat, Albert, 107, 243-44, 256, 266, 268
Finaly, Horace, 43
"Fin de la jalousie, La," 53, 61-62, 65, 229
Fiser, Emeric, 268
Flaubert, 57
Flers, Robert de, 43, 44, 50, 51
France, Anatole, 34, 53, 54, 55, 83, 86, 219, 256, 258, 259, 269
Franck, 150
Freud, 1, 207, 240, 241-42, 243, 266

Gabory, Georges, 257
Gaisberg, E. and P. von, 263
Gallimard, 121, 134
Gaucher, Maxime, 31, 257
Gide, 72, 77, 80, 259, 265
Giotto, 157, 211
Gluck, 53
Gobineau, 96
Goncourt, 148
Gounod, 29
Grasset, 106, 129, 264
Greffuhle, Comtesse, 37-38
Gregh, Fernand, 51, 54, 66, 67, 68, 94, 258, 269
Grévy, 140
Guerne, Comtesse de, 35
Guichard, Léon, 258, 268

Haas, Charles, 19, 20, 25, 149
Hahn, Reynaldo, 44, 53, 54, 68, 69, 90, 105, 119, 126, 259

Halévy, Daniel, 29, 50, 51, 127
Halévy, Jacques, 33
Hartmann, Édouard von, 17, 30
Haussonville, Comte d', 86
Haussonville, Comtesse d', 35
Hayman, Francis, 45
Hayman, Laure, 45-47, 48, 83, 84, 149, 180, 258, 266
Heath, Willie, 44, 52, 58, 79
Hesiod, 53
Hier, Florence, 268
Holmes, Augusta, 69
Hume, 5, 6
Humières, d', 121
Huysmans, J. K., 10, 12, 13, 14

"Impressions de route en automobile," 101, 102, 104, 261
Ingres, 131
"Irreligion d'état, L'," 51

Jäckel, Kurt, 268
Jallifier, 31
Jammes, 234
"Journées de lecture," 256
"Journées en automobile," 261
Joyce, James, 1, 148

Kipling, 16
Klopstock, 57
Kolb, Philip, 268
Krafft-Ebing, 11, 12, 75, 210, 242

La Bruyère, 1, 124, 193
Lacretelle, 257
Lamoureux, 88
La Rochefoucauld, 193, 202
Larsen, J. Anker, 248-50, 263
La Salle, Louis de, 43, 50, 51
Lauris, Georges de, 86, 94, 104, 105, 119, 233, 260, 261, 264
Lavallée, Pierre, 31, 35, 52, 62, 68, 89, 119, 257, 258
Lazard, Jean, 43
Lebon, André, 49

Lemaire, Madeleine, 34, 35, 36, 37, 48, 52, 53, 83, 87
Lemaire, Mlle, 48
Lemaître, Jules, 59
Lennox, Cosmo Gordon, 41
Léon, Princesse de, 37
Leroy-Beaulieu, 49
Lorrain, Jean, 83
Louis XIV, 31, 193
Luynes, Duc de, 125
Lytton, Lord, 34

Maeterlinck, 31, 104
Mâle, Emile, 91-92
Mallarmé, 12, 31
Malthus, 6
Martino, Pierre, 257
Massis, Henri, 269
Mathilde, Princesse, 34
Maugny, Comte de, 119, 120-21, 125, 261
Maugny, Comtesse de, 125
Maurras, Charles, 54, 55, 258
Meissières, René de, 259, 269
Meissonier, 29
"Mélancolique Villégiature," 61, 64, 65
Michelet, 75
Mill, John Stuart, 30
"Mondanité et Mélomanie de Bouvard et Pechuchet," 57
Monet, 220
Montaigne, 193
Montesquiou - Fezensac, Comte de, 35-41, 78, 79, 83, 85, 94, 96, 99, 104, 105, 118, 149, 181, 243, 257, 260, 261, 267, 270
Morand, Paul, 129
Mornand, Louisa de, 84-85, 90, 180, 259, 266
"Mort de Baldassare Silvande, La," 53, 55, 65
"Mort des cathédrales, La," 86, 94

Mozart, 29, 53
Musset, 29, 31, 55, 57, 58

Nietzsche, 105
Noailles, Comtesse de, 22, 35, 87, 92, 93, 104, 113, 117, 130, 256
Nordlinger, Marie, 69, 89, 90, 91, 260, 264

O'Brien, Justin, 269
Olivier (of the Ritz), 126
Ollendorff, 106

Pascal, 133
Pastiches et Mélanges, 93, 127-28, 255, 257, 260, 261, 262
Pater, Walter, 9, 93
Paul, Saint, 250
Péguy, 230
"Pèlerinages ruskiniens en France," 89
Petronius, 55
Picquart, Colonel, 86
Pierhal, Armand, 267, 269
Pierre-Quint, Léon, 258, 264, 269
Plaisirs et les Jours, Les, 25-26, 27, 32, 41, 51, 52-66, 67, 68, 70, 71, 74, 75, 79, 81, 82, 96, 98, 111, 124, 255, 257, 258
Plato, 17, 18, 32, 51
Pliny, 181
Poe, 9, 256
Polignac, Princesse de, 35
Portraits de peintres, 53
Potocka, Comtesse, 35
Potter, 53
Pouquet, Jeanne, see Armand de Caillavet, Mme Gaston
"Présence réelle," 60
Prisonnière, La, 83, 111, 114, 121, 122, 132, 133, 134, 136, 144, 146, 147, 149, 169, 172, 176, 178, 181, 204, 236, 238, 240, 242, 255

"Professeur de beauté, Un," 94
Proust, Adrien, 21, 24, 49, 50, 82, 92-93, 98
Proust, Jeanne Weil (Mme Adrien), 19, 20, 21, 23, 24, 25, 26, 35, 46, 89, 90, 92-93, 97, 98-99, 150
Proust, Robert, 20, 23, 24, 119, 121, 133, 134, 256

Rabaud, Henri, 51
Racine, 55
Radziwill, Prince, 28
Radziwill, Princesse, see Benardahy.
"Rayon de soleil sur le balcon," 256-57
Régnier, Henri de, 31, 104
Reinach, 86
Renan, 8
Reybaud, Louis, 57
Ribot, 6, 18, 95, 256, 260
Richmond, Duke of, 41
Riefstahl, Marie, see Nordlinger
Rivière, Jacques, 269
Robert, Louis de, 85, 234, 259, 260, 263, 265, 269
Rod, Edouard, 15
Rothschild, 191
Rouquès, Amédée, 51
Rousseau, 56
Ruskin, 88-97, 103, 219, 260

Sachs, Maurice, 270
Saint-Saëns, 150
Saint-Simon, Duc de, 1, 125, 193
Sainte-Beuve, 105
Salignac de la Mothe-Fénelon, François de, 87
Salignac-Fénelon, Bertrand de, 87, 94, 120-21, 122-23, 149
Sand, George, 29, 31
Sansovino, 131
Santayana, 270
Sassoon, Sir Philip, 131

Scheikévitch, Mme, 115, 116, 119, 124, 251, 261, 262, 270
Schiff, Sidney, 126
Schopenhauer, 16, 17, 18, 246, 247
Schumann, 53
Sesame and Lilies (Proust translation), 93, 96, 229, 256
Sévigné, Mme de, 55
Shakespeare, 156
Silva Ramos, G. da, 264
Socrates, 75
Sodome et Gomorrhe, 72, 75, 79, 80, 86, 112, 121, 124, 130-31, 132, 133, 143-44, 146, 147, 152, 207, 210, 236, 240, 242, 251, 255, 262
Sollier, Dr., 99-100, 260
"Sonate Clair de Lune," 64
Sorel, Albert, 49
Souday, Paul, 230
Soutzo, Princesse, 125-26, 180
Spencer, Herbert, 30
Stendhal, 1, 156, 246
Straus, Emile, 112, 113, 118
Straus, Mme Emile, 33, 34, 39, 47-48, 49, 51, 69, 71, 74, 102, 105, 108, 124, 126, 127, 149, 229, 261
"Sur la lecture," 93

Taine, 5-6, 7, 15, 18, 30, 255, 256
Temps retrouvé, Le, 70, 106, 110, 122, 129, 135, 145, 147, 148, 181, 182, 190, 195, 207, 210, 224, 232, 235, 240, 243, 248, 255
Tennyson, 93
Thierry, Augustin, 29
Tissot, 149
Titian, 131
Tolstoi, 31, 120
Trarieux, Gabriel, 50, 51
Turenne, de, 83
Turner, 94

Ulrichs, K. H., 11, 207, 242

Van Dyck, 41, 53
Vaudoyer, J. L., 110, 113, 119, 126, 131
Vaugelas, 193
Verlaine, 55
Vermeer of Delft, 35, 131, 132, 238
Vernes, Jules, 123
Vettard, Camille, 234, 240-41, 270
Vigneron, Robert, 257, 259, 260, 261, 270
Vignot, Abbé, 79
Vigny, 209
Vincent de Beauvais, 92
"Violante," 54, 56, 71, 72
Viollet-le-Duc, 92

Vogüé, M. de, 14
Voltaire, 54, 56

Wagner, 64, 88, 150, 238, 269
Wagram, Princesse de, 34, 37
Watteau, 53
Weil, Louis, 19, 22, 45, 46, 81, 84, 100
Weil, Nathée, 19, 81
Wells, H. G., 123
Whistler, 91, 220, 260
Wilde, Oscar, 9, 10
Wilson, Edmund, 270

Yeatman, 89
Yturri, Gabriel d', 39, 40

Zola, 7, 14, 15